America's Education Deficit and the War on Youth

America's Education Deficit and the War on Youth

by HENRY A. GIROUX

MONTHLY REVIEW PRESS
New York

KH

Library of Congress Cataloging-in-Publication Data
available from the publisher—

ISBN: 978-1-58367-344-7 pbk
ISBN: 978-1-58367-345-4 cloth

Monthly Review Press
146 West 29th Street, Suite 6W
New York, New York 10001

www.monthlyreview.org

5 4 3 2 1

10/6/14

Contents

*For teachers everywhere who are struggling for a more
just and democratic world.*

To the memory of Roger Simon, my brother and dearest friend.

Acknowledgments

I WANT TO THANK Susan Searls Giroux for both her editorial help and the numerous conversations we had about this book, all of which provided new insights and ideas. My colleague Grace Pollock provided indispensable editorial help with this project, and as a result the book is much improved. My administrative assistant, Danielle Martak, read every page of this book endless times and offered invaluable insights and editorial suggestions when I needed to revise and keep going with the manuscript. Victoria Harper, my editor at *Truthout*, provided me with unwavering backing in publishing shorter versions of many of the chapters included in this book. I would also like to thank Michael Yates for his probing questions and superb editing of the manuscript. Finally, I would like to thank the Social Sciences and Humanities Research Council of Canada for their financial help in supporting the research that made this book possible.

Introduction: Challenging Casino Capitalism and Authoritarian Politics in the Age of Disposability

THERE IS BY NOW an overwhelming catalogue of evidence revealing the depth and breadth of the corporate- and state-sponsored assaults being waged against democracy in the United States. Indeed, it appears that the nation has entered a new and more ruthless historical era, marked by a growing disinvestment in the social state, public institutions, and civic morality. The attack on the social state is of particular importance because it represents an attempt to shift social protections to the responsibility of individuals while at the same time privatizing investments in the public good and undermining the bonds of communal solidarity. The renowned sociologist Zygmunt Bauman makes this clear in his definition and defense of the social state:

> A state is "social" when it promotes the principle of the communally endorsed, collective insurance against individual misfortune and its consequences. . . . And it is the same principle which lifts members of society to the status of citizens—that is, makes them

stake-holders in addition to being stock-holders, beneficiaries but also actors responsible for the benefits' creation and availability, individuals with acute interest in the common good understood as the shared institutions that can be trusted to assure solidity and reliability of the state-issued "collective insurance policy." The application of that principle may, and often does, protect men and women from the plague of poverty—most importantly, however, it stands a chance of becoming a profuse source of solidarity able to recycle "society" into a common, communal good, thanks to the defense it provides against the horror of misery, that is, of the terror of being excluded, of falling or being pushed over the board of a fast-accelerating vehicle of progress, of being condemned to "social redundancy" and otherwise designed to "human waste."[1]

Matters of politics, power, ideology, governance, economics, and policy now translate unapologetically into a systemic disinvestment in those public spheres that traditionally provided the minimal conditions for social justice, dissent, and democratic expression. The reign of the commodity, with its growing economy of individualism, privatization, and deregulation, offers a market solution for all of society's problems. Yet, given that the apostles of neoliberalism work tirelessly to destroy with naked power the numerous essential institutions of social justice and social protections that exemplify the social state, it is clear that solving society's problems is not their goal. Neoliberalism aims to enhance the wealth and power of those already rich. No longer responsive to the social contract and the preservation of labor, neoliberalism "shifts into a mode of elimination that targets most of us—along with our environment—as waste products awaiting managed disposal."[2] Unfortunately, neoliberalism, or what might better be called "casino capitalism," has become the new normal.

Unabashed in its claim to financial power, self-regulation, and a survival of the fittest value system, neoliberalism not only undercuts the formative culture necessary for producing critical citizens and the public spheres that nourish them, it also facilitates the conditions for producing a bloated defense budget, the prison-industrial complex, environmental degradation, and the emergence of "finance as a criminalized, rogue industry."[3] It is clear that an emergent authoritarianism haunts a defanged democracy now shaped and structured largely by corporations.[4] Money dominates politics; the gap between the rich and poor is ballooning; urban spaces are becoming armed camps; militarism is creeping into every facet of public life; and civil liberties are in shreds.[5] Neoliberalism's ideology of competition now dominates policies that define public spheres such as schools, allowing them to be stripped of a civic and democratic project and handed over to the logic of the market.[6] Regrettably, it is not democracy, but authoritarianism, that remains on the rise in the United States as we move further into the twenty-first century.

The Politics of Fraud

The 2012 U.S. presidential election took place at a pivotal moment in this transformation away from democracy, a moment in which formative cultural and political realms and forces, including the rhetoric used by election candidates, appeared saturated with celebrations of war and social Darwinism. Accordingly, the possibility of an even more authoritarian and ethically dysfunctional leadership in the White House in 2013 caught the attention of a number of liberals and other progressives in the United States. American politics in general, and the 2012 election in particular, presented a challenge to progressives, whose voices in recent years have been increasingly excluded from both the mainstream media and the corridors of political power. Instead, the media played up the apocalyptic view of the Republican Party's fundamentalist warriors, who seemed fixated on translating issues previously seen as non-religious—such as sexual orientation, education, identity, and participation in public life—into the language of a religious revival and militant crusade against evil.[7]

How else to explain Republican vice-presidential nominee Paul Ryan's claim that the struggle for the future is a "fight of individualism versus collectivism," with its nod to McCarthyism and the cold war rhetoric of the 1950s?[8] Or former senator Rick Santorum's assertion that "President Obama is getting America hooked on 'the narcotic of government dependency,'" promoting the view that government has no responsibility to provide safety nets for the poor, disabled, sick, and elderly.[9]

There is more at work here than simply a ramped-up version of social Darwinism, with its savagely cruel ethic of "reward the rich, penalize the poor, [and] let everyone fend for themselves."[10] There is also a full-scale attack on the social contract, the welfare state, economic equality, and any viable vestige of moral and social responsibility. As Robert O'Self argues, the social contract is crucial to what it means for Americans to lead a decent life. At the same time, he wonders if there is a place for women in the Republican Party's view of the contract. Of course, he could easily have added youth, people of color, immigrants, the elderly, and the unemployed. He writes:

> The social contract is supposed to bind us together. It's everything from Medicare to the Americans with Disabilities Act to Social Security to the Equal Pay Act. It is the basic architecture of our collective responsibility to ensure that Americans share in a decent life. The social contract says that though our individual fates differ, we have a collective destiny, too. Many of us respond viscerally to comments from politicians like Mr. Akin because he leaves us wondering what place for women Republicans see in that collective future.[11]

The Romney-Ryan appropriation of Ayn Rand's ode to selfishness and self-interest is of particular importance because it offers not only a glimpse of a ruthless form of extreme capitalism in which the social contract is shredded, but also provides a testimony to a logic of cruelty and disposability in which the poor are considered "moochers," viewed with contempt, and singled out to be punished. But this theocratic economic fundamentalist ideology does more. It destroys any viable notion of civic virtue in which the social contract and common good provide the basis for creating meaningful social bonds and instilling in citizens a sense of social and civic responsibility. The idea of public service is viewed with disdain just as the work of individuals, social groups, and institutions that benefit the citizenry at large are held in contempt.

As George Lakoff and Glenn W. Smith point out, casino capitalism creates a culture of cruelty, with "its horrific effects on individuals—death, illness, suffering, greater poverty, and loss of opportunity, productive lives, and money."[12] But it does more by crushing any viable notion of the common good and public life by destroying "the bonds that hold us together."[13] Under casino capitalism, the spaces, institutions, and values that constitute the public are now surrendered to powerful financial forces and viewed simply as another market to be commodified, privatized, and surrendered to the demands of capital.[14] With market-driven zealots in charge of both parties, politics becomes an extension of war, and greed and self-interest trump any concern for the well-being of others. For the extremists who now control the Republican Party, in particular, reason is trumped by emotions rooted in absolutist certainty and militaristic aggression, and skepticism and dissent are viewed as the work of Satan.

At the same time, both Republicans and Democrats embrace the logic of casino capitalism in which Wall Street creates an economy focused on speculative, short-term investments "designed to make a killing rather than expanding the productive base of the economy."[15] Casino capitalism is the true religion of America and provides a common ground for both major parties, in spite of their differences on the role of government and the welfare state. Casino capitalism does not make tangible products needed to address basic human needs or foster broad-based prosperity as much as it "creates an infinite amount of paper assets that can be traded between individuals."[16] It is an economy that has become a playground for gamblers and bettors in which the dice are loaded in favor of the ultra-rich, bankers, hedge fund managers, and financial elite who operate on the assumption that "society's resources are best allocated by profit-seeking individuals betting on short-term price movements in intangible or paper assets."[17] Casino capitalism thrives on a deregulated and ascendant financial sector that

offers easy credit (particularly evident before the 2007 economic recession), cheap mortgages, and the seductive lure of a promising lifestyle
built on ever burdening debt.

Appeals to religion often provide a rationalization for the culture
of greed, war, repression, and cruelty that drives casino capitalism,
but both parties support unfettered capital accumulation, the endless
search for short investments, and the criminalization of dissent. What
is new in American politics in the current historical conjuncture is the
emergence of a casino capitalism largely unchecked by massive social
movements, the religionization of politics, and the intense role that
religion increasingly plays as a formative register in legitimating the
very parameters of politics.

The Religionization of Politics

It is also the case that something far more serious and dangerous is
unfolding in American politics than the politicization of religion and
the march toward authoritarianism. We are witnessing what Zygmunt
Bauman has called the "religionization of politics," whereby secular
politics and policymaking will be reshaped by the logic and certitude of
religious fundamentalism. As Bauman points out in a different context:

> Much too little attention is paid to . . . the "religionization of poli-
> tics," arguably still more dangerous and often much more gory in
> its consequences [than the politicization of religion]. A conflict of
> interests calling for negotiation and compromise (the daily bread
> of politics) is then recycled into an ultimate showdown between
> good and evil that renders any negotiated agreement inconceivable
> and from which only one of the antagonists can emerge alive (the
> liminal horizon of monotheistic religions).[18]

If the Republican candidacy race of 2012 is any indication,
then political discourse in the United States has not only moved to
the right—it has introduced totalitarian values and ideals into the

mainstream of public life. Religious fanaticism, consumer culture, and the warfare state work in tandem with neoliberal economic forces to encourage privatization, corporate tax breaks, income and wealth inequality, and the further merging of the financial and military spheres in ways that diminish the authority and power of democratic governance.[19] Neoliberal interests in freeing markets from social constraints, fueling competitiveness, destroying education systems, producing atomized subjects, and loosening individuals from any sense of social responsibility prepare the populace for a slow embrace of social Darwinism, state terrorism, and the mentality of war—not least of all by destroying communal bonds, dehumanizing the other, and pitting individuals against the communities they inhabit.

The Dark Shadows of Authoritarianism

Totalitarian temptations now saturate the media and larger culture in the language of austerity as political and economic orthodoxy. What we are witnessing in the United States is the normalization of a politics that exterminates not only the welfare state, and the truth, but all those who bear the sins of the Enlightenment—that is, those who refuse a life free from doubt. Reason and freedom have become enemies not merely to be mocked, but to be destroyed. And this is a war whose totalitarian tendencies are evident in the assault on science, immigrants, women, the elderly, the poor, people of color, and youth.[20] What too often goes unsaid, particularly with the media's focus on inflammatory rhetoric, is that those who dominate politics and policymaking, whether Democrats or Republicans, do so largely because of their disproportionate control of the nation's income and wealth

Increasingly, it appears that these political elite choose to act in ways that sustain their dominance through the systemic reproduction of an iniquitous social order. In other words, big money and corporate power rule while electoral politics are rigged.[21] The secrecy of the voting booth becomes the ultimate expression of democracy, reducing politics to an individualized purchase—a crude form of economic action and a claim to hermetic power. A politics willing to invest in such ritualistic pageantry only adds to the current dysfunctional nature of our social order while reinforcing a profound failure of political imagination. The issue should no longer be how to work within the current electoral system, but how to dismantle it and construct a new political landscape capable of making a claim on equity, justice, and democracy for all of its inhabitants. Obama's once inspiring call for hope has degenerated into a flight from responsibility. The Obama administration has worked to extend the policies of the George W. Bush administration by legitimating a range of foreign and domestic policies that have shredded civil liberties (going so far as to claim the authority to kill Americans without recourse to due process), expanding the permanent warfare state, and increasing the domestic reach of the punitive surveillance state. And if Romney and his ideological cohorts, now viewed as the most extreme faction of the Republican Party, had come to power, surely the existing totalitarian and anti-democratic tendencies at work in the United States would very likely have been dangerously intensified.

The War against Youth

One measure of the increasing move toward authoritarianism in the United States is evident in that the war against democracy and for neoliberalism is now being directed with special force and intensity against young people, especially low-income youth and poor minorities. We now live during an era in which obscene violence is directed with impunity against young protesters, and youth increasingly serve as targets of myriad forms of public and state-sanctioned punishment.[22] The purpose of this book is to bring into the realm of consciousness the degree to which U.S. public spheres, institutions, and values have been hijacked by a politics of distraction and by violent spectacles whose alleged entertainment value conceals an underlying culture of degradation, state-sponsored repression, and an unrelenting depravity that, while it affects everyone, has the most damaging effects on today's and tomorrow's youth. A catalogue of indicting evidence reveals the depth and breadth of the war being waged against the social state, and particularly against young people. Beyond exposing the moral depravity of a nation that fails to protect its young, such a war speaks to nothing less than a perverse death wish, a barely masked desire for self-annihilation. The willful destruction of an entire generation not only transforms U.S. politics into pathology but is sure to signal the death knell for America's future. How much longer will the American public have to wait before the nightmare comes to an end?

For these dire reasons, the time has come for progressives and others to shift the critique of Obama (or the Romney-Ryan platform for that matter) away from an exclusive focus on the policies and practices of his administration and instead develop a new language for politics—one with a longer historical purview and a deeper understanding of the ominous forces that now threaten any credible notion of the United States as an aspiring democracy. Democracy in this case serves not only as a referent for engaging the gap between the existing reality and the promise of its principles and ideals, but also as a site of ongoing struggle that is never finished or completed.[23]

Toward a New Political Project

The first part of this book examines the trends and forces that are contributing to a widespread shift in American life toward authoritarianism. An awareness of the material and cultural elements that have produced these conditions is important; however, it is simply not enough. The collective response here must be to refuse to enter the current political discourse of compromise and accommodation—to think well beyond the discourse of facile concessions and to conduct struggles on the mutually informed terrains of civic literacy, education, and power. A rejection of traditional forms of political mobilization must be accompanied by a new political discourse, one that uncovers the hidden practices of neoliberal domination while developing rigorous models for critical reflection and fresh forms of intellectual and social engagement. As discussed in the second part of this book, young people across the United States and the globe are certainly doing so, despite the barbaric treatment to which they have been subjected over the past two decades, and particularly since the economic collapse of 2008.

Finding our way to a more humane future demands a new politics, a new set of values, a new understanding of politics, and a renewed sense of the fragile nature of democracy. In part, this means that the militant rhetorical war being waged by social conservatives guided by a distorted notion of religion or austerity under the guise of sound fiscal policy must be understood as a facet of contemporary authoritarianism. These tendencies have a long legacy in American history. But the current historical moment seems at an utter loss to create a massive social movement capable of addressing the totalitarian nature and social costs of a religious and political fundamentalism that is merging with an extreme market fundamentalism. In this case, a fundamentalism whose idea of freedom extends no further than personal financial gain and endless consumption.

Under such circumstances, progressives should focus their energies on working with the Occupy movement and other social movements to develop a new language of radical reform and to create new public spheres that will make possible the modes of critical thought and engaged agency that are the very foundations of a truly participatory and radical democracy. Such a project must work to develop vigorous educational programs, modes of public communication, and communities that promote a culture of deliberation, public debate, and critical exchange across a wide variety of cultural and institutional sites. Ultimately, it must focus on the end goal of generating those formative cultures and public spheres that are the preconditions for political engagement and vital for energizing democratic movements for social change—movements willing to think beyond the limits of a savage global capitalism. Pedagogy in this sense becomes central to any substantive notion of politics and must be viewed as a crucial element of organized resistance and collective struggles.

The deep regressive elements of neoliberalism constitute both a pedagogical practice and a legitimating function for a severely oppressive social order. Pedagogical relations that make the power relations of casino capitalism disappear must be uncovered and challenged. Under such circumstances, politics becomes transformative rather than accommodating and aims at abolishing a capitalist system marked by massive economic, social, and cultural inequalities. A politics that uncovers the harsh realities imposed by casino capitalism should also work toward establishing a society in which matters of justice and freedom are understood as the crucial foundation of a substantive democracy. This book draws hope from youth movements doing this very thing, despite the intensification of emerging social and political forces that are relentlessly damaging young people and any prospects they might have for the future.

Rather than invest in electoral politics, it would be more worthwhile for progressives to develop formative conditions that make a real democracy possible. Central to such a project is the development of a new radical imagination that operates in the service of a broad-based social movement that can move beyond the legacy of a fractured left/ progressive culture and politics in order to address the totality of society's problems. As Angela Davis has suggested, this means engaging "in difficult coalition-building processes, negotiating the recognition for which communities and issues inevitably strive [and coming] together in a unity that is not simplistic and oppressive, but complex and emancipatory, recognizing, in June Jordan's words, that 'we are the ones we have been waiting for.'"[24] Developing a broad-based social movement means finding a common ground upon which challenging diverse forms of oppression, exploitation, and exclusion can become part of a wider effort to create a radical democracy. Language is crucial here, particularly language that addresses what it means to sustain a broad range of commitments to others and build more inclusive notions of community. Appeals to social and economic injustice are important, but do not go far enough. There is a need to invent modes of communication that connect learning to social change and foster modes of critical agency through which people assume responsibility for each other. This is not merely about skill sharing or democratizing education and politics; it is about generating a new vision of democracy and a radical project in which people can recognize themselves, a vision that connects with and speaks to the American public's desires, dreams, and hopes.

Reclaiming a Discourse of Ethics and Social Responsibility

Questions of what it means to be a critical and engaged member of society (and how these are linked to the ways people understand themselves, their relations to others, and their relation to the world) are at the heart of a politics wedded to the primacy of the radical imagination. In part, this necessitates, as media scholar Nick Couldry has argued, reclaiming a discourse of ethics and morality, elaborating a new model of democratic politics, and developing fresh analytical concepts for understanding and engaging the concept of *the social*. The social has to be reconfigured so as to expose and eliminate a market-driven project—or what I refer to as the Big Lie—that individualizes responsibility while also silencing claims made in the name of democracy. Reclaiming a democratic notion of the citizen-subject goes hand-in-hand with inventing a new understanding of social conditions, civic responsibility, and critical citizenship.

Matters of education and *how* the public is educated (what I call public pedagogy) are central to a new understanding of politics. Issues of identity, desire, and agency must be considered as part of an energized struggle to reclaim the promise of a substantive global democracy. This entails teaching people to feel a responsibility toward others and the planet, to think in a critical fashion, and to act in ways that support the public good. In this instance, progressives need to create public spheres of engagement using new technologies and other tools that open up new modes of communication and social relations. These efforts should be situated in a larger project rooted in an understanding that critical education and democracy are the primary and mutually constituting elements of any society that can make a claim to promoting the health, justice, and equality of its citizenry. The radical imagination rejects the notion that a corporate-dominated market society represents the essence of democracy. In doing so, it connects economics to social costs and measures the political and spiritual life of a nation by the degree to which it offers collective security, justice, equality, and hope to existing and future generations. At the same time, it refuses the seductions of the prevailing economic and political system, whether in the form of an appeal to the virtues of the electoral system or the call for acting within the existing framework of reform. Young people have "experienced a lifetime of betrayal" and what they need is more "than protection from uncontrolled market forces."[25] Instead of reformist blabber, what is needed are critical viewpoints, modes of governance, and policymaking that address matters of democracy, public life, equality, and the redistribution of wealth and power. Crucial here is the development of new critical vocabularies, modes of knowledge, theoretical resources, and a far-reaching and visionary political project capable of informing and empowering those who have been reduced to the margins of society, barely surviving, while the upper 1 percent accrues highly disproportionate amounts of wealth, income, and power.

This means that progressives must take a cue from youth protesters the world over and develop new ways to challenge the corporate values that shape American and, increasingly, global politics. It is especially crucial to provide alternative values that challenge market-driven ideologies that equate freedom with radical individualism, privatization, and deregulation, while undermining democratic social bonds, the public good, and the welfare state. Such actions can be further addressed by recruiting young people, teachers, labor activists, religious leaders, and other engaged citizens to become public intellectuals who are willing to use their skills and knowledge to make visible how power works and to address important social and political issues. Of course, the American public needs to do more than talk. It also needs to bring together educators, students, workers, and anyone else interested in real democracy in order to create a social movement—a well-organized movement capable of changing the power relations and vast economic inequalities that have created the conditions for symbolic and systemic violence in American society.

Building New Educational Spaces

Regarding policy interventions, progressives can explore a variety of options to build coalitions with labor unions, environmental organizations, and public servants in order to develop a broad-based alternative party to push for much-needed reforms, including paid family and medical leave, a new equal rights amendment for women, literacy and civic engagement programs, a guaranteed minimum income, ecological reform, free child care, new finance laws for funding public education, the cancellation of higher education debt obligations for middle- and working-class students, health care programs, and a massive jobs program in conjunction with a Marshall Plan–like program to end poverty and inequality in the United States. But, to achieve these goals, progressives will invariably need to take on the role of educational activists. One option would be to create micro-spheres of public education that further modes of critical learning and civic agency, and thus enable young people and others to learn how to govern rather than be governed. This could be accomplished through a network of free educational spaces developed among diverse faith communities and public schools, as well as in secular and religious organizations affiliated with higher educational institutions. These new educational spaces, focused on cultivating both dialogue and action in the public interest, can look to past models in those institutions developed by socialists, labor unions, and civil rights activists in the early twentieth century and later in the 1950s and 60s. Such schools represented oppositional public spheres and functioned as democratic public spheres in the best educational sense and ranged from the early networks of radical Sunday Schools to the later Brookwood Labor College and Highlander Folk School in Tennessee.[26] Stanley Aronowitz rightly insists that the current system "survives on the eclipse of the radical imagination, the absence of a viable political opposition with roots in the general population, and the conformity of its intellectuals who, to a large extent, are subjugated by their secure berths in the academy, less secure private sector corporate jobs, and centrist and center-left media institutions."[27]

From the Four Fundamentalisms to the Suicidal State

At a time when critical thought has been flattened, it becomes imperative to develop a discourse of critique and possibility—one that recognizes that without an informed citizenry, collective struggle, and dynamic social movements, hope for a viable democratic future will slip out of our reach. Threatening the future of not only youth, but any group marginalized by virtue of age, gender, race or class, is a growing democratic deficit among developed countries as the gap widens between the people and institutions elected to govern and the citizenry they represent. Chapter 1 of this book provides the contexts for understanding how democratic decline in America now works in tandem with a national *education deficit*, whereby the critical and civic literacies needed for people to engage as active citizens are undermined by both educational policies and practices in schools and the weakening of the public-political culture in broader society. If left unchecked, then tomorrow's concern will be less a persistent democratic deficit than the rise of a new authoritarianism.[28] Chapter 2 reviews how the forces of authoritarianism have evolved from neoliberal-infused political culture, which is driven to restructure society to empower the wealthy and erode the state's ability to act as a defense on behalf of citizens. This is especially dire for society's most vulnerable, who suffer disproportionately from the set of orthodoxies characterizing the dominant pedagogy of late twentieth-century neoliberal capitalism with respect to market deregulation, extreme patriotic and religious fervor, the instrumentalization of education, and the militarization of the entire society. These four fundamentalisms marshal a set of pernicious forces that fuel inequality, unemployment, cultures of cruelty and violence, a harsh penal system, the suppression of dissent, and a lack of access to education, among other ruinous social and economic conditions.

The permanent state of warfare abroad and at home has resulted in cultures of violence across several public spheres beyond the military. Chapter 3 focuses in more detail on U.S. popular culture and a growing celebration of military-like values, which has led not only to an infusion of militaristic technologies and ways of thinking across society, but also to the militarization of public spaces, such as schools. The normaliza-tion of violence is accomplished through the reproduction of violent pedagogies in contexts that lack (and sometimes actively destroy) the critical apparatuses by which the public becomes sensitized and thus resists the dehumanization, suffering, and social costs entailed by acts of violence. A mass culture of violence leads to the gradual acceptance of violence in everyday life—seen in, for example, grotesque specta-cles such as *The Hunger Games* and the television series *The Following*. Chapter 4 turns to the tragic death of the African American youth Trayvon Martin, and the way media coverage fixated on the "hoodie" and its alleged symbolic power to trigger life-threatening fear and brutal violence supposedly apart from persistent forms of racism. Analysis of the "color-blind" media suggests that mass spectacles along with fan-tasies of post-racialism have diverted public attention away from the hidden modes through which neoliberal racism and social inequal-ity continue to operate in American society, particularly through the criminalization of poor minority youth.

Through the alienation and isolation of increasing numbers of young people, the United States is moving ever closer to self-annihilation. Chapter 5 expands further on the war on youth through connecting it to Paul Virilio's notion of a "suicidal state"—defined as a state that "works to destroy its own defenses against anti-democratic forces."[29] Capitulating to authoritarian tendencies, the government works systematically to disenfranchise its own youth, thus attacking the very elements of a soci-ety that allow it to reproduce itself. In the United States, but increasingly everywhere, youth are subject to social conditions that are based on mistrust and fear; they are isolated by society and considered expend-able or redundant. Chapter 5 also explores how the demonization of young people in the broader culture and neoliberal values rooted in a virulent social Darwinism have now joined forces with increasingly pervasive forms of state-sanctioned cruelty—all of which escalate the violence used against young people and threatens to culminate in an unprecedented and disastrous *global* war on youth.

Pointing to the challenges inherent in opposing the warfare state and its culture of cruelty is important, but mere vilification of these ideologies is not enough. Political and pedagogical interventions that enter the conversation in ways that offer both critique and hope should be central in the struggle to create the conditions for a more critical and engaged citizenry. In chapter 6, educators committed to cultivating students as thoughtful citizens are called upon to engage with broader public discourse over the vital importance of public education, as well as the ongoing challenges besetting it, among which are a host of frightening projects rooted in totalitarian logic. There is an urgent necessity in such dark times for intellectuals and various cultural workers to bring the fruits of their scholarship to bear on the crucial issues of the day. In part, this suggests a pressing need for progressives to oppose the right-wing agenda to privatize (and thus demolish) one of the few remaining spaces where critical thinking can be fostered among all young people regardless of privilege and wealth: the public school system and the system of higher education. Religious fundamentalists, in particular, are attempting to steamroll democracy by limiting people's access to critical education—democracy's strongest pillar. Through appeals to moral superiority and self-interest, proponents of privatization like Paul Ryan, Mitt Romney, and Newt Gingrich work to disarm the citizenry and prevent people from seeing the most pernicious impacts triggered by privatization on educational policy and practices, most notably the expansion of charter schools, the narrowing of the teaching curriculum, the dismantling of financial and other supports for students, and the skyrocketing costs of higher education, much of which the Obama administration opposes. Most alarming is how the far-right arm of the Republican Party is using private religious schools to destroy the democratic edifice built on the separation of church and state, and ultimately to marshal support for a theocracy in the United States.

Since the emergence of the Occupy movement in 2011, the potential for collective resistance has grown exponentially. Chapter 7 encourages critical educators to join with Occupiers and other youth in supporting a collective cultural campaign that links the defense of accessible public and higher education to progressive social movements and independent media sources. What must be resisted are the "disappearing acts" of corporate-funded, anti-public intellectuals who erect walls around knowledge, while simultaneously rendering invisible those disadvantaged populations who are deserving of compassion and social protections. These gated intellectuals, often abetted by the dominant media, use privilege and ideological narrowness to divorce themselves from understanding the systemic elements that contribute to social and economic injustice. Their views reduce citizenship to consumption, support corporate greed and private interests, and fuel hyper-individualized notions of equality and freedom. In contrast, engaged public intellectuals might adopt a "borderless pedagogy" that crosses zones of knowledge control and policing and aims to democratize power and knowledge. These new modes of resistance are necessary because a sustainable democratic future will require more than electoral democracy or democracy in name only. It will require a multitude of public and free access forums along with the broad mobilization of traditional and new educational sites in which public intellectuals can do the work of resistance, engagement, and policymaking to support a democratic politics.

Chronicling how the Occupy Wall Street movement has broadly impacted political discourse, chapter 8 explains in detail why a movement that foregrounds the importance of critical education is especially necessary in the current historical moment. The Occupy movement initiated such a task by challenging the fatalism inherent in the capitalist system and developing a new vision of politics. Through the practical translation of theoretical discourses into action for social change, the hope produced by the Occupy movement extends its life to new movements and causes. In the face of police brutality leveled against peaceful protesters with impunity, generations both young and old have a duty to reverse the pressures of the punishing state and develop social movements that not only restore the principles and practices of democracy but build and sustain institutions and formative cultures that can provide a safe, dignified future to young people everywhere. As neoliberal educational policies organize schools today in alignment with punitive and market cultures, the abilities of educators to carry out pedagogies that will ignite students' social responsibility and political consciousness are being stifled. In this new, corporatized climate, teachers are consigned to the role of technicians and are allowed to do little more than robotically carry out assigned curriculum, teaching-to-the-test mandates, or uphold harsh disciplinary policies. In response to this crisis of pedagogical agency among educators, chapter 9 unravels the current neoliberal attacks being waged on teachers in today's culture of consumerism and violence. Taking up the media's momentary celebration of teachers as protectors of youth after the shootings at Sandy Hook Elementary School in Connecticut in the fall of 2012, this chapter addresses the heightened difficulty teachers face in safeguarding the futures of young people. At this specific historical conjuncture teachers are subject to an onslaught of attacks against their role as public servants and critical intellectuals. In addition, the very concept of educator should be *continually* conceptualized as a defender of youth, rather than being celebrated as such only after this kind of tragedy—a short-lived praise quickly lost in the sea of assaults teachers remain subjected to at the hands of advocates for school privatization and market-based education. Importantly, this chapter calls for educators to fight against this anti-democratic configuration of education by reconceptualizing themselves as engaged citizens and public intellectuals committed to making the pedagogical more political and the political more pedagogical, nurturing the critical and civic capacities of the next generation that will challenge the emergent authoritarianism.

Chapter 10 focuses further on the educational foundations of a truly democratic society and the vital role of critical pedagogy for any democratizing movement. Unfortunately, the growing popularity of neoliberal narratives coincides with a trend of thinking about society through a strictly *economic* lens, and this has produced a generation that views education as a form of technical training whereby a student's skills only matter if they can be commodified and traded in the marketplace. As the reigning market orthodoxy translates all aspects of our personal and social lives into the context of commerce, the mode of critique that searches for the gaps between the sociopolitical configuration of the moment and the ideal of democracy to come is quickly becoming a thing of the past, replaced by a desire not for our collective betterment and the public good, but for private gain of a distinctly self-ish bent. When political engagement disappears, how can a movement toward equality and social justice even begin to emerge? This final chapter explains the crucial responsibility and pivotal role that critical educators as public intellectuals can assume in resisting the neoliberal-ization of society by using new political and pedagogical languages to recontextualize democracy outside of market values, while equipping young people with the critical skills and sense of agency they need to play an active role in struggling for and shaping a genuinely democratic future. Central to addressing the education deficit in America will be a robust, broad-based social movement that prioritizes a defense of public and higher education as the crucibles out of which engaged citizenship and democracy are forged.

As a whole, this book provides a context for understanding the war on youth through an examination of the regressive educational apparatuses and culture of cynicism that are now dominating the United States as well as Canada, all of which indicate how both societies are increasingly infused with violence. These real and symbolic forms of violence are promoted by a range of intersecting forces, including neoliberal policymaking, militarization, religious fanaticism, corporate elitism, and persistent racism. Despite widespread calls for electoral reform, the United States, in particular, has arrived at such a crisis in governance that it cannot possibly begin to engage prevailing issues through political reform alone. Education—and critical education in particular—must be taken seriously as a matter of primary importance among all who believe in the promise of U.S. democracy. The education deficit will require wholesale cultural and policy change if the United States is going to redress its devastating impact across all levels of society, particularly on young people. But with the emergence of Occupy Wall Street and other social movements, there *is* hope on the horizon. Indeed, abandoned by an increasingly punitive state and a generation of adults, youth are taking matters into their own hands and are asserting the power of democratic expression and collective struggle in a society that has all but relinquished its claim to equity, justice, social responsibility, and public life.

1.

Beyond the Politics of the Big Lie: The Education Deficit and the New Authoritarianism

Nothing in the world is more dangerous than sincere
ignorance and conscientious stupidity.
—MARTIN LUTHER KING, JR.

THE AMERICAN PUBLIC is suffering from an education deficit. By this I mean it exhibits a growing inability to think critically, question authority, be reflective, weigh evidence, discriminate between reasoned arguments and opinions, listen across differences, and engage the mutually informing relationship between private problems and broader public issues. This growing political and cultural illiteracy is not merely a problem of the individual, which points to simple ignorance. It is a collective and social problem that goes to the heart of the increasing attack on democratic public spheres and supportive public institutions that promote analytical capacities, thoughtful exchange, and a willingness to view knowledge as a resource for informed modes of individual and social agency. One of the major consequences of the current education deficit and the pervasive culture of illiteracy that sustains it is what I call the ideology of the big lie—which propagates the myth that the free market system is the only mechanism to ensure human freedom and safeguard democracy.

The education deficit, along with declining levels of civic literacy, is also part of the American public's collective refusal to know—a focused resistance to deal with knowledge that challenges common sense or to think reflectively about facts and truths that are unsettling in terms of how they disturb some of our most cherished beliefs. Such beliefs are firmly embedded in the national psyche and include, among others: denouncing the sins of big government, legitimating existing levels of economic insecurity, accepting social inequality as part of the natural order, and embracing "minimal government intervention in the field of welfare legislation."[1] The decline of civility and civic literacy in American society is a political dilemma, the social production of which is traceable to a broader constellation of forces deeply rooted in the shifting nature of education and the varied cultural apparatuses that produce it, extending from new digital technologies and online journals to the mainstream media of newspapers, magazines, and television. Politics is now held hostage to what the late Raymond Williams called the "force of permanent education," a kind of public pedagogy spread through a plethora of teaching machines that are shaping how our most powerful ideas are formed.[2] For Williams, the concept of "permanent education" was a central political insight:

> What it valuably stresses is the educational force of our whole social and cultural experience. It is therefore concerned not only with continuing education, of a formal or informal kind, but with what the whole environment, its institutions and relationships, actively and profoundly teaches. . . . [Permanent education also refers to] the field in which our ideas of the world, of ourselves and of our possibilities, are most widely and often most powerfully formed and disseminated. To work for the recovery of control in this field is then, under any pressures, a priority. For who can

doubt, looking at television or newspapers, or reading the women's magazines, that here, centrally, is *teaching*, and teaching financed and distributed in a much larger way than is formal education.[3]

Williams's insight about the relationship between education and politics is more important today than it was in the 1960s, when he developed the idea. The educational force of the wider culture is now one of the primary, if not most powerful, determinants of what counts as knowledge, agency, politics, and democracy itself. Diverse modes of communication are now produced through a range of cultural and pedagogical technologies and distributed in a vast range of new sites extending from computer screens and iPads to mobile phones. The machinery of permanent education and the public pedagogical relationships these create have become the main framing mechanisms in determining what information gets included, who speaks, what stories are told, what representations translate into reality, and what is considered normal or subversive. The cultural apparatuses of popular education and public pedagogy play a powerful role in framing how issues are perceived, what values and social relations matter, and whether any small ruptures will be allowed to unsettle the circles of certainty that now reign as common sense. But education is never far from the reach of power and ideology. As the major cultural apparatuses and technologies of public pedagogy are concentrated in a few hands, the educational force of the culture becomes a powerful ideological tool for legitimating market-driven values and social relations, based on omissions, deceptions, lies, misrepresentations, and falsehoods benefiting the apostles of a range of economic, educational, and religious fundamentalisms.

For the first time in modern history, centralized commercial institutions that extend from traditional broadcast culture to the new interactive screen cultures—rather than parents, churches, or schools—tell most of the stories that shape the lives of the American public. This is no small matter, since the stories a society tells about its history, civic life, social relations, education, children, freedom, and human imagination are a measure of how it values itself, the ideals of democracy, and its future. Most of the stories now told to the American public are about the necessity of neoliberal capitalism, permanent war, and the virtues of a never-ending culture of fear. The domestic front revels in the welcome death of the social state, the necessary all-embracing reach of the market to determine every aspect of our lives, the reduction of freedom to the freedom to consume, placing social relations under the rule of commodities and finance capital, and the notion that everyone is ultimately responsible for their own fate in a world that now resembles a shark tank. The freedom to shop has become the major obligation of citizenship, as George W. Bush reminded the nation after the tragic events of 9/11. Individuals are relentlessly told by advertisers to develop a brand, as if they were just another commodity. We are also constantly reminded by reality TV that life is primarily a theater of cruelty and that only one person can be left on the island. Moreover, illiteracy finds its ultimate legitimation in making role models out of celebrities, encouraging a growing public fondness for ignorance and self-indulgence.

Democracies need informed citizens to make them work, and can only survive amid a formative culture that produces individuals willing to think critically, imagine otherwise, and act responsibly. America seems to have moved away from that possibility, that willingness to think through and beyond the systemic production of the given, the pull of conformity, the comforting assurance of certainty, and the painless retreat into a world of common sense. The time-honored concepts of literacy and critical thinking are under assault by those on the right who view education at best as a profit-making and training organization and at worst as a disciplinary apparatus and object of repression. For instance, in 2006 members of the Florida state legislature outlawed historical interpretation in public schools, arguing that American history must be taught as a series of facts, rather than as a matter of interpretation, reasoned debate, and accumulation of evidence.[4] Of course, what is really being taught is that critical thinking has no place in the classroom. It gets worse. In 2012, the Texas Republican Party included in their platform a ban on what they termed "higher-order thinking skills" and "critical thinking skills."[5] In addition, a number of states have introduced legislation that calls for the teaching of climate change denial in the public schools under the guise of "balanced" teaching.[6]

Hannah Arendt understood the danger of such a state of ignorance, which she famously called the "banality of evil" and described as a "curiously quite authentic inability to think."[7] For Arendt, this was more than mere stupidity, it was a mode of manufactured thoughtlessness that pointed to the disappearance of politics, constituting one of the most serious threats facing democracy. That threat is no longer merely a despairing element of philosophical reflection—it has become the new reality in American life. The political, economic, and social coordinates of authoritarianism are all around us, and, through the educational force of the broader culture, they are becoming more normalized and more dangerous.

There is little distance between what I call an education deficit and the reigning market authoritarianism, with its claim to be both synonymous with democracy and unquestionable in its assumptions and policies. The education deficit, a hallmark achievement of neoliberal capitalism, has produced a version of authoritarianism with a soft edge, a kind of popular authoritarianism that spreads its values through gaming, reality TV, celebrity culture, TV news, talk radio, and a host of other media outlets aggressively engaged in producing subjects, desires, and dreams that reflect a world order dominated by corporations and the alleged "free markets." This is a world that only values narrow, selfish interests; isolated, competitive individuals; finance capital; the reign of commodities; and the alleged "natural" laws of free-market fundamentalism. Freedom in this neoliberal worldview is about the freedom to choose, mainly understood as an abstract market concept removed from matters of power, politics, and social provisions. This message permeates American society and can be seen in the ongoing attempts to define public education as an individual right rather than a public good. The normalizing, if not normative legitimation of neoliberal values of competition, egoism, narrow self-interest, and materialism are pervasive in mainstream television shows such as *American Idol, Real Housewives, Damages, Revenge,* and *House of Cards,* as well as in a plethora of Hollywood films that extend from *American Psycho* to *Up in the Air.*

Using Isaiah Berlin's terminology, freedom in market-driven societies becomes a negative force, largely manifested as freedom from the state. This translates into a highly depoliticized notion of freedom in that it produces "a weakening of democratic pressures, a growing inability to act politically, a massive exit from politics and from responsible citizenship."[8] The only element of positive freedom in the neoliberal ideology is the right to consume. There is no talk of freedom as the right to challenge authority, to refuse to conform, and to dissent. This type of market-driven freedom appeals to formal political and personal freedoms largely as a type of freedom from government interference. The neoliberal conception of freedom focuses on individual initiatives and consumer skills, and in doing so diminishes any viable notion of citizen skills. It says nothing about the freedom of individual and collective action that comes with social rights—that is, a vigorous set of state-sponsored social protections and collective insurance policies "that include the right not only to biological survival but also to social respect and human dignity."[9]

Turbo capitalism rejects the merging of personal, social, and political freedoms. By doing so, it rejects creating the conditions enabled by a robust social state that guarantees free health care, free education, and a decent social wage, as well as housing, food, and other basic necessities for all members of society to live free from material deprivations that make political and personal freedoms dysfunctional. There is more at issue here than a mode of neoliberalism that accelerates the impoverishment of human agency and experience, while it strips freedom and democracy to a thin, if not flattened, conception of consumerism. There is also the emergence of a new mode of authoritarianism in which "the image of progress seems to have moved from the discourse of shared improvement to that of individual survival."[10]

Turbo capitalism with its crushing cultural apparatuses of legitimation does more than destroy the public good and deny too many people the most basic social rights and freedoms; it empties democracy of any substance and renders authoritarian politics and culture an acceptable state of affairs. As the boundaries between markets and democratic values collapse, civil life becomes warlike and the advocates of market fundamentalism rail against state protections as they offer an unbridled confirmation of the market as a template for all social relations.

Notwithstanding the appeal to formalistic election rituals, democracy as a substantive mode of public address and politics is all but dead in the United States. The forces of authoritarianism are on the march, and they seem at this point to be gaining power politically, economically, and educationally. Politicians at every level of government are in collusion with corporate power, many of them bought by industry lobbyists. This despicable state of affairs was particularly evident in the 2010 elections. Commenting on the colonization of politics by big money in that election, Charles Pierce captures the power dynamic and ideological relations that were in effect then and have intensified since:

> In 2010, in addition to handing the House of Representatives over to a pack of nihilistic vandals, the Koch Brothers and the rest of the sugar daddies of the Right poured millions into various state campaigns. This produced a crop of governors and state legislators wholly owned and operated by those corporate interests and utterly unmoored from the constituencies they were elected to serve. In turn, these folks enacted various policies, and produced various laws, guaranteed to do nothing except reinforce the power of the people who put them in office.[11]

More recently, the *New York Times* reported that soon after President Obama took office, "he cut a closed-door deal with the powerful pharmaceutical lobby [abandoning] his support for the reimportation of prescription medicines at lower prices."[12] For the *Times*, this backdoor deal signified "to some disillusioned liberal supporters a loss of innocence, or perhaps even the triumph of cynicism."[13] In actuality, it signified a powerful new mode of capitalism that not only controls the commanding heights of the economy but now replaces political sovereignty with an aggressive form of corporate governance. The state and elite market forces, perhaps inseparable before, have become today both inseparable and powerfully aligned.

From Reagan's assault on the values of the welfare state to Obama's bailout of the mega-banks and the refusal to end the Bush tax cuts, corporate sovereignty as the preeminent mode of U.S. politics is hard to miss. And the surrender of politics to corporate rule and an amalgam of anti-democratic forces is not a one-party affair. As Bill Moyers and Michael Winship have argued, "Since 1979, 377 members of the *Forbes 400* list of richest Americans have given almost half a billion dollars to candidates of both parties, most of it in the last decade. The median contribution was $355,100 each."[14]

As is well known, President Clinton implemented deregulation policies that led directly to the economic crisis of 2008, at the same time enacting welfare reforms that turned a war on poverty into a war on the poor. In fact, the most radical economic measures that Clinton undertook "related to further deregulation of the economy [amounting to] some of the most comprehensive deregulatory reforms of the twentieth century."[15] Similarly, the Bush tax cuts for the wealthy not only increased the power of mega-corporations and financial services to influence policy for the benefit of Wall Street titans and the rich more generally, but also largely punished the middle class and the poor. The *Citizens United* Supreme Court ruling made especially visible the hidden operations behind contemporary politics: big money translates into political power. The economist Joseph Stiglitz is correct in insisting that "we've moved from a democracy, which is supposed to be based on one person, one vote, to something much more akin to one dollar, one vote. When you have that kind of democracy, it's not going to address the real needs of the 99%."[16] Stiglitz's point is right in one sense, though the current political system has nothing substantively to do with democracy and everything to do with a new form of authoritarianism shaped by the converging interests of the financial elite, religious fundamentalists, anti-public intellectuals, and corporate political power brokers.

This new mode of authoritarian governance is distinct from the fascism that emerged in Germany and Italy in the mid-part of the twentieth century. As Sheldon Wolin has pointed out, big business in this new mode of authoritarianism is not subordinated to a political regime and the forces of state sovereignty, but now replaces political sovereignty with corporate rule. In addition, the new authoritarianism does not strive "to give the masses a sense of collective power and strength, [but] promotes a sense of weakness, of collective futility [through] a pervasive atmosphere of fear abetted by a corporate economy of ruthless downsizing, withdrawal or reduction of pension and health benefits; a corporate political system that relentlessly threatens to privatize Social Security and the modest health benefits available, especially to the poor."[17] According to Wolin, all the elements are in place today for a contemporary form of authoritarianism, which he calls "inverted totalitarianism."

> Thus the elements are in place: a weak legislative body, a legal system that is both compliant and repressive, a party system in which one party, whether in opposition or in the majority, is bent upon reconstituting the existing system so as to permanently favor a ruling class of the wealthy, the well connected and the corporate, while leaving the poorer citizens with a sense of helplessness and political despair, and, at the same time, keeping the middle classes dangling between fear of unemployment and expectations of fantastic rewards once the new economy recovers. That scheme is abetted by a sycophantic and increasingly concentrated media; by the integration of universities with their corporate benefactors; by a propaganda machine institutionalized in well-funded think tanks and conservative foundations; by the increasingly closer cooperation between local police and national law enforcement agencies aimed at identifying terrorists, suspicious aliens, and domestic dissidents.[18]

The democratic deficit is not, as many commentators have argued, reducible to the growing (and unparalleled) inequality gap in the United States, pervasive lending fraud, favorable tax treatment for the wealthy, or the lack of adequate regulation of the financial sector. These are important issues, but they are more symptomatic than causal in relation to the democratic decline and rise of an uncivil culture in America. The democratic deficit is closely related, however, to an unprecedented deficit in critical education. The power of finance capital in recent years has not only targeted the realm of official politics but also directed its attention toward a range of educational apparatuses—a vast and complex ideological ecosystem that reproduces itself through nuance, distraction, innuendo, myths, lies, and misrepresentations. This media ecosystem not only changes our sense of time, space, and information, it also redefines the very meaning of the social, and this is far from a democratic process, especially as the architecture of the Internet and other media platforms is largely in the hands of private interests.[19] The educational pipelines for corporate messages and ideology are everywhere and for the last twenty-five years have successfully drowned out any serious criticism and challenge to market fundamentalism.[20]

The current corrupt and dysfunctional state of American politics is about a growing authoritarianism tied to economic, political, and cultural formations that have hijacked democracy and put in place structural and ideological forces that constitute a new regime of politics, not simply a series of bad policies. The solution in this case does not lie in promoting piecemeal reforms, such as a greater redistribution of wealth and income, but in dismantling all the institutional, ideological, and social formations that make gratuitous inequality and other antidemocratic forces possible at all. Even the concept of reform has been stripped of its democratic possibilities and has become a euphemism to "cover up the harsh realities of draconian cutbacks in wages, salaries, pensions and public welfare and the sharp increases in regressive taxes."[21]

Instead of reversing progressive changes made by workers, women, young people, and others, the American public needs a new understanding of what it would mean to advance the ideological and material relations of a real democracy, while removing American society from the grip of "an authoritarian political culture."[22] This will require new conceptions of politics, social responsibility, power, civic courage, civil society, and democracy itself. If we do not safeguard the remaining public spaces that provide individuals and social movements with new ways to think about and participate in politics, then authoritarianism will solidify its hold on the American public. In doing so, it will create a culture that criminalizes dissent, and those who suffer under anti-democratic ideologies and policies will be both blamed for the current economic crisis and punished by ruling elites.

What is crucial to grasp at the current historical moment is that the fate of democracy is inextricably linked to a profound crisis of contemporary knowledge, characterized by its increasing commodification, fragmentation, privatization, and its turn toward racist and jingoistic conceits. As knowledge becomes abstracted from the rigors of civic culture and is reduced to questions of style, ritual, and image, it undermines the political, ethical, and governing conditions for individuals to construct those viable public spheres necessary for debate, collective action, and solving urgent social problems. As public spheres are privatized, commodified, and turned over to the crushing forces of turbo capitalism, the opportunities for openness, inclusiveness, and dialogue that nurture the very idea and possibility of a discourse about democracy cease to exist.

The lesson to be learned in this instance is that political agency involves learning how to deliberate, make judgments, and exercise choices, particularly as the latter are brought to bear on critical activities that offer the possibility of change. Civic education as it is experienced and produced throughout an ever-diminishing number of institutions provides individuals with opportunities to see themselves as capable of doing more than the existing configurations of power in any given society would wish to admit. And it is precisely this notion of civic agency and critical education that has been under aggressive assault within the new and harsh corporate order of casino capitalism. For example, billionaires such as Dick and Betsy DeVos, Bill Gates, and others are using their wealth to enact voucher programs and charter schools in a number of cities across the United States.[23] For these educational (mis) reformers, public values, civic agency, and critical thinking are viewed as antithetical to school reform, if not dangerous.[24] Market values dominate their talk about educational reform. There is no mention in this discourse about the connection between education and democracy. Public and higher education are not seen as a public good and consumer choice is not viewed as the most important determinant in deciding what is taught in the classroom. Intellectual activity has little to do with critical thinking and expanding the imagination. Instead, high-stakes testing, memorization, empirical accountability, choice, and curricula standardization provide the foundation for what it means to educate young people.[25]

Anti-Public Intellectuals and the Conservative Reeducation Machine

The conservative takeover of public pedagogy has a long history, extending from the work of the "Chicago Boys" at the University of Chicago to the various conservative think tanks that emerged after the publication of the "Powell Memo" in the early 1970s.[26] The Powell Memo was particiularly significant in the development of what can be called a conservative public pedagogy machine. Authored by Lewis F. Powell, who would later be appointed as a member of the Supreme Court of the United States, it was designed to develop a broad-based right-wing strategy not only to counter dissent but also to develop a material and ideological infrastructure with the capability to transform the American public consciousness through a conservative pedagogical commitment to reproduce the knowledge, values, ideology, and social relations of the corporate state. Central to such efforts was Powell's insistence that conservatives nourish a new generation of scholars who would inhabit the university and function as public intellectuals actively shaping the direction of policy issues. He also advocated the creation of a conservative speaker's bureau, staffed by scholars capable of evaluating "textbooks, especially in economics, political science and sociology."[27] In addition, he advocated organizing a corps of conservative public intellectuals who would monitor the dominant media, publish their own scholarly journals, books, and pamphlets, and invest in advertising campaigns to enlighten the American people on conservative issues and policies.

Political scientist Frances Fox Piven rightly argues: "We've been at war for decades now—not just in Afghanistan or Iraq, but right here at home. Domestically, it's been a war against the poor [and as] devastating as it has been, the war against the poor has gone largely unnoticed until now."[28] This war at home now includes more than attacks on the poor, as campaigns are increasingly waged against the rights of women, students, workers, people of color, and immigrants, especially Latino Americans. As the social state collapses, the punishing state expands its power and targets larger portions of the population. The war in Afghanistan is now mimicked in the war waged on peaceful student protesters at home. It is evident in the environmental racism that produces massive health problems for African Americans. The domestic war is even waged on elementary-school children, who now live in fear of the police handcuffing them in their classrooms and incarcerating them as if they were adult criminals.[29] This issue was brought home in a shocking photograph published by the *New York Post* in which a seven-year-old was shown handcuffed to a rail in a Bronx police station. He apparently stepped far outside of the bounds of the law by getting into a playground fight over $5.00.[30] The war at home is also being waged on workers and public servants such as teachers and firefighters by taking away their pensions, bargaining rights, and dignity. The spirit of militarism is also evident in the war waged on the welfare state and any form of social protection that benefits the poor, disabled, sick, elderly, and other groups now considered disposable, including children.

The soft side of authoritarianism in the United States does not need to put soldiers in the streets, though it certainly follows that script. As it expands its control over the commanding institutions of government, the armed forces, and civil society in general, it hires anti-public intellectuals and academics to provide ideological support for its gated communities, institutions, and modes of education. As Yasha Levine points out, it puts thousands of dollars in the hands of corporate shills such as Malcolm Gladwell, who has become a "one-man branding and distribution pipeline for valuable corporate messages, constructed on the public's gullibility in trusting his probity and intellectual honesty."[31] Gladwell (who is certainly not alone) functions as a bought-and-paid-for mouthpiece for "Big Tobacco, Pharma, and defend[s] Enron-style financial fraud . . . earning hundreds of thousands of dollars as a corporate speaker, sometimes from the same companies and industries that he covers as a journalist."[32]

Corporate power uses these "pay-to-play" academics, anti-public intellectuals, the mainstream media, and other educational apparatuses to discredit the very people it simultaneously oppresses, while waging an overarching war on all things public. As Charles Ferguson has noted, an entire industry has been created that enables the "sale of academic expertise for the purpose of influencing government policy, the courts, and public opinion, [and] is now a multibillion-dollar business."[33] It gets worse, in that "academic, legal, regulatory, and policy consulting in economics, finance, and regulation is dominated by a half-dozen consulting firms, several speakers' bureaus, and various industry lobbying groups that maintain large networks of academics for hire specifically for the purpose of advocating industry interests in policy and regulatory debates."[34]

Such anti-public intellectuals create what William Black has called a "criminogenic environment" that spreads disease and fraud in the interest of bolstering the interests, profits, and values of the super-wealthy.[35] There is more at work here than carpet-bombing the culture with lies, deceptions, and euphemisms. Language in this case does more than obfuscate or promote propaganda. It creates framing mechanisms, cultural ecosystems, and cultures of cruelty, while closing down spaces for dialogue, critique, and thoughtfulness. At its worst, it engages in the dual processes of demonization and distraction. The rhetoric of demonization takes many forms, for example, calling firefighters, teachers, and other public servants greedy because they want to hold on to their paltry benefits. It labels students as irresponsible because of the large debts they are forced to incur as states cut back funding to higher education (this too is part of a broader effort by conservatives to hollow out the social state). Poor people are insulted and humiliated because they are forced to live on food stamps, lack decent health care, and collect unemployment benefits because there are no decent jobs available. Poor minorities are now subject to overt racism in the right-wing media and outright violence in the larger society.

Anti-public intellectuals rail against public goods and public values; they undermine collective bonds and view social responsibility as a pathology, while touting the virtues of a survival-of-the-fittest notion of individual responsibility. Fox News and its embarrassingly blowhard pundits tell the American people that Governor Scott Walker's victory over Tom Barrett in the Wisconsin recall election was a fatal blow against unions (which often get co-opted by the same values driving the apostles for casino capitalism), while in reality "his win signals less a loss for the unions than a loss for our democracy in this post–Citizens United era, when elections can be bought with the help of a few billionaires."[36] How else to explain that Tea Party favorite Walker raised over $30.5 million during the election—more than seven times Barrett's reported $3.9 million—largely from thirteen out-of-state billionaires?[37] This was corporate money enlisted for use in a pedagogical blitz designed to carpet-bomb voters with the rhetoric of distraction and incivility.

The same pundits who rail against the country's economic deficit fail to connect it to the generous tax cuts they espouse for corporations and the financial institutions and services that take financial risks and sometimes generate capital but more often produce debts and instability that only serve to deepen the national economic crisis. Nor do they connect the U.S. recession and global economic crisis to the criminal activities enabled by an unregulated financial system marked by massive lending fraud, high-risk speculation, a corrupt credit system, and pervasive moral and economic dishonesty. The spokespersons for the ultra-rich publish books arguing that we need even more inequality because it benefits not only the wealthy, but everyone else.[38] This is a form of authoritarian delusion that appears to meet the clinical threshold for being labeled psychopathic given its proponents' extreme investment in being "indifferent to others, incapable of guilt, [and] exclusively devoted to their own interests."[39] Nothing is said in this pro-market narrative about the massive human suffering caused by a growing inequality in which society's resources are squandered at the top, while salaries for the middle and working classes stagnate, consumption dries up, social costs are ignored, young people are locked out of jobs and any possibility of social mobility, and the state reconfigures its power to punish rather than protect the vast majority of its citizens.

The moral coma that appears characteristic of the elite has attracted the attention of scientists, whose studies recently reported that "members of the upper class are more likely to behave unethically, to lie during negotiations, to drive illegally and to cheat when competing for a prize."[40] But there is more at stake here than the psychological state of those who inhabit the boardrooms of Wall Street. We must also consider the catastrophic effects produced by the elites' values and policies. In fact, Joseph Stiglitz has argued that "most Americans today are worse off than they were fifteen years ago. A full-time worker in the U.S. is worse off today then he or she was 44 years ago. That is astounding—half a century of stagnation. The economic system is not delivering. It does not matter whether a few people at the top benefited tremendously—when the majority of citizens are not better off, the economic system is not working."[41] The economic system may not be working for most people, though it is working very well for those who control it, and the ideological rationales used to justify its current course appear immensely successful, managing as they do to portray a market fundamentalism that transforms democracy into its opposite— a form of authoritarianism with a soft edge—as utterly benign, if not also beneficial, to society at large.

Democratic Decline and the Politics of Distraction

Democracy withers, public spheres disappear, and the forces of authoritarianism grow when a family, such as the Waltons of Wal-Mart fame, is allowed "to amass a combined wealth of some $90 billion, which is equivalent to the wealth of the entire bottom 30 percent of U.S. society."[42] Such enormous amounts of wealth translate into equally vast amounts of power, as is evident in the current attempts of a few billionaires to literally buy local, state, and federal elections. Moreover, a concentration of wealth deepens the economic divide among classes, rendering more and more individuals incapable of the most basic opportunities to move out of poverty and despair. This is especially true in light of a recent survey indicating that "nearly half of all Americans lack economic security, meaning they live above the federal poverty threshold but still do not have enough money to cover housing, food, health care and other basic expenses. . . . Forty-five percent of U.S. residents live in households that struggle to make ends meet. That breaks down to 39 percent of all adults and 55 percent of all children."[43] The consequential impacts on civic engagement are more difficult to enumerate, but it does not require much imagination to think about how democracy might flourish if access to health care, education, employment, and other public benefits was ensured equally throughout a society, and not restricted to the rich and wealthy alone. And yet, as power and wealth accrue to the upper 1 percent, the American public is constantly told that the poor, the unions, feminists, critical intellectuals, and public servants are waging class warfare to the detriment of civility and democracy.

The late Tony Judt stated that he was less concerned about the slide of American democracy into something like authoritarianism than American society moving toward something he viewed as even more corrosive: "a loss of conviction, a loss of faith in the culture of democracy, a sense of skepticism and withdrawal" that diminishes the capacity of a democratic formative culture to resist and transform those anti-democratic ideologies that benefit only the mega-corporations, the ultra-wealthy, and ideological fundamentalists.[44] Governance has turned into a legitimation for enriching the bankers, hedge fund managers, and executive members of the financial service industries. Americans now live in a society in which only the thinnest conception of democracy frames what it means to be a citizen—one that equates the obligations of citizenship with consumerism and democratic rights with alleged consumer freedoms. Anti-democratic forms of power do not stand alone as a mode of force or the force of acting on others; they are also deeply aligned with the cultural apparatuses of persuasion, extending their reach through social and digital media, sophisticated technologies, the rise of corporate intellectuals, and a university system that now produces and sanctions intellectuals aligned with private interests—all of which, as Randy Martin, a professor at NYU, points out, can be identified with a form of casino capitalism that is about "permanent vigilance, activity, and intervention."[45]

Indeed, many institutions that provide formal education in the United States have become co-conspirators in a savage casino capitalism that promotes the narrow world of commodity worship, celebrity culture, bare-knuckle competition, and a "war of all against all" mentality that destroys any viable notion of the common good and political, social, and economic rights. University presidents now make huge salaries sitting on corporate boards, while faculty sell their knowledge to the highest corporate bidder and, in doing so, turn universities into legitimation centers for free-market fundamentalism.[46] Of course, such academics also move from the boardrooms of major corporations to talk shows and op-ed pages of major newspapers, offering commentary in journals and other modes of print and screen culture. They are the new traveling intellectuals of neoliberalism, doing everything they can to make the ruthless workings of power invisible, to shift the blame for society's failures onto the very people who are its victims, and to expand the institutions and culture of anti-intellectualism and distraction into every aspect of American life.

Across all levels, politics in the United States now suffers from an education deficit that enables a pedagogy of distraction to dictate, with little accountability, how crucial social problems and issues are named, discussed, and acted upon. The conservative reeducation machine appears shameless in its production of lies, which include insane assertions such as Obama's health care legislation would create "death panels"; liberals are waging a war on Christmas; Obama is a socialist trying to nationalize industries; the Founding Fathers tried to end slavery; and Obama is a Muslim sympathizer and not a U.S. citizen. Other misrepresentations and distortions include the denial of global warming; the government cannot create jobs; cuts in wages and benefits create jobs; Obama has created massive deficits; Obama wants to raise the taxes of working and middle-class people; Obama is constantly "apologizing" for America; and the assertion that Darwinian evolution is a myth.[47] Republican presidential candidate Mitt Romney continued spinning this spiderweb of lies unapologetically, even when members of his own party pointed out the inconsistencies in his claims. For instance, he claimed that "Obamacare increases the deficit," [48] argued that Obama has "increased the national debt more than all other presidents combined," and insisted that Obama has lied about "his record on gay rights."[49] Diane Ravitch rightly argued that in making a case for vouchers Romney made false claims about the success of the Washington, D.C., voucher program.[50]

Robert Reich claims he is "struck by the baldness of Romney's repetitive lies about Obama—that Obama ended the work requirement under welfare . . . or that Obama's Affordable Care Act cuts $716 billion from Medicare benefits."[51] Reich argues that he "cannot recall a presidential candidate lying with such audacity, over and over again."[52] But he goes further and moves from an attack on Romney's character to exposing the power relations behind a massively financed public relations "lying machine" that is heavily bankrolled by at least thirty-three billionaires wedded to the dark ethic and politics of an unchecked model of casino capitalism.[53]

The politics of distraction should not be reduced merely to a rhetorical ploy used by the wealthy and influential to promote their own interests and power. It is a form of market-driven politics, in which the educational force of the broader culture is used to create individuals who lack the knowledge, critical skills, and discriminatory judgment to question the rule of neoliberalism and the values, social practices, and power formations it legitimates. Politics and education have mutually informed each other as pedagogical sites proliferate and circulate throughout the cultural landscape.[54] But today distraction is the primary element used to suppress democratically purposeful education, pushing critical thought to the margins of society. As a register of power, distraction becomes central to a pedagogical landscape inhabited by rich conservative foundations, an army of well-funded anti-public intellectuals from both major parties, a growing number of amply funded conservative campus organizations, increasing numbers of academics who hock their services to corporations and the military-industrial complex, and others who promote the neoliberal ideology. Academics who make a claim to producing knowledge and truth in the public interest are increasingly being replaced by academics for hire who move effortlessly between industry, government, and academia.

Extreme power is now showcased through the mechanisms of ever proliferating cultural/educational apparatuses and the anti-public intellectuals who support them and are rewarded by the elites who finance such apparatuses. The war at home is made currently visible in the show of force aimed at civilian populations, including students, workers, the elderly, immigrants, and others considered disposable or a threat to the new authoritarianism. Its most powerful allies appear to be the intellectuals, institutions, cultural apparatuses, and new media technologies that constitute the sites of public pedagogy that produce the formative culture necessary for authoritarianism to thrive.

Although a change in consciousness does not guarantee a change in either one's politics or society, it is a crucial precondition for connecting what it means to think otherwise about conditions that make it possible to act otherwise. The education deficit must be seen as intertwined with a political deficit, serving to make many oppressed individuals complicit with oppressive ideologies. As the late Cornelius Castoriadis made clear, democracy requires "critical thinkers capable of putting existing institutions into question . . . while simultaneously creating the conditions for individual and social autonomy."[55] Nothing will change politically or economically until new and emerging social movements take seriously the need to develop a language of radical reform and create new public spheres that support the knowledge, skills, and critical thought that are necessary features of a democratic formative culture.

Getting beyond the big lie as a precondition for critical thought, civic engagement, and a more realized democracy will mean more than correcting distortions, misrepresentations, and falsehoods produced by politicians, media's talking heads, and anti-public intellectuals. It will also require addressing how new sites of pedagogy have become central to any viable notion of agency, politics, and democracy itself. This is not a matter of elevating cultural politics over material relations of power as much as it is a rethinking of how power deploys culture and how culture as a mode of education positions power.

James Baldwin, the legendary African American writer and civil rights activist, argued that the big lie points to a crisis of American identity and politics and is symptomatic of "a backward society" that has descended into madness, "especially when one is forced to lie about [an] aspect of anybody's history, [because you then] must lie about it all."[56] He goes on to argue that "one of the paradoxes of education [is] that precisely at the point when you begin to develop a conscience, you must find yourself at war with your society. It is your responsibility to change society if you think of yourself as an educated person."[57] What Baldwin recognizes is that learning has the possibility to trigger a critical engagement with oneself, others, and the larger society—education becomes in this instance more than a method or tool for domination but a politics, a fulcrum for democratic social change. Tragically, in our current climate, "learning" merely contributes to a vast reserve of manipulation and self-inflicted ignorance. Our education deficit is neither reducible to the failure of particular types of teaching nor the descent into madness by the spokespersons for the new authoritarianism. Rather, it is about how matters of knowledge, values, and ideology can be struggled over as issues of power and politics. Surviving the current education deficit will depend on progressives using history, memory, and knowledge not only to reconnect to the everyday needs of ordinary people, but also to jump-start social movements by making education central to organized politics and the quest for a radical democracy.

2.

The Scorched-Earth Politics of America's Four Fundamentalisms

AMERICANS SEEM CONFIDENT in the mythical notion that the United States is a free nation dedicated to reproducing the principles of equality, justice, and democracy. What has been ignored in this delusional view is the growing rise of an expanded national security state since 2001,[1] and an attack on individual rights that suggests the United States has more in common with authoritarian regimes like China and Iran "than anyone may like to admit."[2] I want to address this seemingly untenable notion that the United States has become a breeding ground for authoritarianism by focusing on four fundamentalisms: market fundamentalism, religious fundamentalism, educational fundamentalism, and military fundamentalism. This is far from a detailed and exhaustive list, but it does raise serious questions about how the claim to democracy in the United States has been severely damaged, if not made impossible.

The broader contours of the attack on democratic freedoms have become obvious in recent years. Whereas the Bush administration engaged in torture, shamelessly violated civil liberties, and put a host of Christian extremists in high-ranking governmental positions, the Obama administration has not only continued many of these policies but has further institutionalized them.[3] As Glenn Greenwald reminds us, Obama has continued the Bush-Cheney terrorism and civil liberties policies, further undermining constitutional rights by promoting indefinite detention, expanding the massive surveillance of American citizens, weakening the rights of *habeas corpus* for prisoners in Afghanistan, extending government power through the state secrets privilege, asserting the right to target American citizens for assassination, and waging war on whistle-blowers.[4] More specifically, there are the ongoing revelations about the Obama administration's decision under the National Defense Authorization Act to allow American citizens to be held indefinitely without charge or trial; the government's increased role in using special operations forces and drones in targeted assassinations; the emergence and use of sophisticated surveillance technologies to spy on protesters; the invocation of the state secrecy practices; the suspension of civil liberties that allow various government agencies to spy on Americans without first obtaining warrants; and the stories about widespread abuse and torture by the U.S. military in Afghanistan, not to mention the popular support for torture among the American public.[5]

As the war on terror degenerated into a war on democracy, a host of legal illegalities have been established that put the rule of law, if not the very principle of Western jurisprudence, into a choke hold. How such assaults on the rule of law, justice, and democracy could take place without massive resistance represents one of the most reprehensible moments in American history. Most Americans caught in the grip of trying to survive the brutalizing effects of the economic recession or paralyzed in a relentless culture of fear ignored the assaults on democracy unleashed by a burgeoning national security state. The assaults loom large and are evident in the passage of the Use of Military Force Act, the Patriot Act, the 2002 Homeland Security Act, the Military Commission Act of 2006, and the 2012 National Defense Authorization Act. Jim Garrison rightly raises the question about whether these acts inspired by 9/11 and the war on terror are worth sacrificing the Republic. He writes:

> The question screaming at us through [these bills] is whether the war on terror is a better model around which to shape our destiny than our constitutional liberties. It compels the question of whether we remain an ongoing experiment in democracy, pioneering new frontiers in the name of liberty and justice for all, or have we become a national security state, having financially corrupted and militarized our democracy to such an extent that we define ourselves, as Sparta did, only through the exigencies of war?[6]

The Growing Culture of Cruelty

The rise of the national security state is no longer an abstraction and can also be seen in the collapse of the traditional distinction between the military and the police, as weapons such as microwave guns, drones, and taser shotguns move freely from the military to local police forces and contribute to the rise of pervasive police abuse against students, African Americans, and immigrants.[7] We also have to include in this list a growing culture of manufactured indifference and cruelty, intensified through a commercially driven spectacle of violence that saturates every element of American society. The culture of cruelty is intensified daily by a language of hate aimed indiscriminately by the right-wing media, many conservative politicians, and an army of anti-public pundits against those who suffer from a number of misfortunes including unemployment, inadequate health care, poverty, and homelessness. Think of Rush Limbaugh's cruel and hateful attack on Sandra Fluke, insisting that she was a prostitute because she believed that contraception was a woman's right and should be covered by insurance companies as part of her health coverage. Or for that matter, think about the ongoing attempts on the part of Republican politicians to cut food stamp programs that benefit over 45 million people. Another act of cruelty would be the call to eliminate child labor laws.

Jonathan Schell highlights how this culture of cruelty manifests itself in "a steadily growing faith in force as the solution to almost any problem, whether at home or abroad."[8]

The governing-through-crime model that now imposes violence on schoolchildren all across the country is a particularly egregious example.[9] How else to explain that in 2010 "the police gave close to 300,000 'Class C misdemeanor' tickets to children as young as six in Texas for offenses in and out of school, which result in fines, community service and even prison time"?[10] Infractions as trivial as a dress code violation or being late for class now translate into criminal acts and are symptomatic of what attorney Kady Simpkins insists is a growing trend in which "we have taken childhood behavior and made it criminal."[11] Some of the most shocking examples of the increasing tendency to use excessive forms of punishment on students and process them through what is called the "school-to-prison pipeline" is on full display in two recent reports. One *StateImpact*.org report stated that public schools in Florida and Ohio often used a disciplinary practice called "seclusion."[12] That is, they repeatedly locked "children away in cell-like rooms, closets or old offices, sometimes without their parents' knowledge."[13] In Ohio, "which sent students to seclusion rooms 4,236 times in the 2009–2010 school year, sixty percent of these students had disabilities."[14]

Such practices boggle the mind and have no educational value whatsoever. In fact, seclusion has been found to be deeply traumatizing to some students, and in some cases children have tried to hurt themselves or commit suicide. *ThinkProgress* reported that "in one special education school in Georgia, a 13-year-old boy hung himself in a seclusion room in November 2004."[15] It gets worse. A Department of Justice report uncovered a "school-to-prison pipeline" in Mississippi that revealed that principals and teachers in the schools in Meridian sent largely black and disabled students "to prison for minor disciplinary problems [such as] dress code violations, flatulence, profanity and disrespect."[16] These disciplinary practices suggest that students who are poor, disabled, and vulnerable now inhabit schools that have become "zones of abandonment" that exist beyond the formal rules of school governance where students "become unknowable with no human rights."[17] Under such circumstances, students become voiceless and thus powerless, subject to disciplinary procedures that erase any vestige of agency, subjectivity, or self-recognition.

All of these violations point to the ongoing and growing fundamentalisms and "rule of exceptions" in the American polity that bear witness to a growing militarization of American society. Such disciplinary practices also point to a society that is not only at war with its children, but is also in thrall to a galloping authoritarianism in which the chief function of schooling is repression, especially for low-income and poor minority students as well as those with disabilities and special needs.[18] Public schools for low-income and poor minority children have become what João Biehl calls a "machinery of social death" where young people considered disposable are "often placed in a state of 'terminal exclusion.'"[19]

Those governing the United States no longer have a moral compass or a democratic vision, nor do they have a hold on the social values that would engage modes of governance beneficial to the broader public. Governance is now in the hands of corporate power, and the United States increasingly exhibits all the characteristics of a failed state. As many notable and courageous critics ranging from Sheldon Wolin to Chris Hedges have pointed out, American politics is being shaped by extremists who have shredded civil liberties, lied to the public to legitimate sending young American troops to Iraq and Afghanistan, alienated most of the international community with a blatant exercise of arrogant power and investment in a permanent warfare state, tarnished the highest offices of government with unsavory corporate alliances, used political power to unabashedly pursue legislative policies that favor the rich and punish the poor, and perhaps irreparably damaged any remaining public spheres not governed by the logic of the market.[20] They have waged a covert war against poor young people and people of color who are being either warehoused in substandard schools or incarcerated at alarming rates.[21]

Academic freedom is increasingly under attack by ideological extremists such as former Republican presidential candidate Rick Santorum.[22] Homophobia and racism have become the poster ideologies of the Republican Party; war and soldiers have become the most endearing models of national greatness; and a full-fledged assault on women's reproductive rights is being championed by Republicans at all levels of government. While people of color, the poor, youth, the middle class, the elderly, LGBT communities, and women are being attacked, the Republican Party is supporting a campaign to collapse the boundaries between the church and state, and even liberal critics such as Frank Rich believe that the United States is on the verge of becoming a fundamentalist theocracy.[23] Let me develop this further by examining four of the most serious fundamentalisms that now constitute the new authoritarianism in the United States.

Market Fundamentalism

A number of powerful anti-democratic tendencies now threaten American democracy, and at least four of these are guaranteed to entail grave social and economic consequences. The first is a market fundamentalism that not only trivializes democratic values and public concerns, but also enshrines a rabid individualism, an all-embracing quest for profits, and a social Darwinism in which misfortune is seen as a weakness and a Hobbesian "war of all against all" replaces any vestige of shared responsibilities or compassion for others. Free-market fundamentalists now wage a full-fledged attack on the social contract, the welfare state, any notion of the common good, and those public spheres not yet defined by commercial interests. Within neoliberal ideology, the market becomes the template for organizing the rest of society. Everyone is now a customer or client, and every relationship is ultimately judged in bottom-line, cost-effective terms. Freedom is no longer about equality, social justice, or the public welfare, but about the trade in financial capital, market driven values, and commodities.

As market fundamentalism ensures that the logic of capital trumps democratic sovereignty, low-intensity warfare at home chips away at democratic freedoms while high-intensity warfare abroad delivers democracy with bombs, tanks, and chemical warfare. The cost abroad is massive human suffering and death. At home, as Paul Krugman points out, "The hijacking of public policy by private interests" parallels "the downward spiral in governance."[24] With the rise of market fundamentalism, economics is accorded more respect than politics, and the citizen is reduced to being only a consumer—the buying and selling of goods is all that seems to matter. Even children are now targeted as a constituency from which to make money, reduced to commodities, sexualized in endless advertisements, and shamelessly treated as a market for huge profits. Market fundamentalism not only makes time a burden for those without health insurance, child care, a decent job, and adequate social services, but it also commercializes and privatizes public space, undermining both the idea of citizenship and those very spaces (schools, media, etc.) needed to produce a formative culture that offers vigorous and engaged opportunities for dialogue, debate, reasoned exchange, and discriminating judgments. Under such circumstances, hope is foreclosed, and it becomes difficult either to imagine a life beyond capitalism or to believe in a politics that takes democracy seriously.

When the market becomes the template for all social relations, the obligations of citizenship are reduced merely to consumption and investments in human capital, and production is valued only insofar as it contributes to obscene levels of inequality. Not only the government but all the commanding institutions of society are now placed in the hands of powerful corporate interests, as market fundamentalism works hard to eliminate government regulation of big business and celebrates a ruthless competitive individualism. This type of strangulating control renders politics corrupt and cynical. Robert Kuttner gets it right when he observes:

> One of our major parties has turned nihilist, giddily toying with default on the nation's debt, revelling in the dark pleasures of fiscal *Walpurgisnacht*. Government itself is the devil.... Whether the tart is the Environment Protection Agency, the Dodd-Frank Law or the Affordable Care Act, Republicans are out to destroy government's ability to govern ... the administration trapped in the radical right's

surreal logic plays by Tea Party rules rather than changing the game
... the right's reckless assault on our public institutions is not just
an attack on government. It is a war on America.[25]

Both major parties are deeply conservative and serve as cheerleaders for hyper-capitalism, but the Republican Party seems to be waging
a war not only on the welfare state, women, and immigrants but on
reason itself, given its hatred of the legacy of the Enlightenment and
the most informative aspects of modernity. In the land of the isolated
individual, everything is privatized and public issues collapse into
individual concerns so there is no way of linking private woes to social
problems—the result is thus a dog-eat-dog world. Moreover, when all
things formerly linked to the public good are so aggressively individualized and commercialized, few places are left in which a critical language
and democratic values can be developed to defend institutions as vital
public spheres.

Religious Fundamentalism

The second fundamentalism is religious fervor, championed by a
Republican Party that not only serves up creationism instead of science,
but substitutes unthinking faith for critical reason, and intolerance for a
concern with and openness toward others. This is a deeply disturbing
trend in which the line between the state and religion is being erased as
radical Christians and evangelicals embrace and impose a moralism on
Americans that is largely bigoted, patriarchal, uncritical, and insensitive
to real social problems such as poverty, racism, the crisis in health care,
and the increasing impoverishment of America's children. Instead of
addressing these problems, a flock of dangerous and powerful religious
fanatics who have enormous political clout are waging a campaign to
ban same-sex marriages, undermine scientific knowledge, eliminate
important research initiatives such as those involving embryonic stem
cells, deny the human destruction of the ecological system, overturn
Roe v. Wade, and ban contraceptives for women. This Taliban-like

moralism now boldly translates into everyday cultural practices and political policies as right-wing evangelicals live out their messianic view of the world. For instance, in the last decade conservative pharmacists have refused to fill birth control prescriptions for religious reasons and many states have for all practical purposes banned abortions.

Mixing medicine, politics, and religion means that some women are being denied products designed to prevent conception; sex education in some cases has been limited to "abstinence-only" programs inspired by faith-based institutions; and scientific research challenging these approaches has disappeared from government websites. But the much exalted religious fundamentalism touted by fanatics such as Rick Santorum and many of his Tea Party followers does more than promote a disdain for critical thought and reinforce retrograde forms of homophobia and patriarchy. It also inspires a wave of criticism and censorship against all but the most sanitized facets of popular culture. Remember the moral outrage of the religious right over the allegedly homoerotic representations attributed to the animated cartoon character SpongeBob SquarePants?[26] There was also the conservative Texas lawmaker who jumped onto the moral bandwagon by introducing a bill that would put an end to "sexually suggestive" performances by cheerleaders at sports events and other extracurricular competitions. In another startling example, Cynthia Dunbar, a member of the Republican Texas State Board of Education, has claimed that "public education [is] a subtly deceptive tool of perversion" and is on record imploring "Jesus to 'invade' public schools."[27]

Progressives, as well as any decent conservatives, should be alarmed at the size of the following achieved by Santorum in the 2012 Republican primary. Not only did Santorum reject the separation of church and state, he also made clear his belief that it is better to live under the rule of a theocratic state than in a democracy. Santorum's religious fundamentalism is far from out of step with that of many of his right-wing Republican allies or for that matter of some members of the Democratic Party. Of course, religious fanatics do not ponder these issues seriously because they get their information straight from God. One example comes from Santorum's wife, Karen, who told conservative talk show host Glenn Beck that it was "God's will" that her husband was running in the 2012 Republican presidential primary and that she felt that "God had big plans for Rick."[28] And, of course, Santorum will not doubt his wife's claim because he believes that the ultimate confrontation between good and evil is akin to a religious crusade and that he is the man to lead it (at least before he dropped out of the race). After all, Santorum has stated publicly many times that he is on a moral crusade to snuff out the work of Satan in a variety of areas extending from higher education to health care and women's reproductive rights. Paul Ryan, Mitt Romney's vice-presidential running mate, has been labeled as "one of the most extreme members of the Republican Party on women's health," and rightly so.[29] He opposes abortion regardless of the circumstances, including cases that involve rape, incest, and situations in which an expectant mother's health or life may be in danger.

For many moderate and even right-wing conservatives such as Rudy Giuliani, the likes of Rick Santorum, Newt Gingrich, Rick Perry, and Michelle Bachmann represent the flight of the current Republican Party from the real world. For Giuliani, the party has become anti-modernist. For Ed Rollins, a CNN regular and Republican Party strategist, the party has fatally turned itself into the party of Wall Street and country clubbers, leading them to eventual extinction. Liberals such as Maureen Dowd and Robert Reich view the Republican leadership as either "barking mad" or simply loony. As Reich points out, this is a party "of birthers, creationists, theocrats, climate-change deniers, nativists, gay-bashers, anti-abortionists, media paranoids, anti-intellectuals, and out of touch country clubbers [who] cannot govern America."[30] Of course, there is a semblance of truth in all of these positions, but terms such as "loony," "out of touch," "anti-modernist," and "the politicization of religion," though offering a categorical referent that highlights the extremism and fundamentalism, run the risk of reinforcing a fatal psychologizing or a dead-end collapse into a narrow definition of religious fanaticism. Instead, what must be recognized is that politicians such as Rick Santorum represent a clear and present danger to the promise of a real democracy in the United States.

Educational Fundamentalism

The third related anti-democratic dogma is a virulent form of anti-intellectualism visible in the relentless attempt on the part of the Obama administration and his Republican Party allies to destroy critical education as a foundation for an engaged citizenry and a vibrant democracy. The attack on all levels of education is evident in the attempts to corporatize education, standardize curricula, privatize public schooling, and use the language of business as a model for governance. More extreme assaults in Texas and other conservative states have resulted in policies that have rewritten curricula so as to erase any vestige of progressive history, groups, individuals, conflicts, and democratic values. Words such as "slavery" and "democracy" are now replaced in textbooks with more ideologically benign terms such as "Atlantic triangular trade" and "constitutional republic." Science, evolutionary theory, and reasoned arguments are now erased from the curricula, replaced by creationism and narratives about America as a Christian nation. In line with the flight from secular ethics, public values, which are so crucial to the underlying formative culture that produces an engaged citizenry and substantive democracy, have been transformed into religious values, filtered through endless homilies about individual responsibility concerning the virtues of the free market.

The attack on critical thinking is also evident in the ongoing effort to weaken the autonomy of higher education, undercut the power of faculty, and turn full-time academic jobs into contractual labor. Public schools are increasingly reduced to training grounds and modeled after prisons—with an emphasis on criminalizing student behavior and prioritizing security over critical learning. For instance, security hardware such as video camera surveillance technology, metal detectors, retina detectors, and student-locator ID badges are widespread in American public schools.[31] Students, rather than viewed as potential learners and engaged citizens, are increasingly viewed as suspects, whose education is largely focused on cultivating a sense of fear and insecurity.[32] But there is more at stake here than transforming the school into an adjunct of the national security state; there are also millions to be made by corporations that are part of a security-industrial complex that "has set its sights on the schools as a 'vast rich market'—a $20 billion market."[33] Moreover, while students are viewed as suspects, educators are defined largely as de-skilled technicians, depoliticized professionals, paramilitary forces, hawkers for corporate goods, or money and grant chasers.[34]

At the same time as democracy is removed from the purpose and meaning of schooling, those larger educational forces in the culture are handed over to a small group of corporate interests. The dominant media engage in a form of public pedagogy that appears to legitimate dominant power rather than hold it accountable to any ethical or political standard. Operating in tandem with market fundamentalism, the dominant media deteriorate into a combination of commercialism, propaganda, crude entertainment, and an obsession with celebrity culture.[35] Giant media conglomerates such as Fox News have become advertising appendages for dominant political and corporate interests. Under the sway of such interests, the media neither operate in the interests of the public good nor provide the pedagogical conditions necessary for producing critical citizens or defending a vibrant democracy. Instead, as Robert McChesney and John Nichols have pointed out, concentrated media depoliticize the culture of politics, commercially carpet-bomb citizens, and denigrate public life.[36]

Such media restrict the range of views to which people have access and, as a result, do a disservice to democracy by stripping it of the possibility for debate, critical exchange, and civic engagement. Rather than perform an essential public service, mainstream media become the primary pedagogical tool for promoting a culture of consent and conformity in which citizens are misinformed and public discourse is debased. As the critical power of education within various public spheres is reduced to the official discourse of compliance, conformity, and reverence, it becomes more difficult for the American public to engage in critical debates, translate private considerations into public concerns, and recognize the distortions and lies that underlie much of current government policy. Really, how else is one to explain the popularity of certified liars such as Michelle Bachmann, Sarah Palin, the entire Fox network, and Rush Limbaugh? [37]

Military Fundamentalism

The fourth anti-democratic dogma shaping American life, one that is most disturbing, is the ongoing militarization of public life. Americans are not only obsessed with military power, but "it has become central to our national identity."[38] What other explanation can there be for the fact that the United States has over 725 official military bases outside the country and 969 at home? Or that it spends more on defense than all the rest of the world put together? As Tony Judt states emphatically, "This country is obsessed with war: rumors of war, images of war, 'preemptive' war, 'preventive' war, 'surgical' war, 'prophylactic' war, 'permanent' war."[39] War is no longer a state of exception, but a permanent driving force in American domestic and foreign policy. Cornel West points out that such aggressive militarism is fashioned out of an ideology that supports a foreign policy based on "the cowboy mythology of the American frontier fantasy," while also producing domestic policy that expands "police power, augments the prison-industrial complex, and legitimates unchecked male power (and violence) at home and in the workplace. It views crime as a monstrous enemy to crush (targeting poor people) rather than as an ugly behavior to change (by addressing the conditions that often encourage such behavior)."[40]

The influence of militaristic values, social relations, and ideology now permeates American culture. For example, major universities aggressively court the military establishment for Defense Department grants and, in doing so, become less open to either academic subjects or programs that encourage rigorous debate, dialogue, and critical thinking. In fact, as higher education is pressured by both the Obama administration and its jingoistic supporters to serve the needs of the military-industrial complex, universities increasingly deepen their connections to the national security state in ways that are boldly celebrated. As David Price has brilliantly illustrated, the university is emerging as a central pillar of the national security state.[41] Another index of the growing presence of military values in higher education is the ways in which the curriculum now includes terrorism studies programs, security programs, and training programs that lead to low-level employment in the various layers of the national security complex. Unfortunately, public schools are faring no better. Public schools not only have more military recruiters occupying their halls, they also have more military personnel teaching in the classrooms. Schools now adopt the logic of "tough love" by implementing zero tolerance policies that effectively model urban public schools after prisons, just as students' rights increasingly diminish under the onslaught of a military-style discipline. Students in many schools, especially those in poor urban areas, are routinely searched, frisked, subjected to involuntary drug tests, maced, and carted off to jail. The not-so-hidden curriculum here is that kids can't be trusted; their actions need to be regulated preemptively; and their rights are not worth protecting.

Children and schools are not the only victims of a growing militarization of American society. The civil rights of people of color and immigrants, especially Arabs and Muslims, are being violated, often resulting in either imprisonment and deportation or government harassment. Similarly, black and brown youth and adults are being incarcerated at record levels as prison construction outstrips the construction of schools, hospitals, and other life-preserving institutions. As Michael Hardt and Antonio Negri point out in *Multitude*, war and savage market forces have become the organizing principles of society and the foundation for politics and other social relations.[42] As modes of public pedagogy that increasingly shape all aspects of social life, the growing disciplinary practices of militarized society give rise to a growing authoritarianism that encourages profit-hungry monopolies, the ideology of faith-based certainty, and the undermining of any vestige of critical education, dissent, and dialogue. Abstracted from the ideal of public commitment, the new authoritarianism represents political and economic practices and a form of militarism that loosen any connections among substantive democracy, critical agency, and critical education. Education becomes severely narrowed and trivialized in the media, or is converted into training and character reform in schools. Within higher education, democracy appears as an excess, if not a pathology, as right-wing ideologues and corporate wannabe administrators increasingly police what faculty say, teach, and do in their courses. And it is going to get worse.

The Centrality of Public Pedagogy and the Need
for New Social Movements

In opposition to the rising tide of authoritarianism, there is a need for a vast social movement capable of challenging the basic premises of an ever-expanding systematic attack on democracy. The elements of authoritarianism must be made visible not simply as concepts, but as practices. The Occupy Wall Street movement along with the Quebec student strike movement and others arising globally need to build a network of new institutions that can offer a different language, history, and set of values, knowledge, and ideas. There is a need for free schools, universities, public spheres, and other spaces where learning can be connected to social change and understanding translated into the building of social movements.

As I stress throughout this book, young people, parents, community workers, educators, artists, and others must make a case for linking learning to social change. They must critically engage with and construct anew those diverse sites where critical pedagogy takes place. Educators need to develop a new discourse whose aim is to foster a democratic politics and pedagogy that embody the legacy and principles of social justice, equality, freedom, and rights associated with the democratic concerns of history, space, plurality, power, discourse, identity, morality, and the future. They must make clear that every sphere of social life is open to political contestation and comprises a crucial site of political, social, and cultural struggle in the attempt to forge the knowledge, identifications, affective investments, and social relations capable of constituting political subjects and social agents who will energize and spread the call for a global radical democracy.

Under such circumstances, pedagogy must be embraced as a moral and political practice, one that is both directive and the outgrowth of struggles designed to resist the increasing depoliticization of political culture that is one hallmark of contemporary American life. Education is the terrain where consciousness is shaped; needs are constructed; and the capacity for self-reflection and social change is nurtured and produced. Education across a variety of spheres has assumed an unparalleled significance in shaping the language, values, and ideologies that legitimate the structures and organizations supporting the imperatives of global capitalism. Rather than being simply a technique or methodology, education has become a crucial site for the struggle over those pedagogical and political conditions that offer up the possibilities for people to believe they can develop critical agency—one that will enable them individually and collectively to intervene effectively in the processes through which the material relations of power shape the meaning and practices of their everyday lives.

Within the current historical moment, struggles over power take on a symbolic and discursive as well as material and institutional form. The struggle over education, as most people will acknowledge, involves the struggle over meaning and identity, but it also involves struggling over how meaning, knowledge, and values are produced, legitimated, and operationalized within economic and structural relations of power. Education is not at odds with politics; it is an important and crucial element in any definition of the political and offers not only the theoretical tools for a systemic critique of authoritarianism but a language of possibility for creating actual movements for democratic social change. At stake here is combining an interest in symbolic forms and processes conducive to democratization with broader social contexts and the institutional formations of power itself. The key point is to understand and engage educational and pedagogical practices from the point of view of how they are bound up with larger relations of power. Educators, students, and parents need to be clearer about how power works through and in texts, representations, and discourses, and at the same time recognize that power cannot be limited to the study of representation and discourse.

Changing consciousness is not the same as altering the institutional basis of oppression, and institutional reform cannot take place without a change in consciousness that recognizes the need for such reform and the need to reinvent the conditions and practices that would make it possible. In addition, it is crucial to raise questions about the relationship between pedagogy and civic culture. What would it take for individuals and social groups to believe they have a responsibility to address the realities of class, race, and gender oppression and other specific forms of domination? For too long, those on the left have ignored that the issue of politics as a strategy is inextricably connected to the issue of political education and entangled with power, ideologies, values, the acquisition of agency, and visions of the future. Fortunately, power is never completely on the side of domination, religious fanaticism, or political corruption. Nor is it entirely in the hands of those who view democracy as an excess or burden. Increasingly, more and more individuals and groups at home and around the globe—including students, workers, feminists, educators, writers, environmentalists, senior citizens, artists, and a host of other individuals and movements—are organizing to challenge the dangerous slide on the part of the United States into the morass of an authoritarianism that threatens not just the *promise* but the very *idea* of democracy in the twenty-first century.

3.

Violence, USA: The Warfare State and the Hardening of Everyday Life

SINCE 9/11, THE WAR ON TERROR and the campaign for homeland security have increasingly mimicked the tactics of the enemies they sought to crush. Violence and punishment as both a media spectacle and a bone-crushing reality have become prominent and influential forces shaping American society. As the boundaries between "the realms of war and civil life have collapsed," social relations and the public services needed to make them viable have been increasingly privatized and militarized.[1] The logic of profitability works its magic in channeling the public funding of warfare and organized violence into universities, market-based service providers, Hollywood cinema, cable television, and deregulated contractors. The metaphysics of war and associated forms of violence now creep into every aspect of American society.

As the preferred "instrument of statecraft,"[2] war and its intensifying production of violence crosses borders, time, space, and places. The result is that the United States "has become a 'culture of war' . . .

engulfed in fear and violence [and trapped by a military metaphysics in which] homeland security matters far more than social security."[3] Seemingly without any measure of self-restraint, state-sponsored violence now flows and regroups effortlessly, contaminating both foreign and domestic policies. The criticism of the military-industrial complex, along with its lobbyists and merchants of death, that was raised by President Eisenhower seems to have been relegated to the trash can of history. Instead of being disparaged as a death machine engaged in the organized production of violence, the military-industrial complex is defended as a valuable jobs program and a measure of national pride and provides a powerful fulcrum for the permanent warfare state.

It gets worse. One consequence of the permanent warfare state is evident in the recent public revelations concerning war crimes committed by U.S. government forces. These include the indiscriminate killings of Afghan civilians by U.S. drone aircraft; the barbaric murder of Afghan children and peasant farmers by American infantrymen infamously labeled as "the Kill Team";[4] disclosures concerning four American marines urinating on dead Taliban fighters; and the uncovering of photographs showing "more than a dozen soldiers of the 82nd Airborne Division's Fourth Brigade Combat Team, along with some Afghan security forces, posing with the severed hands and legs of Taliban attackers in Zabul Province in 2010."[5] And, shocking even for those acquainted with standard military combat, there is the case of Army Staff Sgt. Robert Bales, who "walked off a small combat outpost in Kandahar province and slaughtered 17 villagers, most of them women and children, and later walked back to his base and turned himself in."[6] Mind-numbing violence, war crimes, and indiscriminate military attacks on civilians on the part of the U.S. government are far from new and date back to infamous acts such as the air attacks on civilians in Dresden along with the atomic bombings of Hiroshima and Nagasaki during the Second World War.[7]

Military spokespersons are typically quick to remind the American public that such practices are part of the price one pays for combat and are endemic to war itself. State violence wages its ghastly influence through a concept of permanent war, targeted assassinations, an assault on civil liberties, and the use of drone technologies that justifies the killing of innocent civilians as collateral damage. Collateral damage has also come home with vengeance as soldiers returning from combat are killing themselves at record rates and committing mayhem—particularly sexual violence and spousal and child abuse.[8] After more than a decade at war, soldiers in the U.S. military are also returning home and joining the police, thus contributing to the blurring of the line between the military and law enforcement.

The history of atrocities committed by the United States in the name of war need not be repeated here, but some of these incidents have doubled in on themselves and fueled public outrage against the violence of war.[9] One of the most famous events was the My Lai massacre, which played a crucial role in mobilizing protests against the Vietnam War.[10] Even dubious appeals to national defense and honor can provide no excuse for mass killings of civilians, rapes, and other acts of destruction that completely lack any justifiable military objective. Not only does the alleged normative violence of war disguise the moral cowardice of the warmongers, it also demonizes the enemy and dehumanizes soldiers. It is this brutalizing psychology of desensitization, emotional hardness, and the freezing of moral responsibility that is particularly crucial to understand, because it grows out of a formative culture in which war, violence, and the dehumanization of others becomes routine, commonplace, and removed from any sense of ethical accountability.

It is necessary to recognize that acts of extreme violence and cruelty do not represent merely an odd or marginal and private retreat into barbarism. On the contrary, warlike values and the social mindset they legitimate have become the primary currency of a market-driven culture that takes as its model a Darwinian shark tank in which only the strongest survive. In a neoliberal order in which vengeance and revenge seem to be the most cherished values in a "social order organized around the brute necessity of survival," violence becomes both a legitimate mediating force and one of the few remaining sources of pleasure.[11] At work in the new hyper-social Darwinism is a view of the Other as the enemy, an all-too-quick willingness in the name of war to embrace the dehumanization of the Other, and an all-too-easy acceptance of violence, however extreme, as routine and normalized. As many theorists have observed, the production of extreme violence in its various incarnations is now a source of profit for Hollywood moguls, mainstream news, popular culture, the corporate-controlled entertainment industry, and a major market for the defense industries.[12]

This pedagogy of brutalizing hardness and dehumanization is also produced and circulated in schools, boot camps, prisons, and a host of other sites that now trade in violence and punishment for commercial purposes, or for the purpose of containing populations that are viewed as synonymous with public disorder. The mall, juvenile detention facilities, many public housing projects, privately owned apartment buildings, and gated communities all embody a model of a dysfunctional sociality and have come to resemble proto-military spaces in which the culture of violence and punishment becomes the primary order of politics, fodder for entertainment, and an organizing principle for society. All of these spaces and institutions, from malls to housing projects to schools, are beginning to resemble war zones that impose needless frameworks of punishment. This is evident not only in New York City's infamous stop-and-frisk policy, but also in shopping malls that now impose weekend teen curfews, hire more security guards, employ high-tech surveillance tools, and closely police the behavior of young people. Similarly, housing projects have become militarized security zones meting out harsh punishments for drug offenders and serve as battlegrounds for the police and young people.

Even public school reform is now justified in the dehumanizing language of national security, which increasingly legitimates the transformation of schools into adjuncts of the surveillance and police state.[13] The privatization and militarization of schools mutually inform each other as students are increasingly subjected to disciplinary apparatuses that limit their capacity for critical thinking while molding them into consumers, testing them into submission, stripping them of any sense of social responsibility, and convincing large numbers of poor minority students that they are better off under the jurisdiction of the criminal justice system instead of being treated as valued members of the public schools. Schools are increasingly absorbing the culture of prisons and are aggressively being transformed into an extension of the criminal justice system.

Many public schools are being militarized to resemble prisons instead of being safe places that would enable students to learn how to be critical and engaged citizens. Rather than being treated with dignity and respect, students are increasingly treated as if they were criminals, given that they are repeatedly "photographed, fingerprinted, scanned, x-rayed, sniffed and snooped on."[14] As I mentioned in chapter 2, the space of the school resembles a high-security prison with its metal detectors at the school entrances, drug-sniffing dogs in school corridors, and surveillance cameras in the hallways and classrooms. Student behaviors that were once considered child play are now elevated to the status of a crime. Young people who violate dress codes, engage in food fights, hug each other, doodle, and shoot spit wads are no longer reprimanded by the classroom teacher or principal; instead their behavior is criminalized. Consequently, the police are called in to remove them from the classroom, handcuff them, and put them in the back of a police car to be carted off to a police station where they languish in a holding cell. There is a kind of doubling that takes place here between the culture of punishment, on the one hand, and the feeding of profits for the security-surveillance industries.

What has emerged in the United States is a civil and political order structured around the problem of violent crime. This governing-through-crime model produces a highly authoritarian and mechanistic approach to addressing social problems that often focuses on low-income and poor minorities, promotes highly repressive policies, and places undue emphasis on personal security rather than considering the larger complex of social and structural forces that fuels violence in the first place. Far from promoting democratic values, a respect for others, and social responsibility, a governing-through-crime approach criminalizes a wide range of behaviors and in doing so often functions largely to humiliate, punish, and demonize. The abuse and damage that is being imposed on young people as a result of the ongoing militarization and criminalization of public schools defy the imagination. And

the trivial nature of the behaviors that produce such egregious practices is hard to believe. A few examples will suffice:

> In November 2011, a 14-year-old student in Brevard County,
> Florida, was suspended for hugging a female friend, an act which
> even the principal acknowledged as innocent. A 9-year-old in
> Charlotte, North Carolina, was suspended for sexual harassment
> after a substitute teacher overheard the child tell another student
> that the teacher was "cute." A 6-year-old in Georgia was arrested,
> handcuffed and suspended for the remainder of the school year
> after throwing a temper tantrum in class. A 6-year-old boy in San
> Francisco was accused of sexual assault following a game of tag on
> the playground. A 6-year-old in Indiana was arrested, handcuffed
> and charged with battery after kicking a school principal. Twelve-
> year-old Alexa Gonzalez was arrested and handcuffed for doodling
> on a desk. Another student was expelled for speaking on a cell
> phone with his mother, to whom he hadn't spoken in a month
> because she was in Iraq on a military deployment. Four high school
> students in Detroit were arrested and handcuffed for participating
> in a food fight and charged with a misdemeanor with the potential
> for a 90-day jail sentence and a $500 fine. A high school student in
> Indiana was expelled after sending a profanity-laced tweet through
> his Twitter account after school hours. The school had been con-
> ducting their own surveillance by tracking the tweeting habits of all
> students. These are not isolated incidents. In 2010, some 300,000
> Texas schoolchildren received misdemeanor tickets from police
> officials. One 12-year-old Texas girl had the police called on her
> after she sprayed perfume on herself during class.[15]

Public spaces that should promote dialogue, thoughtfulness, and
critical exchange are ruled by fear and become the ideological corol-
lary of a state that aligns its priorities to war and munitions sales while
declaring a state of emergency (under the aegis of a permanent war) as
a major reference for shaping domestic policy. In addition, the media
and other cultural apparatuses now produce, circulate, and validate

forms of symbolic and real violence that dissolve the democratic bonds of social reciprocity. This dystopian use of violence as entertainment and spectacle is reinforced through the media's incessant appeal to the market-driven egocentric interests of the autonomous individual, a fear of the Other, and a stripped-down version of security that narrowly focuses on personal safety rather than collective security nets and social welfare. One consequence is that those who are viewed as disposable and reduced to zones of abandonment are forced "to address the reality of extreme violence . . . in the very heart of their everyday life."[16] Violence in everyday life is matched by a surge of violence in popular culture. Violence now runs through media and popular culture like an electric current. As the *New York Times* reported recently, "The top-rated show on cable TV is rife with shootings, stabbings, machete attacks and more shootings. The top drama at the box office fills theaters with the noise of automatic weapons fire. The top-selling video game in the country gives players the choice to kill or merely wound their quarry."[17]

Under such a warlike regime of privatization, militarism, and punishing violence, it is not surprising that the Hollywood film *The Hunger Games* has become a mega-box-office hit. The film and its success are symptomatic of a society in which violence has become the new lingua franca. It portrays a society in which the privileged classes alleviate their boredom through satiating their lust for violent entertainment, and in this case a brutalizing violence waged against children. Although a generous reading might portray the film as a critique of class-based consumption and violence, given its portrayal of a dystopian future society so willing to sacrifice its children, in the end the film should more accurately be read as depicting the terminal point of what I have called elsewhere the "suicidal society" (a suicide pact literally ends the narrative).[18]

Given Hollywood's rush for ratings, the film gratuitously feeds enthralled audiences with voyeuristic images of children being killed for sport. In a very disturbing opening scene, the audience observes children killing one another within a visual framing that is as gratuitous as it is alarming. That such a film can be made for the purpose of attaining high ratings and big profits, while becoming overwhelmingly popular among young people and adults alike, says something profoundly disturbing about the cultural force of violence and the moral emptiness at work in American society. This is not the type of violence that is instructive about how damaging the spectacle of violence can be. On the contrary, such representations of violence are largely gratuitous, and they create the conditions for a disturbing voyeurism while both mitigating the effects of violence and normalizing it. Of course, the meaning and relevance of *The Hunger Games* rest not simply with its production of violent imagery against children, but with the ways these images and the historical and contemporary meanings they carry are aligned and realigned with broader discourses, values, and social relations. Within this network of alignments, risk and danger combine with myth and fantasy to stoke the seductions of sadomasochistic violence, echoing the fundamental values of the fascist state in which aesthetics dissolves into pathology and a carnival of cruelty. How else to explain the emergence of superhero films that increasingly contain deep authoritarian strains, films that appear to have a deep hold on their dutifully submissive audiences. The film critic A. O. Scott has argued that films such as *Spider-Man, Dark Knight,* and *The Avengers* are marked by a "hectic emptiness," "bloated cynicism," and "function primarily as dutiful corporate citizens . . . serving private interests."[19] But most important, they reinforce the increasingly popular notion that "the price of entertainment is obedience."[20] There is more at work here than what Scott calls "imaginative decadence."[21] There is also the seductive lure and appeal of the authoritarian personality, which runs deep in American culture and finds its emergence in the longing for hyper-masculine superheroes who merge vigilante justice with anti-democratic values.[22] Equally disturbing is the alignment of such films with a corporate-controlled cultural apparatus that legitimates and celebrates a passive embrace of authoritarian values, power, and mythic authoritarian figures.

Within the contemporary neoliberal theater of cruelty, war has expanded its poisonous reach and moves effortlessly within and across America's national boundaries. As Chris Hedges has pointed out brilliantly and passionately, war "allows us to make sense of mayhem and death" as something not to be condemned, but to be celebrated as a matter of national honor, virtue, and heroism.[23] One particularly egregious example of this took place in the summer of 2012 when NBC decided to air *Stars Earn Stripes*, a reality TV show in which celebrities are matched with U.S. military personnel, including former Green Berets and Navy Seals, in carrying out simulated military training, "including helicopter drops in water and long-range weapons fire, all under the direction of retired General Wesley Clark."[24] The various contestants compete against each other to win prizes that are given to various armed forces, charities, and some veterans groups. NBC celebrates the show as a "fast-paced competition" and defends it as a "glorification of service" rather than a "glorification of war."[25] War in this rendering becomes a form of sport, amusement, and entertainment. The violence of war and the human suffering and death it produces is both sanitized and trivialized in this show. Amy Fairweather, a member of the veterans' organization Swords to Ploughshares, rightly criticized the program in stating: "The show 'trivialized' war, whose real consequences were 'not that you were knocked out of the competition next week, the consequences are you don't get to go on with your life'."[26] Nine Nobel Prize winners, including Desmond Tutu, echoed this view in a letter to NBC. They write:

> It is our belief that this program pays homage to no one anywhere and continues and expands on an inglorious tradition of glorifying war and armed violence. . . . Real war is down-in-the-dirt deadly. People—military and civilians—die in ways that are anything but entertaining. Communities and societies are ripped apart in armed conflict and the aftermath can be as deadly as the war itself as simmering animosities are unleashed in horrific spirals of violence. War, whether relatively short-lived or going on for decades as in too many parts of the world, leaves deep scars that can take generations to overcome—if ever. Trying to somehow sanitize war by likening it to an athletic competition further calls into question the morality and ethics of linking the military anywhere with the

entertainment industry in barely veiled efforts to make war and its multitudinous costs more palatable to the public.[27]

Celebrating war, spectacularized violence, and hyper-masculinity reveals more than an ethical descent into barbarism. It also makes visible a market-driven social and economic order that is driven by a financial elite who subordinate all ethical, political, and material considerations to the altar of profitmaking and capital accumulation.[28] War takes as its aim the killing of others and legitimates violence through a morally bankrupt mindset in which just and unjust notions of violence collapse into each other, increasingly in the name of profit and the glorification of celebrity culture. Consequently, it has become increasingly difficult to determine justifiable violence and humanitarian intervention from unjustifiable violence involving torture, massacres, and atrocities, which now operate in the liminal space and moral vacuum of legal illegalities. Even when such acts are recognized as war crimes, they are often dismissed as simply an inevitable consequence of war itself. This view was recently echoed by Leon Panetta, who, responding to the killing of civilians by U.S. Army Staff Sergeant Robert Bales, observed: "War is hell. These kinds of events and incidents are going to take place, they've taken place in any war, they're terrible events, and this is not the first of those events, and probably will not be the last."[29] He then made clear the central contradiction that haunts the use of machineries of war by stating: "But we cannot allow these events to undermine our strategy."[30] Panetta's qualification is a testament to barbarism because it means being committed to a war machine that trades in indiscriminate violence, death, and torture while ignoring the pull of conscience or ethical considerations. Hedges is right when he argues that defending such violence in the name of war is a rationale for "usually nothing more than gross human cruelty, brutality and stupidity."[31]

War and the organized production of violence have also become forms of governance, increasingly visible in the ongoing militarization of police departments throughout the United States. According to the Homeland Security Research Corp., "The homeland security market for state and local agencies is projected to reach $19.2 billion by 2014, up from $15.8 billion in fiscal 2009."[32] The structure of violence is also evident in the rise of the punishing and surveillance state,[33] with its legions of electronic spies and ballooning prison population—now more than 2.3 million. Evidence of state-sponsored warring violence can also be found in the domestic war against "terrorists" (code for young protesters), which provides new opportunities for major defense contractors and corporations to become "more a part of our domestic lives."[34] Young people, particularly poor minorities of color, have already become the targets of what David Theo Goldberg calls "extraordinary power in the name of securitization . . . [They are viewed as] unruly populations . . . [who] are to be subjected to necropolitical discipline through the threat of imprisonment or death, physical or social."[35] The rhetoric of war is now used by politicians not only to appeal to a solitary warrior mentality in which responsibility is individualized, but also to attack women's reproductive rights, limit the voting rights of minorities, and justify the most ruthless cutting of social protections and benefits for public servants and the poor, unemployed, and sick. There is also the day-to-day effects of a hyped and militarized police force that in light of the subordination of individual rights to matters of individual security rarely questions the limits of their own authority. One example of the emerging police state can be found in roadside police stops in which any regard for privacy, individual rights, and human dignity appears to have been abandoned. John W. Whitehead, the director of the Rutherford Institute, provides one disturbing but not unusual example of the police state in action. He writes:

> Consider, for example, what happened to 38-year-old Angel Dobbs and her 24-year-old niece, Ashley, who were pulled over by a Texas state trooper on July 13, 2012, allegedly for flicking cigarette butts out of the car window. First, the trooper berated the women for littering on the highway. Then, insisting that he smelled marijuana, he proceeded to interrogate them and search the car. Despite the fact that both women denied smoking or possessing any marijuana, the police officer then called in a female trooper, who carried out a roadside cavity search, sticking her fingers into the older

woman's anus and vagina, then performing the same procedure on the younger woman, wearing the same pair of gloves. No marijuana was found. [And in a hard to believe second example,] Leila Tarantino was allegedly subjected to two roadside strip searches in plain view of passing traffic during a routine traffic stop, while her two children—ages 1 and 4—waited inside her car. During the second strip search, presumably in an effort to ferret out drugs, a female officer "forcibly removed" a tampon from Tarantino's body. No contraband or anything illegal was found.[36]

The politics and pedagogy of death begins in the celebration of war and ends in the unleashing of violence on all those considered disposable on the domestic front. A survival-of-the-fittest ethic and the utter annihilation of the Other have now become normalized, saturating everything from state policy to institutional practices to the mainstream media. How else to explain the growing taste for violence in, for example, the world of professional sports, extending from professional hockey to extreme martial arts events? The debased nature of violence and punishment seeping into the American cultural landscape becomes clear in the recent revelation that the New Orleans Saints professional football team was "running a 'bounty program' which rewarded players for inflicting injuries on opposing players."[37] In what amounts to a regime of terror pandering to the thrill of the crowd and a take-no-prisoners approach to winning, a coach offered players a cash bonus for "laying hits that resulted in other athletes being carted off the field or landing on the injured player list."[38]

The bodies of those considered competitors, let alone enemies, are now targeted as the war-as-politics paradigm turns America into a warfare state. And even as violence flows out beyond the boundaries of state-sponsored militarism and the containment of the sporting arena, citizens are increasingly enlisted to maximize their own participation and pleasure in violent acts as part of their everyday existence—even when fellow citizens become the casualties. Maximizing the pleasure of violence with its echo of fascist ideology far exceeds the boundaries of state-sponsored militarism and violence. Violence can no longer be defined as an exclusively state function, since the market in its various economic and cultural manifestations now enacts its own violence on numerous populations no longer considered of value. Perhaps nothing signals the growing market-based savagery of the contemporary moment more than the privatized and corporate-fueled gun culture of America.

Gun culture now rules American values and has a powerful influence in shaping U.S. domestic policies. The National Rifle Association is the emerging symbol of what America has come to represent, perfectly captured in T-shirts worn by its followers that brazenly display the messages "I hate welfare" and the biblical-sounding message "If any would not work neither should he eat." [39] The celebration of guns and violence merges in this case with a culture of cruelty, hatred, and exclusion. The National Rifle Association begins to resemble a regime of terror as politics and violence become an inseparable part of its message and the most important mediating force in shaping its identity. The relationship Americans have to guns may be complicated, but the social costs are less nuanced and certainly more deadly. In a country with "90 guns for every 100 people," it comes as no surprise, as Gary Younge points out, that "more than 85 people a day are killed with guns and more than twice that number are injured with them." [40] The merchants of death trade in a formative and material culture of violence that causes massive suffering and despair while detaching themselves from any sense of moral responsibility. Social costs are rarely considered, in spite of the endless trail of murders committed by the use of such weapons and largely inflicted on poor minorities and young people.

With respect to young people, "Each year, more than 20,000 children and youth under age 20 are killed or injured by firearms in the United States. The lethality of guns, as well as their easy accessibility to young people, are key reasons why firearms are the second leading cause of death among young people ages 10 to 19. Only motor vehicle accidents claim more young lives." [41] Violence has become not only more deadly but flexible, seeping into a range of institutions, cannibalizing democratic values, and merging crime and terror. As Jean and John Comaroff point out, under such circumstances a social order emerges that "appears ever more impossible to apprehend, violence appears ever more endemic, excessive, and transgressive, and police come, in the public imagination, to embody a nervous state under pressure."[42] The lethality of gun culture and the spectacle of violence are reinforced in American life as public disorder becomes both a performance and an obsession. The obsession with violence is clearly reflected in advertising and other everyday venues—advertising can even "transform nightmare into desire. . . . [Yet] violence is never just a matter of the circulation of images. Its exercise, legitimate or otherwise, tends to have decidedly tangible objectives. And effects."[43]

An undeniable effect of the warmongering state is the drain on public coffers. The United States has the largest military budget in the world and "in 2010–2011 accounted for 40% of national (federal government) spending."[44] The Eisenhower Study Group at Brown University's Watson Institute for International Studies estimates that the wars in Iraq and Afghanistan have cost the American taxpayers between $3.7 and $4.4 trillion. What is more, funding such wars comes with an incalculable price in human lives and suffering. For example, the Eisenhower Study Group estimated that in these two wars there have been over 224,475 lives lost, 363,383 people wounded, and 7 million refugees and internally displaced people.[45] But war has another purpose, especially for neoconservatives who want to destroy the social state. By siphoning funds and public support away from much needed social programs, war, to use David Rothkopf's phrase, "diminishes government so that it becomes too small to succeed."[46]

The warfare state hastens the dismantling of the social state and its limited safety net, creating the conditions for the ultra-rich, megacorporations, and finance capital to appropriate massive amounts of wealth, income, and power. This has resulted between 2010 and 2012 in the largest ever increase in inequality of income and wealth in the United States.[47] One acute register of the growing inequality in wealth and income is provided by Michael D. Yates:

In the United States in 2007, it is estimated that the five best-paid hedge fund managers "earned" more than all of the CEOs of the

Fortune 500 corporations combined. The income of just the top three hedge-fund managers (James Simon, John Paulson, and George Soros) taken together was nine billion dollars in 2007. . . . Pittsburgh hedge fund manager David Tepper made four billion dollars. . . . If we were to suppose that Mr. Tepper worked 2,000 hours in 2009 (fifty weeks at forty hours per week), he took in $2,000,000 per hour and $30,000 a minute. . . . Others are not so fortunate. In 2010, more than 7 million people had incomes less than 50 percent of the official poverty level of income, an amount equal to $11,245, which in hourly terms (2,000 hours of work per year) is $5.62. At this rate, it would take someone nearly three years to earn what Tepper got each minute. About one-quarter of all jobs in the United States pay an hourly wage rate that would not support a family of four at the official poverty level of income.[48]

Structural inequalities do more than distribute wealth and power upward to the privileged few and impose massive hardships on the poorest members of society. They also generate forms of collective violence accentuated by high levels of uncertainty and anxiety, all of which, as Michelle Brown points out, "makes recourse to punishment and exclusion highly seductive possibilities."[49] The merging of the punishing and financial state is partly legitimated through the normalization of risk, insecurity, and fear in which individuals not only have no way of knowing their fate, but also have to bear the consequences of being left adrift by neoliberal capitalism.

Increasingly, institutions such as schools, prisons, detention centers, and our major economic institutions are being organized for the production of violence. Rather than promote democratic values and a respect for others or embrace civic values, they often function largely to humiliate, punish, and demonize any vestige of social responsibility. Our political system is now run by a financial oligarchy that is comparable to what Alain Badiou calls a "regime of gangsters."[50] And as he rightly argues, the message we get from the apostles of casino capitalism carries with it another form of social violence:

Privatize everything. Abolish help for the weak, the solitary, the sick and the unemployed. Abolish all aid for everyone except the banks. Don't look after the poor; let the elderly die. Reduce the wages of the poor, but reduce the taxes on the rich. Make everyone work until they are ninety. Only teach mathematics to traders, reading to big property-owners and history to on-duty ideologues. And the execution of these commands will in fact ruin the lives of millions of people.[51]

It is precisely this culture of cruelty that has spread throughout America that makes the larger public not merely susceptible to violence but induces it to luxuriate in its alleged pleasures. In American society, the seductive power of the spectacle of violence is fed through a framework of fear, blame, and humiliation that circulates widely in popular culture. The consequence is a culture marked by increasing levels of inequality, suffering, and disposability. There is not only a "surplus of rage," but also a collapse of civility in which untold forms of violence, humiliation, and degradation proliferate. Hyper-masculinity and the spectacle of a militarized culture now dominate American society— one in which civility collapses into rudeness, shouting, and unchecked anger. What is unique at this historical conjuncture in the United States is that such public expression of hatred, violence, and rage "no longer requires concealment but is comfortable in its forthrightness."[52] How else to explain the support by the majority of Americans for state-sanctioned torture, the public indifference to the mass incarceration of poor people of color, the silence on the part of many Americans in the face of the increasing use of police and state-sanctioned violence against peaceful Occupy Wall Street protesters, or the public silence in the face of police violence in public schools against children, even those in elementary schools? As war becomes the organizing principle of society, the ensuing effects of an intensifying culture of violence on a democratic civic culture are often deadly and invite anti-democratic tendencies that pave the way for authoritarianism.

In addition, as the state is hijacked by the financial-military-industrial complex, the "most crucial decisions regarding national policy are not made by representatives, but by the financial and military elites."[53] Such massive inequality and the suffering and political corruption it produces point to the need for critical analysis in which the separation of power and politics can be understood. This means developing terms that clarify how power becomes global even as politics continues to function largely at the national level, with the effect of reducing the state primarily to custodial, policing, and punishing functions—at least for those populations considered disposable.

The state exercises its slavish role in the form of lowering taxes for the rich, deregulating corporations, funding wars for the benefit of the defense industries, and devising other welfare services for the ultra-rich. There is no escaping the global politics of finance capital and the global network of violence it has produced. Resistance must be mobilized globally and politics restored to a level where it can make a difference in fulfilling the promises of a global democracy. But such a challenge can only take place if the political is made more pedagogical and matters of education take center stage in the struggle for desires, subjectivities, and social relations that refuse the normalizing of violence as a source of gratification, entertainment, identity, and honor.

War in its expanded incarnation works in tandem with a state organized around the production of widespread violence. Such a state is necessarily divorced from public values and the formative cultures that make a democracy possible. The result is a weakened civic culture that allows violence and punishment to circulate as part of a culture of commodification, entertainment, distraction, and exclusion. In opposing the emergence of the United States as both a warfare and a punishing state, I am not appealing to a form of left moralism meant simply to mobilize outrage and condemnation. These are not unimportant registers, but they do not constitute an adequate form of resistance.

What is needed are modes of analysis that do the hard work of uncovering the effects of the merging of institutions of capital, wealth, and power, and how this merger has extended the reach of a military-industrial-carceral and academic complex, especially since the 1980s. This complex of ideological and institutional elements designed for the production of violence must be addressed by making visible its vast national and global interests and militarized networks, as indicated by the fact that the United States has over 1,000 military bases abroad.[54] Equally important is the need to highlight how this military-industrial-carceral and academic complex uses punishment as a structuring force to shape national policy and everyday life.

Challenging the warfare state also has an important educational component. C. Wright Mills was right in arguing that it is impossible to separate the violence of an authoritarian social order from the cultural apparatuses that nourish it. As Mills put it, the major cultural apparatuses not only "guide experience, they also expropriate the very chance to have an experience rightly called 'our own.'"[55] This narrowing of experience shorn of public values locks people into private interests and the hyper-individualized orbits in which they live. Experience itself is now privatized, instrumentalized, commodified, and increasingly militarized. Social responsibility gives way to organized infantilization and a flight from responsibility.

Crucial here is the need to develop new cultural and political vocabularies that can foster an engaged mode of citizenship capable of naming the corporate and academic interests that support the warfare state and its apparatuses of violence, while simultaneously mobilizing social movements to challenge and dismantle its vast networks of power. One central pedagogical and political task in dismantling the warfare state is, therefore, the challenge of creating the cultural conditions and public spheres that would enable the American public to move from being spectators of war and everyday violence to being informed and engaged citizens.

Unfortunately, major cultural apparatuses like public and higher education, which have been historically responsible for educating the public, are becoming little more than market-driven and militarized knowledge factories. In this particularly insidious role, educational institutions deprive students of the capacities that would enable them not only to assume public responsibilities, but also to actively participate in the process of governing. Without the public spheres for creating a formative culture equipped to challenge the educational, military, market, and religious fundamentalisms that dominate American society, it will be virtually impossible to resist the normalization of war as a matter of domestic and foreign policy.

Any viable notion of resistance to the current authoritarian order must also address the issue of what it means pedagogically to imagine a more democratically oriented notion of knowledge, subjectivity, and agency and what it might mean to bring such notions into the public sphere. This is more than what Bernard Harcourt calls "a new grammar of political disobedience."[56] It is a reconfiguring of the nature and substance of the political so that matters of pedagogy become central to the very definition of what constitutes the political and the practices that make it meaningful. Critical understanding motivates transformative action, and the affective investments it demands can only be brought about by breaking into the hard-wired forms of common sense that give war and state-supported violence their legitimacy. War does not have to be a permanent social relation, nor the primary organizing principle of everyday life, society, and foreign policy.

The war of all-against-all and the social Darwinian imperative to respond positively only to one's own self-interest represent the death of politics, civic responsibility, and ethics, and set the stage for a dysfunctional democracy, if not an emergent authoritarianism. The existing neoliberal social order produces individuals who have no commitments except to profit, disdain social responsibility, and loosen all ties to any viable notion of the public good. This regime of punishment and privatization is organized around the structuring forces of violence and militarization, which produce a surplus of fear, insecurity, and a weakened culture of civic engagement—one in which there is little room for reasoned debate, critical dialogue, and informed intellectual exchange. Patricia Clough and Craig Willse are right in arguing that we live in a society "in which the production and circulation of death functions as political and economic recovery."[57]

America understood as a warfare state prompts a new urgency for a collective politics and a social movement capable of negating the current regimes of political and economic power, while imagining a different and more democratic social order. Until the ideological and structural foundations of violence that are pushing American society

over the abyss are addressed, the current warfare state will be transformed into a full-blown authoritarian state that will shut down any
vestige of democratic values, social relations, and public spheres. At
the very least, the American public owes it to its children and future
generations, if not the future of democracy itself, to make visible
and dismantle this machinery of violence while also reclaiming the
spirit of a future that works for life rather than death—the future of
the current authoritarianism, however dressed up they appear in the
spectacles of consumerism and celebrity culture. It is time for educators, unions, young people, liberals, religious organizations, and other
groups to connect the dots, educate themselves, and develop powerful social movements that can restructure the fundamental values and
social relations of democracy while establishing the institutions and
formative cultures that make it possible. Stanley Aronowitz is right in
arguing that

> the system survives on the eclipse of the radical imagination, the
> absence of a viable political opposition with roots in the general
> population, and the conformity of its intellectuals who, to a large
> extent, are subjugated by their secure berths in the academy [and
> though] we can take some solace in 2011, the year of the protester
> . . . it would be premature to predict that decades of retreat, defeat
> and silence can be reversed overnight without a commitment to
> what may be termed a "a long march" through the institutions, the
> workplaces and the streets of the capitalist metropoles.[58]

The current protests among young people, workers, the unemployed, students, and others are making clear that this is not—indeed,
cannot be—only a short-term project for reform, but must constitute a
political and social movement of sustained growth, accompanied by the
reclaiming of public spaces, the progressive use of digital technologies,
the development of democratic public spheres, new modes of education, and the safeguarding of places where democratic expression, new
identities, and collective hope can be nurtured and mobilized. Without
broad political and social movements standing behind and uniting the

call on the part of young people for democratic transformations, any attempt at radical change will more than likely be cosmetic.

Any viable challenge to the new authoritarianism and its theater of cruelty and violence must include developing a variety of cultural discourses and sites where new modes of agency can be imagined and enacted, particularly as they work to reconfigure a new collective subject, modes of sociality, and "alternative conceptualizations of the self and its relationship to others."[59] Clearly, if the United States is to make a claim for democracy, it must develop a politics that views violence as a moral monstrosity and war as virulent pathology. How such a claim to politics unfolds remains to be seen. In the meantime, resistance proceeds, especially among the young people who now carry the banner of struggle against an encroaching authoritarianism that is working hard to snuff out all vestiges of democratic life.

4.

Hoodie Politics: Trayvon Martin and Racist Violence in Post-Racial America

THE KILLING OF SEVENTEEN-YEAR-OLD Trayvon Martin was a tragedy that struck the entire nation, but too soon devolved into a media spectacle. The young African American man was shot and killed by an overzealous neighborhood watchman, George Zimmerman, who appeared to have capitulated to the dominant post-racial presumption that equates the culture of criminality with the culture of blackness. While the Florida laws that allowed Zimmerman initially to walk free sparked plenty of moral outrage—including a recognition that racism is alive and well in America and that justice has been hijacked by those who can afford it—the broader and more fundamental questions were not raised. Complex issues get lost when spectacular events are taken over by a media frenzy that feeds on sound bites and simplified answers. Lying beyond the intense spotlight focused on the two individuals were important issues, such as the social and human costs of a corporate-driven gun culture, the privatization of security forces, the price paid by poor minority youth whose every act is criminalized, and how crimes rooted in a pervasive racism are shrouded in darkness, left offstage and invisible. To bolster the incredible claim that we live in a post-racial society, crimes such as these are often isolated from a larger set of socioeconomic forces, which, if examined, would provide a broader understanding of how the needless killing of a seventeen-year-old black youth and a much more encompassing war on youth are causing massive suffering and tragic deaths among many young people in America.[1]

The killing of Trayvon Martin cannot be removed from the history of slavery and a prison-industrial complex that bears down heavily on all black men, both young and old. For instance, "There are more African American adults under correctional control today—in prison or jail, on probation or parole—than were enslaved in 1850, a decade before the Civil War began."[2] The racial underpinnings of the incarceration of young blacks can, in part, be traced to the fact that the war on drugs has essentially become a war on black youth. As Michelle Alexander points out:

> The drug war has been brutal—complete with SWAT teams, tanks, bazookas, grenade launchers, and sweeps of entire neighborhoods—but those who live in white communities have little clue to the devastation wrought. This war has been waged almost exclusively in poor communities of color, even though studies consistently show that people of all colors use and sell illegal drugs at remarkably similar rates. In fact, some studies indicate that white youth are significantly more likely to engage in illegal drug dealing than black youth. Any notion that drug use among African Americans is more severe or dangerous is belied by the data. White youth, for example, have about three times the number of drug-related visits to the emergency room as their African American counterparts. That is not what you would guess, though, when entering our nation's prisons and jails, overflowing as they are with black and brown drug offenders. In some states, African Americans comprise 80%–90% of all drug offenders sent to prison.[3]

The capacious nature of this war becomes evident in a number of startling statistics that indicate that poor minority youth are not just excluded from the American Dream but have become utterly redundant and disposable, waste products of a society that no longer considers them of any value. Many of these youth are pushed out of schools, denied job training opportunities, subjected to rigorous modes of surveillance and criminal sanctions, and viewed less as chronically disadvantaged than as flawed consumers and civic felons. One measure of this war on low-income and poor minority youth is evident in the fact that more youth are incarcerated in the United States than in any other country in the world. Nearly one in every ten of male high school dropouts in the United States is in either jail or juvenile detention.[4] For African American male youth, the incarceration rate jumps to one in four high school dropouts ending up in prison.[5]

The criminalization of poor minority youth is matched by economic deprivations that make it difficult for them to either challenge or escape from the zones of abandonment in which they find themselves. In this instance, the war on poverty has been transformed into a war on the poor, especially young people. This is clear in that nearly half of all U.S. children and 90 percent of black youngsters will be on food stamps at some point during childhood.[6] Nearly 45 percent of black children live below the poverty line and millions lack health insurance. The consequences are often deadly. For example, Deamonte Driver, a seventh-grader in Prince George's County, Maryland, died because his mother did not have the health insurance to cover an $80 tooth extraction. Because of a lack of insurance, his mother was unable to find an oral surgeon willing to treat her son. By the time he was admitted and diagnosed in a hospital emergency room, the bacteria from the abscessed tooth had spread to his brain and, despite the level of high-quality intensive treatment he finally received, he eventually died.[7] In a society in which wealth determines access to the most basic services, some "children are . . . consigned to the coffins of history."[8] Moreover, far too many poor children attend substandard schools, lack jobs, and live in crime-infested neighborhoods. What becomes clear is that social marginalization, poverty, low levels of education, and high unemployment are increasingly driving up already staggering incarceration rates for low-income and poor minority youth. And it is precisely this larger economic and political landscape that is often ignored when Trayvon Martin's death is discussed in the mainstream media. While liberals have the tendency to rush to universalize the deeply felt personal loss that resulted from Trayvon Martin's death, the rosy raceless sentiment was ruptured when President Obama uncharacteristically drew attention to his own racial difference and suggested that if he had a son he would look like Trayvon. But the fact of the matter is that since the dawn of the post–civil rights era, young black and brown youth have been routinely and radically othered as a generation of suspects, if not a dangerous scourge. Though poor minority youth may garner some sympathy when their needless deaths receive public attention, too many of them experience an existential and social death every day that often goes unnoticed. The popular slogan "We are all Trayvon" may be expressed with good intentions, but it bears the burden of hiding more than it reveals. Among liberal white sympathizers, young poor minorities are not "us": they are the excluded, the Other, the excess, and the disposable. What needs to be remembered is that they have been made voiceless, powerless, and invisible in America. Marginalized by race or class and forcibly excluded from the American Dream, they register more as a threat to be contained or eliminated than as an object of compassion and social investment. Poor minority youth are not merely excluded, they are also punished for living outside the power relations that give rise to the corrupt privileges of the second Gilded Age. One notable example is made clear in the questions raised by Rich Benjamin in a *New York Times* op-ed. He writes: "After all, why did the police treat Mr. Martin like a criminal, instead of Mr. Zimmerman, his assailant? Why was the black corpse tested for drugs and alcohol, but the living perpetrator wasn't?"[9]

What is missing in the current debate over the legalities of the case are questions of justice, which require taking a hard look at the underlying economic, racial, and political conditions that make such a senseless act of violence possible. It is easy to ridicule as racist Geraldo Rivera's claim that the boy's "hoodie" was somehow responsible for his death—as if it carried an unequivocal and dangerous signification for all young people, regardless of what their race, neighborhood, or class location might be. But the real question we must ask in this case is what kind of society would allow young black and brown youth to be killed because they are wearing a hoodie? Indeed, the politics of distraction runs deep in American culture. And questions concerning what kind of society we have now become, reflected in such a tragic killing, are simply ignored. Such questions are important because they invoke wider social considerations and prevent us from wallowing in a purely privatized discourse that, in the end, only allows us to focus on the most narrow and restricted of issues such as the personality of the shooter, George Zimmerman. Operating within the parameters of an utterly privatized discourse, the dominant media seem only capable of asking "Who is George Zimmerman and why did he shoot this young man?" Actually, the more purposeful question would be, what kind of society creates a George Zimmerman, along with a formative culture that elevates vigilantism over justice, emotion over reason, fear over shared responsibilities, and violence over compassion? This is not to overlook that Zimmerman should be brought to justice through a fair trial but to look beyond Zimmerman's dreadful act and see it as symptomatic of a larger war being waged on poor and minority youth. In a similar way, the media's narrow focus on the prevalence of a gun culture, gated communities, and private security forces ("Rambos for hire") in the United States does not provide an understanding for why "military force has replaced democratic idealism as the main source of U.S. influence" or why war is a source of national pride rather than alarm.[10] Nor does it tell us why the spectacle of violence has become the greatest source of entertainment in American popular culture, further enabling the process whereby civil society "organizes itself for the production of violence."[11] Within this bigger picture, we quickly discern how the war on youth not only places young people in ongoing conditions of uncertainty regarding their education, health care, employment, and their future, but it does so to the degree that it dictates whether they will live or die.

The Politics of Disposability and the Culture of Cruelty

An echo of the conditions that are responsible for Trayvon Martin's senseless killing can be heard in the words of politicians who embrace a culture of cruelty, suggesting that children who develop chronic illnesses should not be given access to health care. This is evident in laws that sentence young people to adult prisons, and in economic policies that drain income from working families and their children in order to line the pockets of the extremely wealthy and their hedge fund managers. Furthermore, it is also visible in a carceral state that wages a war on the poor rather than on poverty, defunds public schools to hasten their privatization, and demonizes young people while demonstrating that punishing youth remains a higher priority than educating them. Across the entire society, a culture of compassion has been replaced by a culture of fear that radically forestalls future possibility. The manufactured national hysteria over the need for security has become an autoimmune disease, massaged by endless moral panics about poor people, immigrants, minorities, and dangerous youth—all the while making us less safe and ever more vulnerable to violence. A consumer and hyper-militarized society that defines all relationships according to market values and enshrines a survival-of-the-fittest ethic leaves behind a string of abandoned visions, dreams, and hopes for the future. Symptoms of ethical, political, and economic impoverishment are all around us.

Economic Darwinism and the Madness of Gated Communities

When traces of the social contract and our feelings of collective responsibility to present and future generations were still alive in the United States (prior to the late 1970s), many Americans believed it took a social welfare state and strong communities to raise a child. That is, they believed in social safety nets that offered social protections, decent health care, child care, and other important social rights that affirmed the centrality of and shared experience of the common good, if not democracy itself. What many Americans now accept is a society that has turned its back on public values and social justice and in doing so has set the principles of democracy against itself, deforming the language of both freedom and justice that made equality a viable idea and political goal. Community as a metaphor for the common good and social contract is all but dead in America. "Community" is now gated and policed, and responsibility is reduced to a private and privately contracted affair shaped by a set of values that breathe a kind of mad savagery into a new form of economic Darwinism. In this market-driven, hyper-masculine, and militarized society, shared modes of sociality that once provided collective protections and expanded the rights of the social contract are now viewed with disdain. Indeed, for some pundits such as Rick Santorum, who relies on a religiously inflected rhetoric of evil and sin, notions of a secular public sphere are derided as a pathology that poisons the body politic.

Young people now find themselves in a world in which sociality has been reduced to an ideological battleground over materialistic needs waged by an army of disconnected and nomadic individuals, just as more and more people find their behavior criminalized and subject to state violence. Youth, in particular, now find themselves in a social order in which bonds of trust have been replaced by bonds of fear. As Zygmunt Bauman puts it, "Trust is replaced by universal suspicion. All bonds are assumed to be untrustworthy, unreliable, trap-and-ambush-like—until proven otherwise."[12] When all forms of social solidarity and civic values are abandoned to a free market logic, the only thing left will be the obligations of consumer-driven self-interest advanced against all other interests. Once again, how else to explain the fate of generations of young people, especially poor white, brown, and black youth, who find themselves in a society "in which 500,000 young people are incarcerated, 2.5 million are arrested annually, and almost a third . . . have been arrested for a crime" by the age of twenty-three?[13] What kind of society do we live in that allows 1.6 million kids to be homeless at any given time in a year? What country allows massive inequalities in wealth and income to produce a politically and morally dysfunctional social order in which "45 percent of U.S. residents live in households that struggle to make ends meet, [which] breaks down to 39 percent of all adults and 55 percent of all children"?[14] What is clear is that we now live in a society that invests more in what Etienne Balibar calls "the death zones of humanity" than in life itself, at least when it comes to impoverished youth.[15]

A Culture of Hyper-Punitiveness

What the shooting of Trayvon Martin tells us is that too many young people are not only being stripped of their hope and dignity, but also their lives. American society has become what Steve Herbert and Elizabeth Brown refer to as a "political culture of hyper-punitiveness," one in which it has become easier and apparently more acceptable to punish children who do not obey, refuse to be invisible, or question authority—children whose presence reminds us of how far we have moved away from the ideals that once allowed Americans to make a claim on democracy.[16] We now live in a bifurcated country of gated communities organized to protect at all costs their distinct privileges from desperately poor "no-go" zones, also isolated and armed to the teeth. Living in these paranoid lifeworlds, we have become a nation that emulates the fictional Dexter, the much celebrated serial killer in the cable TV series. Crime now drives social policy, and vigilante culture increasingly plays a prominent role in shaping American life. This is a bunker culture where guns rule, even as corporations have learned to capitalize on the growing culture of cruelty and punishment. Hollywood thrives on the spectacle of racial violence, and the American government devolves into a torture state. It is also a society that has intensified its racism behind the cloak of colorblindness and other post-racial myths, while at the same time exercising with more diligence its policing and punishing functions. Glen Ford, the editor at *Black Agenda*, touches on this in his commentary about why the George Zimmermans of the world think that they can get away with assaulting and punishing black youth: "They do these things because they can, and they think they can because they believe they've been given permission by a significant segment of society to carry out these attacks on young black men. And inevitably, if they are given what they believe is the green light, some people are going to take it."[17] Given these contexts and conditions, the issue is not whether a crime takes place because a young person wears a hoodie, but what kind of society do we live in when a child can be shot for emulating a style that is associated with that of black and brown urban youth?

Since the arrival of the Puritans, punishment has been inextricably woven into the fabric of American life, and it increasingly targets young people who have been pushed to the margins of society. Hence, it is not surprising that in America there is a rush to punish individuals for committing crimes, but no longer a passion and a commitment to examine the entrenched social issues that produce them. We now believe that some individuals were just born evil, and our responsibility begins and ends with their expulsion—not their salvation. We gloat over justice being served by sentencing young people such as Dharun Ravi to years in jail for a horrific homophobic crime that prompted the suicide of his roommate Tyler Clementi, but we never raise questions about the forces at work in a society that daily reproduce and reinforce this hateful culture in the first place.

Too many young people have not only been expelled from American society, but are also being punished with a kind of mass vengeance that suggests the emergence of a new political and economic culture in which life has become cheap. Trayvon Martin's death should not be trivialized by the distracting discourse of hoodies, nor is it reducible to the actions of a (possibly) mentally unbalanced shooter. It is not (yet) about a clear-cut act of racial violence, nor for that matter simply about the isolated and shocking death of a young man. It is about the death of the ideal of justice and the extinguishing of democratic values. It is symptomatic of the way in which an entire generation of poor minority youth are being punished, excluded, and starved in the elimination system of a violent, self-mutilating social order. It is about the stench and scope of death being promulgated throughout a society that has become cruelly deranged, corporately owned, politically corrupt, and morally bankrupt. Trayvon Martin's death is symptomatic of a war on young people intent on the destruction of youthful minds and bodies. It is also about the slide of a hyper-market-driven country into a moral and political coma that enables it to function without apology, without ethical considerations, in a world of power relations, values, and practices that are as punishing in their effects as they are cruel in their conception.

For many young people, the hoodie is not the central danger. Rather, violence is the central force in their lives, and the rhetoric and metaphors through which it gains legitimacy extend from the ever-pervasive reality of police brutality to the modes of punishment that creep from their schools and the streets to their homes. Violence is now the major force for producing identities, desires, and social policies. Unfortunately, for too many young people, violence has become the normal condition of their lives, the only space left where many of them can even recognize how their agency might be defined and what their future has to offer them. What Trayvon Martin's death tells the American public is, as Patricia Ticento Clough and Craig Willse have pointed out in a different context, that we live in a society "in which the production and circulation of death functions as political and economic currency."[18] And the price paid for that extends from the tragic death of a young African American man to an ongoing assault on millions of poor youth in this country. The cost is high, and with it comes the tragic violation of human life and the death of democracy itself. Surely, in remembering the death of Trayvon Martin, we can and must do more than don a hoodie to prop up the superficial solidarity of an alleged post-racial world order.

5.

The "Suicidal State" and the War on Youth

IN SPITE OF BEING discredited by the economic recession of 2008, unfettered free-market capitalism has once again become a dominant force in American society. This pervasive regime of neoliberalism is producing unprecedented inequalities in wealth and income, runaway environmental devastation, egregious amounts of human suffering, and what Alex Honneth has called an "abyss of failed sociality."[1] The Gilded Age is back with big profits for the ultra-rich and large financial institutions, and increasing impoverishment and misery for middle and working classes. Political illiteracy and religious fundamentalism have cornered the market on populist rage, providing support for a country in which, as Robert Reich points out, "the very richest people get all the economic gains [and] routinely bribe politicians" to cut their taxes and establish policies that eliminate public goods.[2] At the same time, students are being assaulted by the police for engaging in peaceful protests against the harshest elements of the neoliberal order while low-income and poor minority youth are placed increasingly under the authority of the criminal justice system. Everywhere we look, the rich and powerful use their authority to undermine the social state. Corporate elites now use their unchecked power to lay off millions of workers, simultaneously cutting the benefits and rights of those on the job in order to increase their own exorbitant profits. Social protections are dismantled; public servants are denigrated; and public goods such as schools, infrastructure, health care services, and public transportation deteriorate beyond repair. Meanwhile, the neoliberal social order embraces the ruthless and punishing values of economic Darwinism and a survival-of-the-fittest ethic and wages an ongoing war on women's rights, the welfare state, workers, students, and anyone who has the temerity to speak out against such attacks. Relatively unchecked in imposing its values, social relations, and forms of social death upon all aspects of civic life, neoliberalism[3] has given rise to what Paul Virilio has called a "suicidal state."[4] The United States now resembles a society in which governments work to destroy their own defenses against anti-democratic forces.[5] As Jacques Derrida explained, such states offer no immunity against authoritarianism; rather, they emulate "that strange behavior where a living being, in quasi-suicidal fashion 'itself' works to destroy its own protection, to immunize itself against its 'own' immunity." What is "put at risk by this terrifying autoimmunity logic," Derrida grimly stated, "is nothing less than the existence of the world."[6] Susan Searls Giroux follows up this logic with a series of important questions:

> I've wondered about the troubling figure of societal suicide. How is it possible that a free and democratic society, precisely in the act of securing itself, or claiming to secure itself, could quicken its own demise? Where does the suicidal urge come from—is it a function of a deep, abiding illness in the collective psyche or a fleeting impulse linked to traumatic loss, or some imagined heroism? Is this really the future we face and, if so, how do we determine our degree of risk? Do we invoke the same assessment scale used for individual suicides? Gender, for example, is a factor; males are at greater risk, but how does one determine the gender of a society—by its masculinist inclination? Evidence of depression is another sign. Does one look to dips in the stock market

or consumer confidence indices? Sales of anti-depressant medications? How about recent suicide attempts? Derrida describes the Cold War as a "first moment," a "first autoimmunity." Recent significant trauma or loss? Without question. Capacity for rational thinking lost? So it would seem. Little or no social support? Would loss of global support work here? Going down such a list, the signs don't look promising.[7]

For over thirty years, the North American public has been reared on a neoliberal dystopian vision that legitimates itself through a set of largely unchallenged claims: there are no alternatives to a market-driven society; economic growth should not be constrained by considerations of social costs or moral responsibility; war is a permanent condition of society; and democracy and capitalism are virtually synonymous. While there are many variants of neoliberalism, what links these diverse strands is a "fundamental preference for the market over the state as a means of resolving problems and achieving human ends."[8]

At the heart of this market-driven regime is an instrumental rationality that sells off public goods and services to the highest bidders in the private sector, and simultaneously dismantles those public spheres, social protections, and institutions serving the larger society. As economic power succeeds in detaching itself from government regulations, social costs, and ethical considerations, a new global financial class reasserts the prerogatives of capital and systematically destroys those public spheres—including public and higher education—that traditionally advocate for social equality and contribute to the creation of an educated citizenry that is a fundamental condition for a viable democracy.

In the current moment, the bloated financial class and their lobbyists do their magic by buying off politicians who are only too willing to squander the public coffers on wars abroad, attempting to establish across the globe what can be called death zones inhabited by drones, high-tech weaponry, and, increasingly, private armies.[9] Andrew Bacevich captures the expanding parameters of this militarized death march in the following commentary:

[With] Pentagon outlays running at something like $700 billion annually, the United States spends as much or more money on its military than the entire rest of the world combined. The United States currently has approximately 300,000 troops stationed abroad, again more than the rest of the world combined (a total that does not even include another 90,000 sailors and marines who are at sea); as of 2008, according to the Department of Defense, these troops occupied or used some 761 "sites" in 39 foreign countries, although this tally neglected to include many dozens of U.S. bases in Iraq or Afghanistan; no other country comes even remotely close to replicating this "empire of bases"—or to matching the access that the Pentagon has negotiated to airfields and seaports around the world.[10]

Empire now provides the salutes, spectacles, and high drama that offer a distraction from the predatory violence that shapes domestic politics. Unfortunately, as I have mentioned elsewhere in this book, despite our knowledge of the corrupt profiteering practices that instigated a global financial meltdown, free-market fundamentalism does not appear to be losing either its legitimacy or its claims on democracy. On the contrary, in this new era in which we live, consumerism and profit making are defined as the essence of democracy, and freedom has been reconceived as the unrestricted ability of markets to govern economic relations free from government regulation or moral considerations.

As the principle of economic deregulation gradually merges with a notion of unregulated self-interest, one consequence is that people— eager to protect what they believe is their freedom—become all too willing to relinquish their power, civil rights, and social protections to unaccountable and unchecked forms of authoritarian corporate and state control. Of course, since September 2011, the paralyzing fog of depoliticization in a post-9/11 world has been ruptured by the Occupy movement, the roar of angry workers, and young people refusing to cede their futures to the new oligarchs, bankers, the Koch brothers, hedge fund managers, Christian extremists, and the corporate-controlled liberal and conservative media apparatuses.[11]

As a result of the triumph of corporate power over democratic values—made visible recently in the *Citizens United* Supreme Court case that eliminated all controls on corporate spending on political campaigns—the authority of the state now defends the market and powerful financial interests, even as it expands its disciplinary control over the rest of society. There is more at work here, as David Harvey points out, than merely a political project designed "to reestablish the conditions for capital accumulation and to restore the power of economic elites."[12] There is also a reconfiguration of the state by a merging of the warfare and punishing state, the endpoint of which is undoubtedly a "suicidal state."[13]

Lending muscle to corporate initiatives, the suicidal state becomes largely responsible for managing and expanding mechanisms of control, containment, and punishment over a vast number of public institutions. As a weakened social contract comes under sustained attack, the model of the prison, along with its practices and accelerating mechanisms of punishment, emerges as a core institution and mode of governance under the suicidal state—and a hyper mode of punishment is consequently seeping into a variety of institutions.[14] Agencies and public services that once offered relief and hope to the disadvantaged are now being replaced with a police presence, along with other elements of the criminal justice system.[15] The brutal face of the emerging police state is also evident in the attacks on young black people and youthful protesters, and in the stop-and-frisk policies initiated in major urban cities that contain large black, brown, and immigrant populations. In Bloomberg's New York City, a "Clean Halls" program allows the police to conduct searches in private apartment buildings, stopping people in hallways and demanding an ID, and in many cases harassing and arresting people needlessly. The extent of the brazenly illegal legalities have prompted Matt Taibbi of *Rolling Stone* to state that he has just discovered that the punishing state is as much a threat to democracy as white-collar corruption:

> Stories like this "Clean Halls" program are beginning to make me
> see that journalists like myself have undersold the white-collar

corruption story in recent years by ignoring its flip side. We have two definitely connected phenomena, often treated as separate and unconnected: a growing lawlessness in the financial sector, and an expanding, repressive, increasingly lunatic police apparatus trained at the poor, and especially the non-white poor.[16]

Democracy and Youth on Life Support

Democracy is on life support, and the list of casualties in the war to empty it of any substance is long. We are witnessing the ongoing privatization of public schools, health care, prisons, transportation, the military, public airwaves, public lands, and other crucial elements of the commons along with the undermining of our most basic civil liberties. Privatization in this case not only turns public goods over to the savage interests of the corporate elite, but puts such goods in the hands of market-based fundamentalists who exercise increasing control over the production of identities, values, modes of agency, and dissent in the United States. Homeschooling, vouchers, charter schools, and the rhetoric of "school choice" all serve as code for privatizing public goods, public spheres, and non-commodified institutions. Similarly, the bridges between public and private life are being dismantled, while the market—with its disregard for the complex web of systemic forces that bear down on people's lives, not to mention its disregard for human life itself—becomes the template for structuring all social relations. As public spheres dedicated to the public good shrink, the language of community, public values, and social responsibility disappears from the public imagination just as the ability to translate private troubles into larger social problems disappears as a basic tool of civic literacy. This political and educational deficit is particularly damaging for young people who no longer symbolize a crucial and long-term social investment in the future.

Since the 1970s, there has been an intensification of the anti-democratic pressures of neoliberal modes of governance, ideology, and policies. What is particularly new is the way in which young people

are increasingly denied any place in an already weakened social contract and the degree to which they are no longer seen as central to
how the United States defines its future. Youth is no longer the place
where society reveals its dreams but where it increasingly hides its
nightmares. Within neoliberal narratives, youth are either defined as
a consumer market or stand for trouble.[17] This shift in representations
of how American society talks about young people betrays a great deal
about what is increasingly new about the economic, social, cultural,
and political constitution of American society and its growing disinvestment in young people, the social state, and democracy itself.[18] The
promises of modernity regarding progress, freedom, and hope have
not been eliminated; they have been reconfigured, stripped of their
emancipatory potential and relegated to the logic of a savage market
instrumentality. Modernity has reneged on its promise, however
disingenuous or limited, to young people of mobility, stability, and collective security. Long-term planning and the institutional structures
that support it are now relegated to the imperatives of privatization,
deregulation, flexibility, and short-term investments. Social bonds
have given way to the collapse of social protections and the welfare
state just as "the emphasis is now on individual solutions to socially
produced problems."[19] As Sharon Stevens points out, what we are now
witnessing is not only the "wide-ranging restructurings of modernity"
but also the effect "these changes have for the concept of childhood
and the life conditions of children."[20]

The severity of the consequences of this shift in modernity under
neoliberalism among youth is evident in the fact that this is the first
generation in which the "plight of the outcast may stretch to embrace
a whole generation."[21] The eminent sociologist Zygmunt Bauman
argues that today's youth have been "cast in a condition of liminal
drift, with no way of knowing whether it is transitory or permanent."[22]
That is, the generation of youth in the early twenty-first century has
no way of grasping if they will ever "be free from the gnawing sense
of the transience, indefiniteness, and provisional nature of any settle-
ment."[23] Neoliberal violence produced in part through a massive shift
in wealth to the upper 1 percent, growing inequality, the reign of

financial services, the closing down of educational opportunities, and the stripping of benefits and resources from those marginalized by race and class has produced a generation without jobs, independent lives, and even the most minimal social benefits. Youth no longer occupy the hope of a privileged place that was offered to previous generations. They now inhabit a neoliberal notion of temporality marked by a loss of faith in progress along with the emergence of apocalyptic narratives in which the future appears indeterminate, bleak, and insecure. Heightened expectations and progressive visions pale and are smashed next to the normalization of market-driven government policies that wipe out pensions, eliminate quality health care, raise college tuition, and produce a harsh world of joblessness while giving millions to banks and the military. Students, in particular, now find themselves in a world in which heightened expectations have been replaced by dashed hopes. The promises of higher education and previously enviable credentials have turned into the swindle of fulfillment as "for the first time in living memory, the whole class of graduates faces a high probability, almost the certainty, of ad hoc, temporary, insecure and part-time jobs, unpaid 'trainee' pseudo-jobs deceitfully rebranded 'practices'—all considerably below the skills they have acquired and eons below the level of their expectations."[24]

What has changed about an entire generation of young people includes not only neoliberal society's disinvestment in youth and the permanent fate of downward mobility, but also the fact that youth live in a commercially carpet-bombed and commodified environment that is unlike anything experienced by those of previous generations. Nothing has prepared this generation for the inhospitable and savage new world of commodification, privatization, joblessness, frustrated hopes, and stillborn projects.[25] The present generation has been born into a throwaway society of consumers in which both goods and young people are increasingly objectified and deemed disposable. As cultural studies theorist Lawrence Grossberg points out, young people now inhabit a world in which there are few public spheres or social spaces autonomous from the reach of the market:

Kids see themselves presented in highly sexualized ways for advertising and entertainment purposes, even while their own sexual
behavior is repressed and criminalized. . . . Kids hear themselves
attacked for their consumerism, even while the media and corporate
interests commercialize and commodify every dimension of their
lives, every pleasure, every need. From the kids' perspective, it looks
as if we are selling, or perhaps we already have sold, our children to
advertisers, to private business, to corporate capitalism. . . . What
can it say to them that as a society we are unwilling to pay for their
education (as ours had been paid for) but we are willing to commercialize education (junk foods, field trips to chain stores, sponsored
lesson materials and textbooks, advertising in hallways)?[26]

The structures of neoliberal modernity do more than disinvest in
young people and commodify them, they also transform the protected
space of childhood into a zone of disciplinary exclusion and cruelty,
especially for those young people further marginalized by race and
class who now inhabit a social landscape in which they are increasingly
disparaged as flawed consumers. With no adequate role to play as consumers, many youth are now considered disposable, forced to inhabit
"zones of social abandonment" extending from bad schools to bulging
detention centers and prisons.[27] In the midst of the rise of the punishing state, the circuits of state repression, surveillance, and disposability
increasingly "link the fate of blacks, Latinos, Native Americans, poor
whites, and Asian Americans" who are now caught in a governing-
through-crime youth complex, which serves as a default solution to
major social problems.[28]

Already disenfranchised by virtue of their age, young people are
under assault today in ways that are entirely new because they now face
a world that is far more dangerous than at any other time in recent history. Not only do they live in a space of social homelessness in which
precariousness and uncertainty lock them out of a secure future, but
they also find themselves living in a society that seeks to silence them
by making them invisible. Victims of a war against economic justice,
equality, and democratic values, young people are now told not to

expect too much and to accept the status of "stateless, faceless, and functionless"[29] nomads, a plight for which they alone will have to accept responsibility. At best, they are told each must assume sole responsibility for their fate. At worst, they are viewed as unproductive, excess, and utterly expendable. But the discourse of redundancy has a darker side, even beyond those signaling that society is no longer willing to invest in poor minority and white youth: hidden behind the careless face of the corporate state is a social order that makes many young people a prime target of an emerging governing-through-crime complex.

Today's young people inhabit an age of unprecedented symbolic, material, and institutional violence—an age of grotesque irresponsibility, unrestrained greed, and unchecked individualism. Youth now constitute a present absence in any talk about democracy. Their disappearance is symptomatic of a society that has turned against itself, punishes its children, and does so at the risk of killing the entire body politic. The suicidal state produces an autoimmune crisis that attacks middle-class, poor minority, and low-income youth, the very elements of a society that allow it to reproduce itself, and at the same time killing off any sense of history, memory, and ethical responsibility. Under such circumstances, all bets are off regarding the future of democracy.

Also lost in the current historical conjuncture is the very idea of the public good, the notion of connecting learning to social change, and the development of modes of civic courage infused by the principles of social justice. Under the regime of a ruthless economic Darwinism that emphasizes an egocentric, win-at-any-cost war against all ethics, the concepts and practices of community and solidarity have been replaced by a world of cutthroat politics, financial greed, media spectacles, and a rabid consumerism. With all public concerns now reduced to private matters, we are witnessing the triumph of individual rights over social rights, nowhere better exemplified than in the gated communities, gated intellectuals, and gated values that have become symptomatic of a society that has lost all claims to democracy.

Zygmunt Bauman is right to insist that "visions have nowadays fallen into disrepute and we tend to be proud of what we should be ashamed of."[30] Politics has become an extension of war, just as state-sponsored violence increasingly finds legitimation in popular culture and a broader culture of cruelty that promotes an expanding landscape of fear—even the fear of democracy itself—and undermines any sense of shared responsibility toward others. Economic insecurity increasingly produces political insecurity, cynicism, and a depoliticized public as the current system of economic terror dehumanizes and atomizes large segments of society. As fear and terror sweep over society, individuals increasingly "live in a state of stupor, in a moral coma. . . . Thinking becomes a stupid crime; it endangers [one's] life."[31] Under these conditions, youth, who have historically posed a challenge to authority, become a lightning rod for all the various perceived threats to society. Poor minority youth, in particular, become targets. They are not just excluded from the American Dream, but have become utterly redundant and disposable, waste products of a society that no longer considers them of any value. Such youth, already facing forms of racial and class-based exclusion, now experience a kind of social death as they are pushed out of schools, denied job training opportunities, subjected to rigorous modes of surveillance and criminal sanctions, and viewed less as chronically disadvantaged than as flawed consumers and civic felons. Some young people, such as Trayvon Martin and Rekia Boyd (shot and killed in 2012 by an off-duty Chicago policeman), experience something more ominous: death by homicide.

The everyday existence of poor white, immigrant, and minority youth has indeed become a matter of survival. No longer tracked into either high- or low-achievement classes, many of these youth are being pushed right out of school into the juvenile criminal justice system.[32] Under such circumstances, the disposability of certain social groups becomes central to the political and social order. Too many young people are not completing high school (barely half of Latino and black men graduate from high school in four years), and are bearing the brunt of a system that leaves them uneducated and jobless, one that ultimately offers them a life of destitution or prison—the only available roles for those individuals who cannot be producers or consumers. When the material foundations of agency and security disappear, hope becomes hopeless, and young people are reduced to the status of waste products to be tossed out or hidden away in the global human waste industry.

Not only have social safety nets and protections unraveled in the last thirty years, but the suffering and hardships many children face have been greatly amplified by both the economic crisis and the austerity policies that are being currently implemented with little justification. Young people now find themselves in a world in which sociality has been reduced to an economic battleground over materialistic needs waged by an army of nomadic and fiercely competitive individuals, just as more and more young people find their behavior pathologized, criminalized, and subject to state violence.[33] Youth now inhabit a social order in which bonds of trust have been replaced by bonds of fear. As Bauman puts it, "Trust is replaced by universal suspicion. All bonds are assumed to be untrustworthy, unreliable, trap-and-ambush-like—until proven otherwise."[34]All forms of social solidarity are now abandoned to a free-market logic that has individualized responsibility and reduced civic values to the obligations of a consumer-driven self-interest advanced against all social considerations and social costs. How else to explain the fate of generations of young people, especially poor white, brown, and black youth, who find themselves in a country that is the world's leader in incarceration, one in which such youth are considered the nexus of crime?

The United States is one of the few countries in the world that puts children in supermax prisons, tries them as adults, incarcerates them for exceptionally long periods of time, defines them as "super predators," pepper-sprays them for engaging in peaceful protests, and describes them as "teenage time bombs."[35] In the aftermath of the war on terror, young people have become the enemy of choice, elevated to the status as an all-pervasive threat to dominant authority. Clearly, the increased militarization of local police forces and their growing use of violence against young protesters signal the threat that young people now pose to the rise of the finance and punishing state. Instead of children being nurtured and educated, they are now tasered, sequestered in dangerous prisons, and demonized in order to divert our attention from real social problems and their potential solutions. At the same time, society engages in a public purification ritual through imposing harsh disciplinary practices on its most vulnerable members. As I have mentioned in previous chapters, statistics paint a bleak picture for young people in the United States: 1.5 million are unemployed, which marks a seventeen-year high; 12.5 million are without food; and, in what amounts to a national disgrace, one out of every five American children lives in poverty. Nearly half of all U.S. children and 90 percent of black youngsters will be on food stamps at some point during childhood.[36] Increasingly, kids are forced to inhabit a rough world where childhood is nonexistent, crushed under the heavy material and existential burdens they are forced to bear.

The deteriorating state of youth may be the most serious challenge facing educators, social workers, youth workers, and others in the twenty-first century. It is a struggle that demands a new understanding of politics, one that demands that we think beyond the given, imagine the unimaginable, and combine the lofty ideals of democracy with a willingness to fight for its realization. But this is not a fight that can be won through individual struggles or fragmented political movements. It demands new modes of solidarity, new political organizations, and a powerful social movement capable of uniting diverse political interests and groups. It is a struggle that is as educational as it is political. It is also a struggle that is as necessary as it is urgent. It is a struggle that *must not* be ignored.

The Promise of Collective Struggle

One way of addressing our collapsing intellectual and moral visions regarding young people is to imagine those policies, values, opportunities, and social relations that invoke adult responsibility and reinforce the ethical imperative to provide young people, especially those marginalized by race and class, with the economic, social, and educational conditions that make life livable and the future sustainable. Clearly such a vision must move beyond what Alain Badiou has called the "crisis of negation,"[37] which is a crisis of imagination, historical possibility, and an aversion to new ideas. Hope for a new vision can be found in the protests of the Occupy and Quebec student movements in North America and other youth resistance movements around the globe. What is evident in this worldwide movement of youth protests is a bold attempt to imagine the possibility of another world, a refusal of the current moment of historical one-dimensionality, and a refusal to settle for reforms that are purely incremental.

The challenge is not insignificant. The United States as a suicidal state is now organized around the primacy of sadistic impulses, with widespread violence and modes of hyper-punishment functioning as part of an anti-immune system that turns the economy of genuine pleasure into a mode of sadism that creates the foundation for sapping democracy of any political substance and moral vitality. The suicidal state devalues any viable notion of rationality, ethics, and democracy, and has given rise to a suicidal society marked by a culture of cruelty in which the ultimate form of entertainment has become the pain and suffering of others, especially those considered throwaways or lacking consumer privileges and rights. High-octane moral panics, a flight from civic responsibility, extreme callousness, and the reproduction of human suffering have become the by-products of a market-driven society marked by an autoimmune disease that destroys its own pro-tections against a creeping authoritarianism.

The prevalence of institutionalized injustice, illegal legalities, and expanding violence in American society suggests that the only way forward to a viable future must begin with a new conversation and pol-itics that address how a truly just and fair world must look. We see the initiation of such a conversation among the protesters who organized the Occupy movement. This is a conversation infused by the need for a new political language that is formulated with great care and self-reflec-tion by intellectuals, artists, workers, unions, parents, educators, young people, and others whose individual protections and social rights are in grave danger from the threat of a creeping fundamentalism that spreads its poison everywhere in the body politic.

The suicidal tendencies of the state with its apparatuses of violence are creeping into all aspects of social life, making clear that too many young people and others marginalized by class, race, and ethnicity have been abandoned by America's claim to democracy, especially in light of the rising forces of militarism, neoliberalism, religious fundamentalism, and state terrorism. The United States has become a suicidal state, indicating a new urgency for a collective politics and social movements capable of both negating the established order and imagining a new one. In these efforts, critique must merge with a sense of realistic hope, and individual struggles must expand into larger social movements. Until we address what Stanley Aronowitz has brilliantly analyzed as "The Winter of Our Discontent," the suicidal state will continue to engage in autoimmune practices that attack the very values, institutions, social relations, and hopes that keep the ideal of democracy alive.[38]

At the very least, the American public owes to its children and future generations an effort to dismantle this machinery of death and to reclaim the spirit of a future that works for life rather than for the death worlds of the current authoritarianism, dressed up as it is with a soft edge of consumer spectacle and celebrity culture. It is time for the 99 percent to connect the dots, educate themselves, and develop social movements that will not only rewrite the language of democracy but put into place the institutions and formative cultures that make it possible. There is no room for failure here, because failure would cast us back into the clutches of a crushing authoritarianism that—though different from previous historical periods—exhibits a similar imperative to proliferate violent social formations and to execute a death-dealing blow to democracy.

6.

Religious Fundamentalism, the Attack on Public Schools, and the Crisis of Reason

RIGHT-WING FUNDAMENTALISTS such as former Republican presidential candidate Rick Santorum loathe public schools (derisively labeled government schools), often suggesting that they are wedded to doing the work of Satan. Santorum, true to his love affair with the secular ideology of privatization, prefers homeschooling. For him, homeschooling enshrines the notion of choice, suggesting that individuals are capable of assuming responsibility for educating themselves. But homeschooling and the notion of choice it enshrines are only two expressions of a broader issue: the government's abandonment of people to whatever social fate or problems they may face—whether it be finding the best education for their children or securing decent health care. Actually, Republicans such as Santorum, Mitt Romney, Newt Gingrich, and Paul Ryan dislike any public institution that enables people to think critically and act with a degree of responsibility toward the public. As stated in the 2012 Texas Republican Party platform, conservatives not only banned critical thinking but any form of analytical thought that challenges "the student's fixed beliefs [or might] undermine parental authority."[1] Such a statement is more than a legitimation of ignorance: it is a celebration of modes of pedagogy that promote conformity, refuse to question authority, and empty out any relationship between education and a critical notion of citizenship.

The Texas State Board of Education, which has as one of its duties the responsibility "to update curriculum standards and textbooks" for Texas students ("4.8 million textbook-reading children in as of 2011") has used that power to impose very conservative standards on what can be included and excluded in "schoolbooks across the country."[2] What has resulted is a pedagogy of censorship and ignorance. For instance, Thomas Jefferson's name was removed from a list of Enlightenment philosophers because he is credited with coining the phrase "separation of church and state."[3] Ideologically charged words such as "democracy" and "capitalism" were replaced with "representative democracy" and "republic," and the term "imperialism" was removed from any association with American foreign policy. It gets worse. Progressive historical figures and social movements, especially during and after the sixties, were either purged from the books or replaced by a lineup of conservatives. For instance, the board also included a statement insisting that students learn about "the conservative resurgence of the 1980s and 1990s, including Phyllis Schlafly, the Contract with America, the Heritage Foundation, the Moral Majority and the National Rifle Association."[4] The gains of the Great Society, particularly affirmative action and the civil rights movements, were disparaged with the assertion that they were "unintended outcomes."[5]

A rhetorical war is being waged by the several members of the Republican Party against not only schools but the whole secular state and culture, the ultimate goal of which is clearly the extermination of dissent, critical thinking, informed judgment, and any vestige of independent agency. How else to explain former Republican presidential candidate Rick Santorum's tirade against higher education, his hatred of Muslims, his suggestion that Obama is not a true Christian, and his disdain for the reproductive rights of women? Another front-row exhibit of such ignorance was evident in the comments by Republican

Todd Akin who claimed that "legitimate rape" rarely leads to pregnancy. And Akin is not some lone political ignoramus filling the media sphere with hateful nonsense. As Frank Rich points out:

> Only a handful of the House's 241 Republican members differ at all from his hardline stand on abortion. And on women's rights, the Senate caucus is barely different: Only one of that chamber's 47 GOP members voted against the so-called Blunt Amendment, another Republican jihad against women's health care this year.[6]

The violence of war in this discourse is sanctioned as a spiritual crusade, or as Santorum once put it: "This is not a political war at all. This is not a cultural war at all. This is a spiritual war."[7] And the spiritual enemies include anyone who does not fit or agree with Santorum's and the Republican Party's fundamentalist worldview. There is more than ignorance at work here; there is also the dangerous demonization of "everybody but white, heterosexual, right-wing Christian males."[8] The mainstream media dress up this discursive fascism as just another opinion, refusing to utilize the civic courage and critical analyses needed to name it for what it is: a form of totalitarian extremism.

Religious political discourse must be seen as part of not only the deeply disturbing emergence of religious fundamentalism, but also as a crucial element of the new authoritarianism emerging in the United States. Analyzing the merging of right-wing religious fundamentalism and a growing corporate and state authoritarianism is an important theoretical and political intervention because it points to a particular rather than general indictment of religion. That is, it distinguishes the more fundamentalist strains of religion from their progressive counterparts, enabling a crucial recognition of the nurturing and progressive work of many religions while confronting a virulent form of totalitarianism that speaks through militant and fundamentalist religious orthodoxy. Santorum and his ilk define themselves as the new warriors attempting to bring morality back to America. In actuality, they are right-wing revolutionaries who want to replace democratic principles with autocratic ones, critical thought with unconditional obedience to a spiritual leader, and justice with a notion of faith rooted in exclusion, disposability, and the annihilation of difference.

The New Anti-Intellectualism

Anti-intellectualism—as an integral facet of the religionization of politics—provides the foundation for both an authoritarian culture and an authoritarian state.[9] This is one reason why religious fundamentalists denounce public education, which harbors the promise of actually educating students to be thoughtful, self-reflective, and capable of not only questioning so-called common sense but also of holding power accountable. Some progressives view the right-wing stance against public education as simply another example of the Republican Party endorsing the notion that being stupid is not merely acceptable but necessary in a social order that views critical analysis and discriminating judgment as a threat to theocratic authority. Others view this anti-public stance against education and for a pedagogy of repression as a misguided flight from rationality and truth. But there is more going on here than the issue of whether right-wing fundamentalists are intellectually and politically challenged. Surely, one reason why radical Christian evangelicals, neoconservatives, and right-wing nationalists in the United States today perceive critical education, especially, to be so threatening is that central to the very definition of critical pedagogy is the task of educating students to become critical agents who can actively question and build the connections between people's individual troubles, such as unemployment, and broader systemic determinants that underlie "personal" problems. In other words, critical education cultivates students who value collective well-being, examine public issues, lead rather than follow, embrace reasoned arguments over opinions, and reject a narrow conception of common sense as the engine of truth.

Any discourse that promotes doubt is dangerous, especially to demagogues who view ignorance as a political advantage. For them, ignorance is a gift that is as self-serving as it is politically useful, since it provides a sense of community for those who wish to be free of social responsibility and live comfortably in a moral coma. It also makes it easier to avoid the messy task of addressing and dealing with informed, skeptical citizens. In fact, one might say that Americans are increasingly proud of what they should in actuality be deeply ashamed about. Mark Slouka points to an ignorance index that captures the disinvestment in education and the illiteracy it produces as a growing part of American national identity and culture. As he puts it, "here is the mirror—look and wince":

> One out of every four of us believes we've been reincarnated; 44 percent of us believe in ghosts; 71 percent, in angels. Forty percent of us believe God created all things in their present form sometime during the last 10,000 years. Nearly the same number—not coincidentally, perhaps—are functionally illiterate. Twenty percent think the sun might revolve around the earth.[10]

Religious fundamentalism is in essence a war on the basic rights, freedom, and institutions of democracy, especially those that create an engaged populace. What religious fundamentalists realize perhaps better than most liberal progressives is that democracy simply cannot function without an informed public and that in the absence of such a citizenry we have a public disinvested from either thinking reflectively or acting responsibly. There is nothing more feared by fundamentalists than individuals who can actually think critically and reflectively and are willing to invest in reason and freedom, rather than a crude moralism and a reductionistic appeal to faith as the ultimate basis of agency and politics. Those who appeal to a theocratic worldview long for a crowd of followers willing to lose themselves in causes and movements that trade in clichés and alleged "common sense."

This loss of rational connection between language and ethical considerations, of course, is characteristic of the Tea Party crowd with their overt racism, dislike for critical thought, and longing for outlets through which they can vent their anger, moral panics, and hatred for those who reject their rigid Manichean view of the world.[11] This is a crowd that embraces the likes of Santorum and other fundamentalists because they provide the outlets in which such groups can fulfill their desire to be amused by what might be called the spectacle of anti-politics. And though Romney, the titular head of the Republican Party, appeared more moderate or at least strategically silent on the issue of religious fundamentalism, the party he led in 2012 is in the hands of political and religious extremists who are clearly more on the side of the deepest strains of ignorance and fundamentalism than on the side of reason and enlightenment. Evangelical extremist votes were a crucial necessity for Romney's control of the Republican Party, and there was little question that he lived in fear of alienating this powerful group.

Censorship, Zero Tolerance Policies, and Punishing-for-Profits Incarceration

In terms of providing young people with a decent education, Arizona politicians and administrative incompetents made clear that critical pedagogy is especially dangerous when they chose to ban ethnic studies classes and censor books in favor of a conflict-free version of American history.[12] Not only does critical pedagogy offer students a way of connecting education to social change, it also brings to light subordinated histories, narratives, and modes of knowledge in an attempt to give students often rendered voiceless the capacities to both read the word and the world critically. Against any notion of education as a form of empowerment, the religious fanatics and privatizing fundamentalists censor critical thought and impose a stifling amnesia over historical inquiry. But they wish to do more. As part of a broader regressive educational project of defining education in disciplinary and repressive terms, they steadfastly attempt to substitute a pedagogy of training and punishment for a pedagogy of critical learning.

As I mention throughout this book, too many children in America now attend schools modeled after prisons. Schools have become places where the challenge of teaching and learning has been replaced by an obsession with crime, punishment, and humiliation. Many young people are being charged with criminal misdemeanors for behaviors that are too trivial to warrant recognition, let alone punishment.[13] What are we to make, for instance, of an incident in a Stockton school where a five-year-old was handcuffed and taken to a hospital for psychiatric evaluation? This hard-to-believe event happened because the child in question pushed away a police officer's hand after he placed it on the child's shoulder. What does it mean when young people are charged with assault for engaging in behaviors that in the past would have barely solicited a teacher's attention? How do we defend a public school system that sanctions the pepper-spraying of a child with an IQ below 70 because "he didn't understand what the police were saying"?[14] This is nothing less than barbarism parading as sound educational and disciplinary practice. As is well known, zero tolerance laws have become a plague imposed on public schooling. They have become a shameless quick-and-easy—and apparently lucrative—fix for defining student misconduct. Texas, for example, served more than one thousand primary school kids over a six-year period with tickets for misbehaving, and in some cases fines ran as high as $500.[15] Such practices, which merge harsh disciplinary measures with a reactionary curriculum and pedagogy infused with the tenets of religious fundamentalism, produce another plank in the growing authoritarianism that has emerged in the public schools since the 1980s.[16]

In Chicago, Noble Street Charter Network schools, run by former felon Michael Milken, set up a dehumanizing discipline system that repeatedly issued demerits and fines to students for "minor infractions" ranging from chewing gum and slouching in a chair to looking away from the teacher.[17] The disciplinary apparatus set up by Noble is called the "SMART" policy and demands the following behaviors: "sitting up straight, making eye contact when addressed by the teacher, articulating in standard English, responding to questions and prompts appropriately, and tracking the teacher with their eyes at all times."[18] Students are not just punished for breaking these rules; they are required to pay a fine. In the course of three years, ten Noble schools netted $386,745 in fines, and if "students failed to pay, they could be held back, regardless of their academic status."[19] The Advancement Project, a multi-racial civil rights organization, has called such disciplinary practices not only ineffective but "pernicious and harmful to youth."[20] They are also most certainly harmful to poor families who have to choose between buying food and paying school administrators for cruel, punishing fines. In many respects, this policy amounts to a tax on poor people—one that Matthew Mayer, a professor in the graduate school of education at Rutgers University, described as "almost medieval in nature. It's a form a financial torture, for lack of a better term . . . because it likely has no bearing on students' academic performance and disproportionately hurts poor families."[21]

Clearly, this practice can neither be defended as a disciplinary measure nor justified in any way as beneficial to students. It is clearly a form of harassment, and one that is aimed at both students and their parents. What could possibly be the pedagogical rationale for this illogical and cruel practice? Students in this scenario are reduced to Pavlovian dogs, while the anti-public privateers extend the reach of the punishing state into the school and make a large profit to boot.

Dangerous Pedagogy

What is it about critical schooling and pedagogy that is so dangerous to religious and ideological fundamentalists? The most obvious answer is that critical pedagogy believes in forms of school governance that respect both teachers and administrators, on the one hand, and students on the other. That is, it supports institutional conditions extending from decent pay to equitable modes of governance that make good teaching possible. It also argues for modes of education that enable teacher autonomy in the classroom and foster the capacities of students to read widely, learn the best that humanity has produced, and develop the skills necessary to both critique existing social forms and institutions and transform them whenever necessary. Put bluntly, critical pedagogy insists that knowledge is crucial to democratic citizenship because it provides young people with the tools to act responsibly in the service of civic courage. What past detractors of critical pedagogy refused to accept is that education is always a moral and political practice, rather than an empty and sterile method. But the religious fundamentalists who despise critical education fully acknowledge the power of schooling to shape people's identities and ways of thinking, and consequently crave replacing it with religious-based education. This is why, for them, critical pedagogy must be utterly and totally eradicated, and not simply tolerated as a marginal practice.

Critical pedagogy offers the promise of educating students to be able to reject the official lies of power and the utterly reductive notion of training as a substitute for informed modes of education. Paraphrasing Bill Moyers, critical pedagogy should be seen as part of a larger project whose purpose is to dignify "people so they become fully free to claim their moral and political agency."[22] In this instance, critical pedagogy opens up a space where students should be able to come to terms with their own power as critical agents; it provides a sphere where the unconditional freedom to question and assert one's voice is central to the purpose of education.[23] But it does not stop there. In the spirit of Paulo Freire, critical pedagogy provides the conditions for students to learn how to read and write as well as master and learn how to interrogate the basic concepts of literature, the arts, science, philosophy, social theory, and the applied disciplines.[24] Dialogue, in this case, exists as both an informed exchange between the teacher and student as well as a dialogue between the everyday experience of students and selective intellectual traditions that are engaged "not in reverence, but always critically."[25] As a political and moral practice, critical pedagogy should make clear both the multiplicity and the complexity of history as a narrative, which students can then engage as part of critical dialogue rather than accept unquestioningly. Similarly, such a pedagogy should cultivate in students a healthy skepticism about power, a "willingness to temper any reverence for authority with a sense of critical awareness."[26] As a performative practice, critical pedagogy should provide the conditions for students to be able to reflectively frame their own relationship to the ongoing project of an unfinished democracy. It is precisely this relationship between democracy and critical pedagogy that is so threatening to conservatives such as Rick Santorum, Sarah

Palin, and other religious advocates of the theocratic modes of political governance and learning.

Education as a moral and political project means, in part, making a commitment to the future, and it remains the task of educators to make sure that the future points the way to a more socially just world—a world in which the discourses of critique and possibility in conjunction with the values of reason, freedom, and equality function to alter, as part of a broader democratic project, the grounds upon which life is lived. This is hardly a prescription for political indoctrination, but it is a project that gives education its most valued purpose and meaning, which in part is "to encourage human agency, not mold it in the manner of Pygmalion."[27] The underlying political project of learning in the service of critical agency and transformation is a position that threatens right-wing groups, neoconservative politicians, and religious extremists because they recognize that such a pedagogical commitment goes to the very heart of what it means to address real inequalities of power at the social level. Such a pedagogical project conceives of education as a project for democracy and critical citizenship, and at the same time foregrounds a series of important and often ignored questions such as: Why do we as educators do what we do in the ways we do it? Whose interests does public education serve? How might it be possible to understand and engage the diverse contexts in which education takes place? In spite of the right-wing view that equates indoctrination with any suggestion of politics, critical pedagogy is not simply concerned with offering students new ways to think critically and act with authority as agents in the classroom: it is also concerned with providing students with the skills and knowledge necessary for them both to question deep-seated assumptions and myths that legitimate the most archaic and disempowering social practices that structure every aspect of society and to intervene in the world they inhabit in ethically conscious ways.

Education is not neutral, but that does not mean it is merely a form of indoctrination. On the contrary, education is a practice that attempts to expand the capacities necessary for human agency, and hence the possibilities for democracy itself. The public should nourish those pedagogical practices that promote "a concern with keeping the forever unexhausted and unfulfilled human potential open, fighting back all attempts to foreclose and pre-empt the further unravelling of human possibilities, prodding human society to go on questioning itself and preventing that questioning from ever stalling or being declared finished."[28] In other words, the kind of education the public should support is one that forges a language of critical agency and future possibility and a culture of openness, debate, and engagement— all elements that are now at risk in the latest and most dangerous attack on public education.

The attack on public schooling and critical pedagogy is, in part, an attempt to de-skill teachers and dismantle teacher authority. Teachers can make a claim to being fair, but not to being either neutral or impartial. Teacher authority can never be neutral, nor can it be assessed in terms that are narrowly ideological. It is always broadly political and interventionist in terms of the knowledge effects it produces, the classroom experiences it organizes, and the future it presupposes in the countless ways in which it addresses the world. Teacher authority at its best means taking a stand without standing still. A critical and directive approach to authority suggests that educators make a sincere effort to be self-reflective about the value-laden nature of their authority, while embracing the fundamental task of educating students to take responsibility for the direction of society. Rather than shrink from political responsibility, educators should embrace one of pedagogy's most fundamental goals: to teach students to believe that democracy is both desirable and possible. Connecting education to the possibility of a better world means the difference between teachers being technicians and teachers being self-reflective educators who are more than the instruments of a safely approved curriculum and officially sanctioned worldview.

The authority that enables educators to teach emerges out of the training, knowledge, research, professional rituals, and scholarly experiences that they bring to their field of expertise and classroom teaching. Such authority provides the space and experience in which pedagogy goes beyond providing the conditions for the simple acts of knowing and understanding and includes the cultivation of the very power of self-definition and critical agency. But teacher authority cannot be grounded exclusively in the rituals of professional standards. Learning occurs in a space in which commitment and passion provide students with a sense of what it means to link knowledge to a sense of direction. Teaching is a practice rooted in an ethico-political vision that attempts to take students beyond the world they already know, in a way that does not insist on a particular fixed set of altered meanings. In this context, teacher authority rests on pedagogical practices that reject the role of students as passive recipients of familiar knowledge and view them instead as producers of knowledge, who not only critically engage diverse ideas but also transform and act on them.[29] Pedagogy is the space that provides a moral and political referent for understanding how what we do in the classroom is linked to wider social, political, and economic forces.

It is impossible to separate classroom experiences from the economic and political conditions that shape them, and that means pedagogy has to be understood as a form of labor in which questions of time, autonomy, freedom, and power become as central to the classroom experience as that which is taught. As an entry point for engaging fundamental questions about democracy, pedagogy gestures to important questions about the political, institutional, and structural conditions that allow teachers to produce curricula, collaborate with colleagues, engage in research, and connect their work to broader public issues. Pedagogy is not about balance, a merely methodological consideration; on the contrary, as philosopher and economist Cornelius Castoriadis reminds us, if education is not to become "the political equivalent of a religious ritual,"[30] then it must do everything possible to provide students with the knowledge and skills they need to learn how to deliberate, make judgments, and exercise choice, particularly as the latter is brought to bear on critical activities that offer the possibility of democratic change.

Educating for Social Change

Democracy simply cannot work if citizens are not autonomous, self-judging, and independent—these are also qualities indispensable for students if they are going to make vital judgments and choices about participating in and shaping decisions that affect their everyday lives, including, but not limited to, institutional reform and policymaking.[31] Hence, pedagogy becomes the cornerstone of democracy in that it provides the very foundation for students to learn not merely how to be governed, but also how to be capable of governing.

One gets the sense that right-wing pundits, politicians, and religious bigots believe that there is no place in the classroom for politics, worldly concerns, social issues, and questions about how to lessen human suffering. In their discourse, the classroom becomes an unworldly parallel of the gated community—a space for conformity and coercion as a tool for perpetuating dominant market-driven values and white-Christian religious values. This cannot truly be called education; it is a flight from self and society. As Erich Fromm has pointed out, this type of education produces authoritarian personalities and punishes those who refuse to live in a society modeled after a fundamentalist theocracy.[32] This type of anti-enlightenment education does not produce students who are willing to assume responsibility for others whose presence in the world matters, but quasi-literate students who consider the presence of diversity and difference, if not thinking itself, an unbearable burden to be contained or expelled. Santorum and his fundamentalist allies argue for a model of education that supports the notion of the teacher as a police officer, clerk, or pitchman for privatization, rather than a model rooted in an understanding of educators as engaged public intellectuals. That is, teachers should identify themselves and be supported by others as intellectuals and civic educators who work under conditions that provide the authority, respect, and autonomy necessary for making education a worldly practice and critical pedagogy an empowering experience.

The current assault on young people, public education, and critical thinking is first and foremost an attack on the conditions that make critical education and democracy possible. It is also a distraction from processes that could raise questions about the real problems facing public education today, which include the lack of adequate financing, the instrumentalization and commodification of knowledge, the increasing presence of police and security in schools, the hijacking of public education by corporate interests, the substitution of standardized testing for substantive forms of teaching and learning, and the increasing attempts by right-wing extremists to turn education into job training or into an extended exercise in patriotic xenophobia and religious fundamentalism. As a right-wing juggernaut attempts relentlessly to destroy the social state, worker protections, unions, and civil liberties, it is easy to forget that a much less visible attack is being waged on young people, and especially on public schools and the possibility of critical forms of teaching. Critical pedagogy, that archenemy of fundamentalists everywhere, must be understood as central to any effort to educate students to be informed, skilled, and knowledgeable critical agents—it must also be understood as the most crucial resource we have for understanding politics and defending all aspects of public schooling as one of the few remaining democratic public spheres in the United States today. Pedagogy that enables students to think critically and hold power accountable is dangerous to those who favor the status quo, and it is precisely because of these so-called dangerous tendencies that it must be embraced as central to any viable democratic political project.

7.

Gated Intellectuals and Fortress America: Toward a Borderless Pedagogy in the Occupy Movement

A GROUP OF RIGHT-WING extremists in the United States would have the American public believe it is easier to imagine the end of the world than it is to imagine the end of a market society. Comprising this group are the Republican Party extremists; religious fundamentalists such as Rick Santorum, Ayn Rand disciples like Paul Ryan; and a host of conservative anti-public foundations funded by billionaires such as the Koch brothers.[1] Their pernicious influence has transformed the landscape of American political discourse into "fortresses of . . . one truth, one way, one life formula—of adamant and pugnacious certainty and self-confidence; the last shelters for the seekers of clarity, purity and freedom from doubt and indecision."[2] Manichean, absolutist visions such as these foster the political and cultural conditions for creating vast inequalities and massive human hardships throughout the globe. The dominant messages being constructed across multiple sectors in the United States all converge in support of a hyper-market fundamentalism and the fortress mentality that increasingly drives the meaning of citizenship and social life. One consequence is that the principles of self-preservation and self-interest undermine, if not completely sabotage, political agency and democratic public life.

Neoliberalism and its army of supporters cloak their interests in an appeal to "common sense" while doing everything possible to deny climate change, massive inequalities, a political system hijacked by big money and corporations, the militarization of everyday life, and the corruption of civic culture by a consumerist and celebrity-driven advertising machine. The financial elite, the 1 percent, and the hedge fund sharks have become the highest-paid social magicians in America. They perform magic on the social by making the structures and power relations of racism, inequality, homelessness, poverty, and environmental degradation disappear. And in doing so they employ deception by seizing upon a stripped-down language of choice, freedom, enterprise, and self-reliance—which works to personalize responsibility, collapse social problems into private troubles, and reconfigure the claims for social and economic justice on the part of workers, poor minorities of color, women, and young people into a species of individual complaint. But this deceptive strategy does more. It also substitutes shared responsibilities for a culture of diminishment, punishment, and cruelty. The social is now a site of combat, infused with a live-for-oneself mentality, and a space where a responsibility toward others is now gleefully replaced by an ardent, narrow, and inflexible responsibility only for oneself.

When the effects of structural injustice become obscured by a discourse of individual failure, human misery and misfortune are no longer the objects of compassion, but of scorn and derision. In the summer of 2012 alone, we have witnessed Rush Limbaugh call Georgetown law student Sandra Fluke a "slut" and "prostitute"; U.S. Marines captured on video urinating on the dead bodies of Afghanistan soldiers; and the public revelation by Greg Smith, a Goldman Sachs trader, that the company was so obsessed with making money that it cheated and verbally insulted its own clients, mockingly referring to them as "muppets."[3] Also frightening is the mass misogynic attack by right-wing extremists against women's reproductive rights, which Maureen Dowd rightly calls an attempt by "Republican men to wrestle American women back into chastity belts."[4] These are not unconnected blemishes on the body of neoliberal capitalism. Rather, these chilling occurrences are symptomatic of an infected political and economic system that has lost touch with any vestige of decency, justice, and ethics.

The Gated Intellectuals

Overlaying the festering corruption is a discourse in which national destiny (coded in biblical scripture) becomes a political theology, drawing attention away from the actual structural forces that decide who has access to health insurance and adequate health care, decent jobs, and quality schooling, and a social contract and state-sponsored protections that ensure that Americans have a decent life.[5] This disappearing act does more than whitewash history, obscure systemic inequalities of power, and privatize public issues. It also creates social automatons, isolated individuals who live in gated communities, along with their resident intellectuals who excite legions of consumer citizens to engage in a survival-of-the fittest ritual in order to climb heartlessly up the ladder of hyper-capitalism. The gated individual, scholar, artist, media pundit, and celebrity—walled off from growing impoverished populations—are also cut loose from any ethical mooring or sense of social responsibility. Such a radical individualism and its shark-like values and practices have become the hallmark of American society. Unfortunately, hyper-capitalism does more than create a market-driven culture in which individuals demonstrate no responsibility for the other and are reduced to zombies worried only about their personal safety and their stock portfolios. It also undermines public values, the centrality of the common good, and any political arenas not yet sealed off from an awareness of our collective fate. As democracy succumbs to the instrumental politics of the market economy and the relentless hype of the commercially driven spectacle, it becomes more difficult to preserve those public spheres, dialogues, and ideas through which private troubles and social issues can inform each other.

The gated intellectuals, pursuing their flight from social responsibility, become obsessed with the privatization of everything. And not content to remain supine intellectuals in the service of corporate hacks, they also willingly, if not joyfully, wage war against what is viewed as the ferocious advance of civil society, public values, and the social. Gated intellectuals such as Thomas Friedman, George Will, Dinesh D'Souza, Norman Podhoretz, Charles Murray, David Brooks, and others voice their support for what might be called a "gated" or "border" pedagogy—one that establishes boundaries to protect the rich, isolates citizens from one another, excludes those populations considered disposable, and renders young people invisible, especially poor youth of color, along with others marginalized by class and race. Such intellectuals play no small role in legitimating what David Theo Goldberg has called a form of neoliberalism that promotes a "shift from the caretaker or pastoral state of welfare capitalism to the 'traffic cop' or 'minimal' state, ordering flows of capital, people, goods, public services, and information."[6]

The gated intellectual works hard to make thinking an act of stupidity, turn lies into truths, builds a moat around oppositional ideas so they cannot be accessed, and destroys those institutions and social protections that serve the common good. Gated intellectuals and the institutions that support them believe in societies that stop questioning themselves, engage in a history of forgetting, and celebrate the progressive "decomposition and crumbling of social bonds and communal cohesion."[7] Policed borders, surveillance, state secrecy, targeted assassinations, armed guards, and other forces provide the imprimatur of dominant power and containment, making sure that no one can trespass onto gated property, spheres of influence locations, protected global resources, and public spheres. On guard against any claim to the common good, the social contract, or social protections for the underprivileged, gated intellectuals spring to life in universities, news programs, print media, charitable foundations, churches, think tanks, and other cultural apparatuses, aggressively surveying the terrain to ensure that no one is able to do the crucial pedagogical work of democracy by offering resources and possibilities for resisting the dissolution of sociality, reciprocity, and social citizenship itself. Moreover, former military, government officials, and business leaders often find their way into colleges and TV networks under the pretense of being "scholars," public intellectuals, and pundits. Needless to say, these are basically anti-public quasi-intellectuals, who trade in ideas that often embrace the politics of a moral coma and the tenets of free-market fundamentalism. Rather than call power into question, they trade in commonsense assumptions and attach themselves to "the seats of power" in an age of conformity.[8]

The gated mentality of market fundamentalism has walled off, if not *disappeared* those spaces where dialogue, critical reason, and the values and practices of social responsibility can be engaged. The armies of anti-public intellectuals who appear daily on television and radio talk shows and other platforms work hard to create a fortress of indifference and manufactured stupidity. Public life is reduced to a host of babbling politicians and pundits, ranging from Sarah Palin and Rush Limbaugh to Sean Hannity, all of whom should have their high school diplomas revoked. Much more than providing idiot spectacles and fodder for late-night comics, the assault waged by the warriors of rule enforcement and gated thought poses a dire threat to those vital public spheres that provide the minimal conditions for citizens who can think critically and act responsibly. This is especially true for public education, where the forces of privatization, philanthropy, and commodification have all but gutted public schooling in America.[9] What has become clear is that the attack on public schools has nothing to do with their failings; it has to do with the fact that they are public. How else to explain the fact that a number of conservative politicians such as Ron Paul refer to them as "government schools"?[10] I think it is fair to say that the massive assault taking place on public education in Arizona, Wisconsin, Florida, Maine, and other Republican Party–led states will soon extend its poisonous attack and include higher education in its sights in ways that will make the current battle look like a walk in the park.

Higher education is worth mentioning here because for gated intellectuals it is one of the last strongholds of democratic action and reasoning, and one of the most visible targets along with the welfare state. As is well known, higher education is increasingly being walled off from the discourse of public values and the ideals of a substantive democracy at a time when it is most imperative to defend the institution against an onslaught of forces that are as anti-intellectual as they are anti-democratic in nature. Universities are now facing a growing set of challenges that collectively pose a dire threat to the status of higher education as a sphere rooted in and fostering independent thought, critical agency, and civic courage. These challenges, to name but a few, include budget cuts, the downsizing of faculty, the militarization of research, alienation from the broader public (which increasingly looks upon academe with suspicion, if not scorn), and the revising of the curriculum to fit market-driven goals. They also include attempts to eliminate tenure, reduce faculty to part-time indentured servants, and fill academic departments with corporate-friendly majors. Many of the problems in higher education can be linked to the evisceration of funding, the intrusion of the national security state, the lack of faculty self-governance, and a wider culture that increasingly appears to view education as a private right rather than a public good. All of these disturbing trends, left unchecked, are certain to make a mockery of the very meaning and mission of the university as a democratic public sphere.

The Challenges Facing the Occupy Movement

The Occupy movement and other social movements are challenging many of these anti-democratic and anti-intellectual forces. Drawing connections between the ongoing assault on the public character and infrastructure of higher education and the broader attack on the welfare state, young people, artists, new media intellectuals, and others are reviving what critical intellectuals such as C. Wright Mills, Tony Judt, Zygmunt Bauman, and Hannah Arendt engaged as "the social question"—now with a growing sense of urgency in a society that appears to be losing a sense of itself in terms of crucial public values, the common good, and economic justice. One of the most important challenges facing educators, the Occupy movement, young people, and others concerned by the fate of democracy is providing the public spaces, critical discourses, and counter-narratives necessary to reclaim higher education and other public spheres from the civic- and capital-stripping policies of free market fundamentalism, the authoritarian politicians who deride critical education, and an army of anti-public intellectuals dedicated to attacking all things collective and sustaining. Public values have for decades been in tension with dominant economic and political forces, but the latter's growing fervor for unbridled individualism, disdain for social cohesion and safety nets, and contempt for the public good appear relentless against increasingly vulnerable communal bonds and weakened democratic resistance. The collateral damage has been widespread and includes a frontal assault on the rights of labor, social services, and every conceivable level of critical education.

Instead of the gated intellectual, there is a dire need for public intellectuals in the academy, art world, business sphere, media, and other cultural apparatuses to move from negation to hope. That is, there is a need to develop what I call *a project of democratization and borderless pedagogy* that moves across different sites—from schools to the alternative media—as part of a broader attempt to construct a critical formative culture in the United States that enables Americans to reclaim their voices, speak out, exhibit moral outrage, and create the social movements, tactics, and public spheres that will reverse the growing tide of authoritarianism in the United States. Intellectuals who take up this task are essential to democracy. In part, this is because social well-being depends on a continuous effort to raise disquieting questions and challenges, use knowledge and analytical skills to address important social problems, alleviate human suffering where possible, and redirect resources back to individuals and communities who cannot survive and flourish without them. Engaged public intellectuals are especially needed at a time when it is necessary to resist the hollowing out of the social state, the rise of a governing-through-crime complex, and the growing gap between the rich and poor that is pushing the United States back into the moral and political abyss of the Gilded Age. This is characterized by what David Harvey calls the "accumulation of capital through dispossession," which he claims "is about plundering, robbing other people of their rights" through the dizzying dream worlds of consumption, power, greed, deregulation, and unfettered privatization that are central to a neoliberal project.[11]

One particular challenge now facing the Occupy movement and the growing numbers of public intellectuals who reject the zombie politics of neoliberalism is that of providing a multitude of public and free access forums—such as *Truthout, Truthdig, AlterNet, Counterpunch, Salon,* and other alternative media spaces as well as free learning centers where knowledge is produced—in which critically engaged intellectuals are able not only to do the work of connecting knowledge, skills, and techniques to broader public considerations and social problems, but also make clear that education takes place in a variety of spheres that should be open to everyone. It is precisely through the broad mobilization of traditional and new educational sites that public intellectuals can do the work of resistance, engagement, policymaking, and supporting a democratic politics. Evidence of a growing number of such spheres can be found on Web papers and websites being produced by young people all over the globe, including the Occupy movement.[12]

Such spheres should also enable young people to learn not just how to read the world critically but to be able to produce cultural and social forms that foster shared practices and ideas rooted in a commitment to the common good. These spheres will provide a sense of solidarity, encourage intellectuals to take risks, and model what it means to engage a larger public through work that provides both a language of critique and a discourse of educated hope, engagement, and social transformation, while shaping ongoing public conversations about significant cultural and political concerns. To echo the great sociologist C. Wright Mills, there is a need for public intellectuals who refuse the role of "sociological bookkeeper," preferring instead to be "mutinous and utopian" rather than "go the way of the literary faddist and the technician of cultural chic." We can catch a glimpse of what such intellectuals do and why they matter in the work of Pierre Bourdieu, Edward Said, Jacques Derrida, Angela Davis, Carol Becker, Noam Chomsky, and, more recently in a younger generation of intellectuals, Arundhati Roy, Naomi Klein, Judith Butler, Chris Hedges, David Theo Goldberg, and Susan Searls Giroux—all of whom have been crucial in helping a generation of young people find their way to a more humane future, one that demands a new politics, a new set of values, and a renewed sense of the fragile nature of democracy. In part, this means educating a new generation that is willing to combine moral outrage, analytic skills, and informed knowledge in order to hold power accountable and expand those public spheres where ideas, debate, critique, and hope continue to matter.

Under the present historical circumstances, it is time to remind ourselves—in spite of idiotic anti-intellectual statements from various conservatives such as Michelle Bachmann, Newt Gingrich, and Ron Paul who condemn higher education and critical thought itself—that critical ideas matter. Those public spheres in which critical thought is nurtured provide the minimal conditions for people to become worldly, take hold of important social issues, and alleviate human suffering as the means of making the United States a more equitable and just society. Ideas are not empty gestures, and they do more than express a free-floating idealism. They provide a crucial foundation for assessing the limits and strengths of our sense of individual and collective agency and what it might mean to exercise civic courage in order not merely to live in the world but to shape it in light of democratic ideals that would make it a better place for everyone. Critical ideas and the technologies, institutions, and public spheres that enable them matter because they offer us the opportunity to think and act otherwise, challenge common sense, cross over into new lines of inquiry, and take positions without standing still—in short, to become border crossers who refuse the silos that isolate the privileged within an edifice of protections built on greed, inequitable amounts of income and wealth, and the one-sided power of the corporate state. And, of course, there is a need to cross not only borders literally by addressing the world as global citizens in order to analyze and work to solve problems and issues that are interrelated

and planetary, but also to create intellectual, social, and political movements that are global in nature.

Gated intellectuals do not work with ideas, but sound bites. They
don't engage in debates; they simply spew off positions in which unsub-
stantiated opinion and sustained argument collapse into each other.
Yet instead of simply responding to the armies of gated intellectuals
and the corporate money that funds them, it is time for the Occupy
movement and other critical-thinking individuals to join with the
independent media and make pedagogy central to any viable notion
of politics. It is time to initiate a cultural campaign in which reason can
be reclaimed, truth defended, and learning connected to social change.
The current attack on public and higher education by the armies of
gated intellectuals is symptomatic of the fear that right-wing reaction-
aries have of critical thought, quality education, and the possibility of a
generation emerging that can both think critically and act with political
and ethical conviction. Let's hope that as time unfolds and new spaces
emerge, the Occupy movement and other acts of resistance engage in
a form of borderless pedagogy in which they willingly and assertively
join in the battle over ideas, reclaim the importance of critique, develop
a discourse of hope, and occupy many quarters and sites so as to drown
out the corporate funded ignorance and political ideologies that strip
history of its meaning, undermine intellectual engagement, and engage
in a never-ending pedagogy of deflection and disappearance. There has
never been a more important time in American history to proclaim the
importance of communal responsibility and civic agency, and to shift
from a democracy of consumers to a democracy of informed citizens.
As Federico Mayor, the former director general of UNESCO, rightly
insisted, "You cannot expect anything from uneducated citizens except
unstable democracy."[13]

The United States has become Fortress America, and its gated
banks, communities, hedge funds, and financial institutions have
become oppressive silos of the rich and privileged designed to keep out
disadvantaged and vulnerable populations. At the same time, millions
of gated communities have been created against the will of their inhabitants, who have no passports to travel and are locked into abandoned

neighborhoods, prisons, and other sites equivalent to human waste dumps. The walls of privilege need to be destroyed and the fortresses of containment eliminated, but this will not be done without the emergence of a new political discourse, a borderless pedagogy, and a host of public spheres and institutions that provide the formative culture, skills, and capacities that enable young and old alike to counter the ignorance discharged like a poison from the mouths of those corporate interests and anti-public intellectuals who prop up the authority of Fortress America and hyper-capitalism. It is time for the Occupy movement to embrace its pedagogical role as a force for critical reason, social responsibility, and civic education. This is not a call to deny politics as we know it, but to expand its reach. The Occupy protesters need to become border crossers, willing to embrace a language of critique and possibility that makes visible the urgency of talking about politics and agency not in the idiom set by gated communities and anti-public intellectuals, but through the discourse of civic courage and social responsibility. We need a new generation of border crossers and a new form of border-crossing pedagogy to play a central role in keeping critical thought alive while challenging the further unraveling of human possibilities. Such a notion of democratic public life is engaged in both questioning itself and preventing that questioning from ever stalling or being declared finished. It provides the formative culture that enables young people to break the continuity of common sense, come to terms with their own power as critical agents, be critical of the authority that speaks to them, translate private considerations into public issues, and assume the responsibility for what it means to live in, shape, and assume power in a democracy.

If gated intellectuals defend the privileged, isolated, removed, and individualized interests of those who decry the social and view communal responsibility as a pathology, then public intellectuals must ensure that their work and actions embody a democratic ideal through reclaiming all those sites of possibility in which dialogue is guaranteed, power is democratized, and public values trump sordid private interests. Democracy must be embraced not merely as a mode of governance, but more important, as Bill Moyers points out, as a means of dignifying people so they can become fully free to claim their moral and political agency.

8.

The Occupy Movement and the Politics of Educated Hope

To be truly radical is to make hope possible
rather than despair inevitable.

—RAYMOND WILLIAMS

HAVING LOST ITS CLAIM on democracy, American society must change direction as a matter of survival. One indication of America's loss of purchase on a democratic future is the discourse of denial surrounding the crises produced on a daily basis by hyper-punitive casino capitalism.[1] Rather than address the ever-proliferating crises produced by market fundamentalism as an opportunity to understand how the United States has arrived at such a point, the dominant classes now use such crises as an excuse for normalizing a growing punishing and warfare state, while consolidating the power of finance capital and the mega-rich. Uncritically situated in an appeal to common sense amid a growing culture of distraction, the merging of corporate and political power is now constructed on a discourse of refusal—a denial of

historical conditions, existing inequalities, and massive human suffering—used to bury alive the conditions of its own making. The notion
that neoliberal capitalism has an enormous stake in the dominance of
public life by corporations apparently no longer warrants recognition
and debate in mainstream apparatuses of power. Hence, the issue of
what happens to democracy and politics when corporations dominate
almost all aspects of American society is no longer viewed as a central
question to be addressed in public life.[2]

As society is increasingly organized around shared fears, escalating
insecurities, and a post-9/11 politics of terror, the mutually reinforcing dynamics of a market-based fundamentalism and a government
that appears incapable of putting in place checks on the power of corporations and financial service industries render democratic politics
both bankrupt and inoperable. The hatred of government on the part
of Republican extremists, with the acquiescence of many liberals, has
resulted not only in attacks on public services, the cutting of worker
benefits, the outsourcing of government services, a hyper-nationalism,
and the evisceration of public goods such as schools and health care,
but also an abdication of responsible and accountable governance. The
language of the market, with its incessant appeal to self-regulation and
the virtues of radical individualism, now offers the primary dysfunctional and poisonous index of what possibilities the future may hold,
while jingoistic nationalism and racism hail its apocalyptic underbelly.

For the apostles of neoliberalism, the notion that democracy
requires modes of economic and social equality as the basis for supportive social bonds, safe communities, and compassionate communal
relations disappears along with the claims traditionally made in the
name of social justice, human rights, and democratic values.[3] Under
the reign of free-market fundamentalism with its shroud of Conradian
darkness, entrepreneurial values such as competitiveness, self-interest,
deregulation, privatization, and decentralization now produce self-
interested actors who have no interest in promoting the public good or
governing in the public interest.[4] Under these circumstances, the One
Percent and the financial, cultural, and educational institutions they
control declare war on government, immigrants, poor youth, women,

the elderly, and other institutions and groups considered disposable. Crony capitalism produces great wealth for the few and massive human suffering for the many around the globe. At the same time, it produces what João Biehl calls "zones of social abandonment" that "accelerate the death of the unwanted" through a form of economic Darwinism "that authorizes the lives of some while disallowing the lives of others."[5] Eric Cazdin is right when he argues: "Accordingly, many are dying not because capitalism is failing but because it is succeeding, because it is fulfilling its logic—a fact that seems more and more visible today than at any other time in recent history."[6] Of course, this logic is that "all ideals are at the mercy of the larger economic logic,"[7] one that views some populations as disposable and state violence as a legitimate instrument of rule. Language now colludes with deception in making state violence unnameable and hence not subject to critique. Joy James states this well:

> If you don't name it and shun the language, then you veil the phenomenon. What is also obscured is state violence, as conventional language maintains that only dictatorships, not democracies, practice racial genocide. Convention assumes that electoral democracies have a fail-safe mechanism—an enlightened and empowered citizenry—that prevents their participation (except as liberators) in genocidal practices. It is thus not surprising that those most targeted by historical and contemporary state excesses are those most likely to crash into its apparatuses: racially fashioned policing and the prison industrial complex, homelessness, substandard schools and housing, foster care for children marred by indifference, inadequate oversight and resources, the poverty draft into an immoral war, and "shoot-to-kill" edicts for (black) survivors of New Orleans's substandard levees designed by the Army Corps of Engineers.[8]

As market relations based on selfish competition become the mechanism for surviving within a market society, democracy becomes both the repressed scandal of neoliberalism and its ultimate fear.[9] In such a society, cynicism is the ideology of choice as public life collapses into the ever-encroaching domain of the private and social ills and human suffering become more difficult to identify, understand, and engage analytically. The result, as Jean Comaroff points out, is that "in our contemporary world, post-9/11, crisis and exception have become routine, and war, deprivation, and death intensify despite ever denser networks of humanitarian aid and ever more rights legislation."[10] In addition, as corporate power and finance capital gain ascendancy over society, the depoliticization of politics and the increasing transformation of the social state into the punishing state have resulted in the emergence of a new form of authoritarianism in which the fusion of corporate power and state violence increasingly permeates all aspects of everyday life.[11]

Such violence, with its expanding machinery of death and surveillance, creates an ever-intensifying cycle, rendering citizens' political activism dangerous and even criminal—as became apparent in the recent assaults waged by the government against youthful protesters on college campuses, in the streets, and in other spaces now colonized by capital and its apparatus of enforcement.[12] More recently, as noted in a report by the Partnership for Civil Justice Fund, assaults against the Occupy Wall Street movement have included massive collusion between financial institutions such as big banks, university presidents, the FBI, the Department of Homeland Security, and local police.[13] Not only was OWS designated repeatedly as a potential criminal and terrorist threat, they were also put under constant surveillance, monitoring, and reporting by banks, universities, and other major corporate institutions.

Beyond the Erosion of Critical Thought and Public Spaces

In opposition to the attacks on critical thought, dissent, and the discourse of hope—or what Jacques Rancière calls the erosion of "the public character of spaces, relations, and institutions"[14]—the Occupy movement has issued a call for and demonstrated a common investment in what Theodor Adorno and Max Horkheimer describe as the need "to hang on to intellectual and real freedom" and ensure that thinking does not lose its "secure hold on possibility."[15] This is evident in the willingness of the movement to make the "challenge to capitalism front and center among its concerns and passions [and] to make economic injustice for the 99 percent and the ruling economic system central, defining issues."[16] Worth noting is that the Occupy protesters believe that intellectuals comprise anyone willing to exercise critical thought and come from a broad range of jobs, fields, and institutions, not just those designated for academic work. Intellectual production is not the privileged preserve of academics, so-called experts, or think tank wonks. The protesters argue that all of us should inhabit the realm of politics, be willing to cross intellectual and physical boundaries, connect questions of understanding to questions of power, and unite passion, commitment, and conscience in new ways in order to reflect on and engage with the larger society. The Occupy intervention is both intellectual and political, and it suggests contesting neoliberal capitalism in several registers.

The protesters, seeking to rescue the political possibilities of ambivalence from the powerful, have succeeded in breaking open the sordid appeal to common sense, unmasking casino capitalism's most pernicious myths—especially the alleged belief that capitalism and democracy are the same—struggling to restage power in productive ways, enacting social agency from those places where it has been denied, and working to provide an accurate historical accounting of the racial state and racial power. What has emerged in the Occupy movement is the refusal on the part of protesters to accept the dominant narratives of official authority and the limitations they impose upon individual and social agency, thus using spaces of critique, dissent, dialogue, and collective resistance as starting points from which to build unfamiliar, potential worlds. In the process of thinking seriously about structures of power, state formation, militarism, capitalist formations, class, and pedagogy, the protesters have refused to substitute moral indignation for the hard work of contributing to critical education and enabling people to expand the horizons of their own sense of agency in order to collectively challenge established structures of financial and political power.

This rethinking of politics bristles with a deeply rooted refusal to serve up well-worn and obvious truths, reinforce existing relations of power, or bid retreat to an official rendering of common sense that promotes "a corrosive and demoralizing silence."[17] What emerges from these distinct but politically allied voices is a pedagogy of disruption, critique, recovery, and possibility. It is a pedagogy that recognizes that there is no viable democracy without will and awareness, and that critical education motivates and provides a crucial foundation for understanding and intervening in the world in a way that fosters more democratic realities. As Stanley Aronowitz argues, "The [current] system survives on the eclipse of the radical imagination, the absence of a viable political opposition with roots in the general population and the conformity of its intellectuals."[18] Although a pedagogy of disruption and possibility offers no guarantees, it does create a formative culture capable of generating the collective imagination and hard work needed to make the "long march . . . through the institutions, the workplaces and the streets of the capitalist metropoles."[19]

Rethinking the Discourse of Politics in a Consumer Society

The Occupy movement has also explored in different ways how politics demands a new language and a broader view of pedagogy that are both critical and visionary. In the historical shadow of the civil rights and anti–Vietnam War movements, the Occupy protesters are attempting to establish a new language for making power visible and organizing modes of direct action. This commitment translates into a pedagogy capable of illuminating the anti-democratic forces and sites that threaten human lives, the environment, and democracy itself; and at the same time its visionary nature cracks open the present to reveal new horizons, different futures, and the promise of a global democracy. And yet, under the reign of neoliberal ideology, racist xenophobic nationalisms, the punitive state, and a range of other forces holding democracy hostage, citizenship is increasingly privatized, commodified, and distorted in ways that feed a sense of powerlessness and disengagement from democratic struggles, if not politics itself. Neoliberalism presents misfortune as a weakness, and the logic of the market instructs individuals to rely on their own wits if they fall on hard times, especially since the state has washed its hands of any responsibility for the fate of its citizens. And it is precisely this marriage between the everyday outcomes and the dictates of capitalism that the Occupy movement is challenging.

If the act of critical translation is crucial to a democratic politics, it faces a crisis of untold proportions in the United States, as the deadening reduction of the citizen to a consumer of services and goods empties politics of substance by stripping citizens of their political skills, offering up only individual solutions to social problems and dissolving all obligations and responsibilities for others into an ethos of hyper-individualism and a narrowly privatized universe. The logic of the commodity penetrates all aspects of life, and the most important questions driving society no longer seem concerned about matters of equity, social justice, and the fate of the common good.[20] As every facet of society becomes privatized and commodified, Americans increasingly find themselves alone, facing withered social bonds and lacking institutional protections from the social state. The most important decision now facing most people is not about living a life with dignity and freedom, but making the grim choice between survival and dying. As the government deregulates, privatizes, and outsources key aspects of governance, turning over the provision of collective insurance, security, and care to private institutions and market-based forces, it undermines the social contract since "the present retreat of the state from the endorsement of social rights signals the falling apart of a community in its modern, 'imagined' yet institutionally safeguarded incarnation."[21]

One consequence is that the reality of human suffering, misfortune, and misery caused by social problems is now buried under the discourses of personal safety and individual responsibility. Increasingly, as social institutions give way to the machinery of surveillance, punishment, and containment, social provisions along with the social state are disappearing. Similarly, the exclusionary logic of ethnic, racial, and religious divisions renders more individuals and groups disposable—languishing away in prisons, dead-end jobs, or the deepening pockets of poverty while effectively prevented from engaging in politics in a meaningful way. Instead of vibrant democratic public spheres, neoliberal capital creates "zones of social abandonment," the new domestic "machineries of inscription and invisibility" that thrive on the energies of the unwanted, unbankable, and unrecognized—who now include more and more groups such as students, women, immigrants, poor people of color, the elderly, and those who refuse to define themselves in terms of consumer culture.[22]

As the machineries of social death expand, politics seems to take place elsewhere—most of all in globalized regimes of power that are indifferent to traditional forms of state-based power and hostile to any notion of addressing human suffering and social problems with a sense of collective responsibility. Chris Hedges succinctly captures the spirit and politics of this mode of corporate colonialism. He writes:

> We are controlled by tiny corporate entities that have no loyalty to the nation and indeed in the language of traditional patriotism are traitors. They strip us of our resources, keep us politically passive and enrich themselves at our expense. . . . The colonized are denied job security. Incomes are reduced to subsistence level. The poor are plunged into desperation. Mass movements, such as labor unions, are dismantled. The school system is degraded so only the elites have access to a superior education. Laws are written to legalize corporate plunder and abuse, as well as criminalize dissent. And the ensuing fear and instability—keenly felt this past weekend by the more than 200,000 Americans who lost their unemployment benefits—ensure political passivity by diverting all personal energy toward survival. It is an old, old game.[23]

As Hedges states, it is an old game, one reinforced by a new authoritarian politics that is unapologetic about its abuses and ongoing production of violence and human misery. It is a politics that owes more to the fascist regimes of Germany, Italy, and Chile than to any notion of democracy. And it is precisely in the renewal of democracy through a politics capable of challenging the current structures of power and ideology that the Occupy movement offers its greatest promise. What is particularly important in this movement is the growing recognition that moral condemnations of greed, corruption, consumerism, and injustice provide only "the minimal positive program for sociopolitical change" and ongoing effort is required to address the more crucial need for systemic transformations in American society.[24]

We live at a time when the crisis of politics is inextricably connected to the crisis of education and agency. Any viable politics or political culture must emerge from a determined effort to provide the economic conditions, public spaces, pedagogical practices, and social relations in which individuals have the time, motivation, and knowledge to engage in acts of translation that reject the privatization of the public sphere, the lure of ethno-racial or religious purity, the emptying of democratic traditions, the crumbling of the language of commonality, and the decoupling of critical education from the unfinished demands of a global democracy. As the Occupy movement increasingly addresses what it means politically and pedagogically to confront the impoverishment of public discourse, the collapse of democratic values, the erosion of civic-oriented institutions, and the corporate colonizing of American society, it puts in place a language for developing new public spheres where critical thought, dialogue, exchange, and collective action can take place. At work here is the attempt to develop a new political language for rescuing modes of critical agency and articulating social grievances that have been aggravated or ignored by the dictates of global neoliberalism, a punishing state, and a systemic militarization of public life. In the midst of such hard times for the promise of democracy, the Occupy movement offers an incisive language of analysis and hope, a renewed sense of political commitment, a different democratic vision, and a politics of possibility.

Political exhaustion and impoverished intellectual visions are fed by the widely popular assumption that there are no alternatives to the present state of affairs. Within the increasing corporatization of everyday life, market values replace social values, while people with the education and monetary means appear more and more willing to retreat into the safe, privatized enclaves of family, religion, and consumption. In such cases, hope is privatized and foreclosed, just as the conditions disappear in which certain kinds of democratic politics are possible. Those without the luxury of combining the individual, political, and social rights that would make their choices meaningful pay a terrible price in the form of material suffering and the emotional hardship and political disempowerment that are its constant companions. Even those who live in the relative comfort of the middle class must struggle within a poverty of time in an era in which the majority must work more than they ever have to make ends meet.

Mainstream theorists, intellectuals, and talk-show pundits revere the thought that politics as a site of contestation, critical exchange, and engagement is in a state of terminal arrest or has simply come to an end. The only politics that matters for this group of extremists is a politics that benefits corporations, the rich, and the servants of finance capital. However, the Occupy movement argues in diverse and often complex ways that too little attention is paid to what it means to think through the realm of the political, particularly how the struggle over radical democracy is inextricably linked to creating and sustaining public spheres where individuals can be engaged as political agents equipped with the skills, capacities, and knowledge they need not only to be autonomous, but also to believe that such struggles are worth taking up. The growing cynicism in American society may say less about the reputed apathy of the populace than about the bankruptcy of old political narratives and the need for a new vocabulary and vision for clarifying intellectual, ethical, economic, and political projects, especially as they work to reframe questions of agency, ethics, and meaning for a substantive democracy.

Toward a Discourse of Educated Hope

For the Occupy movement, there is a pressing need to get beyond the discourse of negation to imagine another world, a future that is not simply a reproduction of the present. Hope, in this instance, is the precondition for individual and social struggles that involve the ongoing practice of critical education in a wide variety of sites and the renewal of civic courage among citizens, residents, and others who wish to address pressing social problems.[25] *Hope* says "no" to the totalizing discourse of the neoliberal present; it contains an activating presence that opens current political structures to critical scrutiny, affirms dissent, and pluralizes the possibilities of different futures. In this sense, hope is a subversive force.

In opposition to those who seek to turn hope into a new slogan or to punish and dismiss efforts to look beyond the horizon of the given, the promise of the Occupy movement lies in its ability to develop the spaces and places where a democratic formative culture and language of collective struggle can be nurtured and thrive. In this way, the movement both embodies and initiates a pedagogical project and the conditions needed for providing a sense of opposition and engaged struggle. As a project, Andrew Benjamin insists, hope must be viewed as "a structural condition of the present rather than as the promise of a future, the continual promise of a future that will always have to have been better."[26] At the same time, as Alain Touraine points out, "Opposition to domination is not enough to create a movement; a movement must put forward demands in the name of a positive attribute."[27] Clearly, hope in this instance is not an individual proclivity or a simple act of outrage, but rather a crucial part of a broader politics that acknowledges the social, economic, spiritual, and cultural conditions in the present that make certain kinds of agency and democratic politics possible.

Hence, hope is more than an instrumentally oriented politics—it is also a pedagogical and performative practice that provides the foundation for enabling human beings to learn about their potential as moral and civic agents. Hope is the outcome of those pedagogical practices and struggles that tap in to memory and lived experiences, while linking individual responsibility with a progressive sense of social change. As a form of utopian longing, educated hope opens up horizons of comparison by evoking not just different histories, but also different futures; at the same time, it substantiates the importance of ambivalence while problematizing certainty. In the words of Paul Ricoeur, hope serves as "a major resource as the weapon against closure."[28] Critical hope is a subversive force when it pluralizes politics by opening up a space for dissent, makes authority accountable, and becomes an activating presence in promoting social transformation.

The current limits of the utopian imagination are related, in part, to the failure of many individuals and social groups to imagine what pedagogical conditions might be necessary to bring into being forms of political agency and social movements that expand the operations of individual rights, social provisions, and democratic freedoms. At the same time, a politics and pedagogy of hope provide neither a blueprint for the future nor a form of social engineering, but a belief, simply, that different futures are possible, which holds open matters of contingency, context, and indeterminacy. It is only through critical forms of education that human beings can learn to "combine a gritty sense of limits [of the present] with a lofty vision of possibility."[29] Hope therefore poses the important challenge of how to reclaim individual and collective agency within a broader struggle to deepen the possibilities for social justice and global democracy. The Occupy movement recognizes that any viable notion of political and social agency is dependent upon a culture of questioning, whose purpose is to "keep the forever unexhausted and unfulfilled human potential open, fighting back all attempts to foreclose and pre-empt the further unravelling of human possibilities, prodding human society to go on questioning itself and preventing that questioning from ever stalling or being declared finished."[30]

The project of asking questions that will hold power accountable and of reclaiming politics from exile must strike a careful balance between leaving itself forever open to future questions and acting decisively to change the lived experience of the ever-expanding ranks of dispossessed and disposable peoples. Reclaiming politics requires a form of educated hope that accentuates how politics is played out on the terrain of imagination and desire as well as in material relations of power and concrete social formations. Freedom and justice, in this instance, have to be mediated through the connection between civic

education and political agency, which presupposes that the goal of educated hope is not to liberate the individual *from* the social—a central
tenet of neoliberalism—but to take seriously the notion that the individual can only be liberated *through* the social.

Central to the Occupy movement is the premise that hope as a
subversive, defiant practice should provide a link, however transient,
provisional, and contextual, between vision and critique, on the one
hand, and engagement and transformation on the other. But for such
a notion of hope to be consequential, it has to be grounded in a pedagogical project that has some hold on the present. Hope becomes
meaningful to the degree that it identifies interventions and processes,
offers alternatives to an age of profound pessimism, reclaims an ethic
of compassion and justice, and struggles for those institutions in which
equality, freedom, and justice flourish as part of the ongoing struggle
for a global democracy. One of the great promises of the Occupy movement is its recognition that the threat to social justice and democracy
is not merely the existence of casino capitalism, but the disappearance
of critical discourses that allow us to think outside of and against the
demands of official power, as well as the spaces where politics can even
occur. It is only in such democratic public spheres where people can
learn and assert a sense of critical agency, embrace the civic obligation
to care for the other, and refuse to take "shelter where responsibility for
one's actions need not be taken."[31]

An inclusive democracy must be responsive to the varied needs of
the citizens who comprise it. In order to facilitate critical thought and
nurture the flexibility it requires, the Occupy movement protesters do
not provide totalizing answers as much as they offer better questions.
They open up conversations in which acts of critical recovery unleash
possibilities that have been repressed by official history or caught in the
trap of existing social realities. In an age when the dominant tendency
among academics is to follow power and fashion, the protesters exhibit
both a strong sense of political conviction and an admirable civic courage in their willingness to speak against the status quo, take risks, and
struggle to give history back to those who are increasingly removed
from the political sphere. They also put their bodies on the line in the

face of a society that is willing to unleash the police on its youthful protesters rather than invest in their future.

There is more at stake here than saying no, making power visible,
and recognizing that our individual and collective experiences are not
dictated by fate. There is also the challenge of confronting the actual
with the possible, of pulling hope down to earth, of making sure that
the possibilities we mobilize are engaging real problems and concrete
expressions of domination and power. In addition, there is the need
to translate theoretical concerns into public action, raise up the level
of discourse in an attempt to connect the academy to the dynamics of
everyday life, and give worldly expression to our critical work. Politics
as an act of translation between theory and practice is essential to the
struggle against the coming darkness that brands critical judgment as
an enemy of the state and destroys the spaces and opportunities for
public dissent, paving the way for existing elements of authoritarianism
to crystallize into new forms that further deform language and make
"despair inevitable." A democratic politics may take many forms, but
central to connecting its diverse expressions is the need for individuals,
groups, and social movements to be able to reveal individual problems
as public concerns, use theoretical resources to change concrete and
systemic relations of power, and challenge "a hateful politics toward the
public realm, toward politics."[32]

Such a challenge is essential to any emancipatory politics of hope
and meaning. Without the ability to see how each of our lives is related
to the greater good, we lack the basis for recognizing ourselves as bear-
ers of rights and responsibilities—the precondition of our human
agency—who should rightfully assume the task of governance rather
than simply be governed. Without an understanding of critical agency,
we lack the basis for raising questions about the goals and aims of our
society and what we want our society as a whole to accomplish, especially given the challenges of creating a global democracy. In short, we
lack what makes a democratic politics viable. The alternative to pursuing a new democratic politics is to allow a national security state to
grow unchecked, along with a species of authoritarianism that encourages profit-hungry monopolies, the ideology of faith-based certainties,

the pursuit of ethno-racial purity, the militarization of everyday life, the destruction of civil liberties, the practice of torture, and the undermining of any vestige of critical education, responsible dissent, critical thought, and collective struggle. The manifold crises facing American society are much too urgent to give up on and so necessitate a resurgence of critique and a discourse of hope premised on the feasibility of a more democratic and just future along with the social movements that will make it possible. There are glimpses of such hope in many of the actions now being taken by Occupy movements. Such actions range from providing aid to Hurricane Sandy victims to creating a movement focused on helping people who are being evicted from their homes. There is also an ongoing movement to build a national organization that would push for debt relief for students. All of these movements face the challenge of not only dealing with specific issues but connecting them to a broader movement in which the very structure of American society can be changed.[33]

9.

Neoliberalism's War against Teachers in Dark Times: Rethinking the Sandy Hook Elementary School Killings

THE TRAGIC DEATHS of twenty-six people shot and killed on December 14, 2012, at Sandy Hook Elementary School in Newtown, Connecticut, included twenty young children and six educators. All of the children were shot multiple times. Many more children might have been killed or injured had it not been for the brave and decisive actions of the teachers in the school. The mainstream media was quick to call them heroes, and there is little doubt that what they did under horrific circumstances reveals not only how important educators are in shielding children from imminent threat, but also how demanding their roles have become in preparing them to negotiate a world that is becoming more precarious, more dangerous—and infinitely more divisive. In this case, teachers not only saved the lives of many young people, they also gave their lives in doing so. Teachers are one of the most important resources a nation has for providing the skills, values, and knowledge that prepare young people for productive citizenship—but more than this, to give sanctuary to their dreams and aspirations for a future of hope, dignity, and justice.

It is indeed ironic, in the unfolding nightmare in Newtown, that only in the midst of such a shocking tragedy are teachers celebrated in ways that justly acknowledge, albeit briefly and inadequately, the vital role they play every day in both protecting and educating our children. What is repressed in these jarring historical moments is that teachers have been under vicious and sustained attack by right-wing conservatives, religious fundamentalists, and centrist Democrats since the beginning of the 1980s. Depicted as the new "welfare queens," their labor and their care has been instrumentalized and infantilized;[1] they have been fired en masse under calls for austerity; they have seen rollbacks in their pensions; and have been derided because they teach in "government schools." Public school teachers too readily and far too pervasively have been relegated to zones of humiliation and denigration.[2] The importance of what teachers actually do, the crucial and highly differentiated nature of the work they perform, and their value as guardians, role models, and trustees only appears in the midst of such a tragic event. If the United States is to prevent its slide into a deeply violent and anti-democratic state, it will, among other things, be required to fundamentally rethink not merely the relationship between education and democracy, but also the very nature of teaching, the role of teachers as engaged citizens and public intellectuals, and the relationship between teaching and social responsibility. This chapter makes one small contribution to that effort.

The War against Public School Teachers

Right-wing fundamentalists and corporate ideologues are not just waging a war against the rights of unions, workers, students, women, the disabled, low-income groups and poor minorities, but also against those public spheres that provide a vocabulary for connecting values, desires, identities, social relations, and institutions to the discourse of social responsibility, ethics, and democracy, if not thinking itself.

Neoliberalism or unbridled free-market fundamentalism employs modes of governance, discipline, and regulation that are totalizing in their insistence that all aspects of social life be determined, shaped, and weighed by market-driven measures.[3] Neoliberalism is not merely an economic doctrine that prioritizes buying and selling, makes the supermarket and mall the temples of public life, and defines the obligations of citizenship in strictly consumerist terms. It is also a mode of pedagogy and set of social arrangements that uses education to win consent, produce consumer-based notions of agency, and militarize reason in the service of war, profits, power, and violence while simultaneously instrumentalizing all forms of knowledge.

The increasing militarization of reason and growing expansion of forms of militarized discipline are most visible in policies currently promoted by wealthy conservative foundations such as the Heritage Foundation and the American Enterprise Institute, along with the high-profile presence and advocacy of corporate reform spokespersons such as Joel Klein and Michelle Rhee and billionaire financiers such as Michael Milken.[4] As Ken Saltman, Diane Ravitch, Alex Means, and others have pointed out, wealthy billionaires such as Bill Gates are financing educational reforms that promote privatization, de-professionalization, online classes, and high-stakes testing, while at the same time impugning the character and autonomy of teachers and the unions that support them.[5] Consequently, public school teachers have become the new class of government-dependent moochers, and the disparaged culture of Wall Street has emerged as the only model or resource from which to develop theories of educational leadership and reform.[6] The same people who gave us the economic recession of 2008, lost billions in corrupt trading practices, and sold fraudulent mortgages to millions of homeowners have ironically become sources of wisdom and insight regarding how young people should be educated.

Attesting to the hard-to-miss fact that political culture has become an adjunct of the culture of finance, politicians at the state and federal levels, irrespective of their political affiliation, advocate reforms that amount to selling off or giving away public schools to the apostles of casino capitalism.[7] More important, the hysterical fury now being waged by the new educational reformists against public education exhibits no interest in modes of education that invest in an "educated public for the culture of the present and future."[8] On the contrary, their relevance and power can be measured by the speed with which any notion of civic responsibility is evaded.

What these individuals and institutions all share is an utter disregard for public values, critical thinking, and any notion of education as a moral and political practice.[9] The wealthy hedge fund managers, think tank operatives, and increasingly corrupt corporate CEOs are panicked by the possibility that teachers and public schools might provide the conditions for the cultivation of an informed and critical citizenry capable of actively and critically participating in the governance of a democratic society. In the name of educational reform, reason is gutted of its critical potential and reduced to a deadening pedagogy of memorization, teaching to the test, and classroom practices that celebrate mindless repetition and conformity. Rather than embraced as central to what it means to be an engaged and thoughtful citizen, the capacity for critical thinking, imagining, and reflection are derided as crucial pedagogical values necessary for "both the health of democracy and to the creation of a decent world culture and a robust type of global citizenship."[10]

This derision is clear by virtue of the fact that testing and punishing have become the two most influential forces that now shape American public education. As Stanley Aronowitz points out:

> Numerous studies have shown the tendency of public schooling to dumb down the curriculum and impose punitive testing algorithms on teachers and students alike. Whether intended or not, we live in an era when the traditional concepts of liberal education and popular critical thinking are under assault. Neoliberals of the center, no less than those of the right, are equally committed to the reduction of education to a mean-spirited regime of keeping its subjects' noses to the grindstone. As the postwar "prosperity" which offered limited opportunities to some from the lower orders to gain a measure of mobility fades into memory, the chief function of schools is repression.[11]

Instead of talking about the relationship between schools and democracy, the new educational reformers call for disinvestment in public schools, the militarization of school culture, the commodification of knowledge, and the privatizing of both the learning process and the spaces in which it takes place. The crusade for privatizing is now advanced with a vengeance by the corporate elite, a crusade designed to place the control of public schools and other public spheres in the allegedly reliable hands of the apostles of casino capitalism.[12] Budgets are now balanced on the backs of teachers and students, while the wealthy get tax reductions and the promise of gentrification and private schools.[13] In the name of austerity, schools are defunded so as to fail and provide an excuse to be turned over to the privatizing advocates of free-market fundamentalism. In this discourse, free-market reformers refuse to imagine public education as the provision of the public good and social right and reduce education to meet the immediate needs of the economy.

For those schools and students that are considered redundant, the assault on reason is matched by the enactment of a militaristic culture of security, policing, and containment, particularly in urban schools.[14] Low-income and poor minority students now attend schools that have more security guards than teachers and are educated to believe that there is no distinction between prison culture and the culture of schooling.[15] The underlying theme that connects the current attack on reason and the militarizing of social relations is that education is both a petri dish for producing individuals who are wedded to the logic of the market and consumerism and a sorting machine for ushering largely poor black and brown youth into the criminal justice system. There is no language among these various political positions for defending the public school as a vital social institution and public good. Public education, in this view, no longer benefits the entire society but only individuals, and rather than being defined as a public good is redefined as a private right.

Within this atomistic, highly individualizing script, shared struggles and bonds of solidarity are viewed as either dangerous or pathological. Power relations disappear, and there is no room for understanding how corporate power and civic values rub up against each other in ways that are detrimental to the promise of a robust democracy and an emancipatory mode of schooling. In fact, in this discourse, corporate power is used to undermine any vestige of the civic good and cover up the detrimental influence of its anti-democratic pressures.

It gets worse. A pedagogy of management and conformity does more than simply repress the analytical skills and knowledge necessary for students to learn the practice of freedom and assume the role of critical agents; it also reinforces deeply authoritarian lessons while reproducing deep inequities in the educational opportunities that different students acquire. As Sara Robinson points out:

> In the conservative model, critical thinking is horrifically dangerous, because it teaches kids to reject the assessment of external authorities in favor of their own judgment—a habit of mind that invites opposition and rebellion. This is why, for much of Western history, critical thinking skills have only been taught to the elite students—the ones headed for the professions, who will be entrusted with managing society on behalf of the aristocracy. (The aristocrats, of course, are sending their kids to private schools, where they will receive a classical education that teaches them everything they'll need to know to remain in charge.) Our public schools, unfortunately, have replicated a class stratification on this front that's been in place since the Renaissance.[16]

As powerful as this utterly reactionary and right-wing educational reform movement might be, educators are far from willingly accepting the role of de-skilled technicians groomed to service the needs of finance capital and produce students who are happy consumers and unquestioning future workers. Public school teachers have mobilized in Wisconsin and a number of other states where public schools, educators, and other public servants are under attack. They have been collectively energized in pushing back the corporate and religious fundamentalist visions of public education and they are slowly mobilizing into a larger social movement to defend both their role as engaged intellectuals and schooling as a public good. In refusing to be fit for domestication, many teachers, such as the brave teachers who rallied recently against the neoliberal assault on public education in Chicago, are committed to fulfilling the civic purpose of public education through a new understanding of the relationship between democracy and schooling, and learning and social change. In the interest of expanding this struggle, educators need a new vocabulary for not only defining schools as democratic public spheres, students as informed and critically engaged citizens, but also teachers as public intellectuals. In what follows, I want to focus on this issue as one important register of individual and collective struggle for teachers. At stake here is the presupposition that a critical consciousness is not only necessary for producing good teachers, but also enables individual teachers to see their classroom struggles as part of a much broader social, political, and economic landscape.

Unlike many past educational reform movements, the present call for educational change presents both a threat and a challenge to public school teachers that appear unprecedented. The threat comes in the form of a series of educational reforms that display little confidence in the ability of public school teachers to provide intellectual and moral leadership for our youth. For instance, many recommendations that have emerged in the current debate across the world either ignore the role teachers play in preparing learners to be active and critical citizens or suggest reforms that ignore the intelligence, judgment, and experience that teachers might offer in such a debate. At the same time, the current conservative reform movement aggressively disinvests in public schooling so as to eliminate the literal spaces and resources necessary for schools to work successfully.

Where teachers do enter the debate, they are objects of educational reforms that reduce them to the status of high-level technicians carrying out dictates and objectives decided by experts far removed from the everyday realities of classroom life. Or they are reduced to the status of commercial salespersons selling knowledge, skills, and values that have less to do with education than with training students for low-wage jobs in a global marketplace. Or, even worse, they are reduced to security officers employed primarily to discipline, contain, and, all too often, turn students who commit infractions over to the police and the criminal justice system.[17] Not only do students not count in this mode of schooling, but teachers are stripped of their dignity and capacities when it comes to critically examining the nature and process of educational reform.

Although the political and ideological climate does not look favorable for the teachers at the moment, it does offer them the challenge to join a public debate with their critics as well as the opportunity to engage in a much needed self-critique regarding the nature and purpose of schooling, classroom teaching, and the relationship between education and social change. Similarly, the debate provides teachers with the opportunity to organize collectively to improve the conditions under which they work and to demonstrate to the public the central role that teachers must play in any viable attempt to reform public schools.

In order for teachers and others to engage in such a debate, it is necessary that theoretical perspectives be developed that redefine the nature of the current educational crisis while simultaneously providing the basis for an alternative view of teacher work. In short, this means recognizing that the current crisis in education cannot be separated from the rise and pernicious influence of neoliberal capitalism and market-driven power relations, both of which work in the interest of disempowering teachers, dismantling teacher unions, and privatizing public schools. At the very least, such recognition will have to come to grips with a growing loss of power among teachers around the basic conditions of their work, but also with a changing public perception of their role as reflective practitioners.

I want to make a small theoretical contribution to this debate and the challenge it calls forth by examining two major problems that need to be addressed in the interest of improving the quality of "teacher work," which includes all the clerical tasks and extra assignments as well as classroom instruction. First, it is imperative to examine the ideological and material forces that have contributed to the de-skilling and commodification of teacher work; that is, the tendency to reduce teachers to the status of specialized technicians within the school bureaucracy, whose function then becomes one of managing and implementing curricular programs rather than developing or critically appropriating curricula to fit specific pedagogical concerns and the particular needs of students. Second, there is a need to defend schools as institutions essential to maintaining and developing a critical democracy and also to defending teachers as public intellectuals who combine scholarly reflection and practice in the service of educating students to be thoughtful, active citizens.

Devaluing and De-skilling Teacher Work

One of the major threats facing prospective and existing teachers within the public schools is the increasing development of instrumental and corporate ideologies that emphasize a technocratic approach to both teacher preparation and classroom pedagogy. At the core of the current emphasis on the instrumental and pragmatic factors in school life are a number of important pedagogical assumptions. These include: a call for the separation of conception from execution; the standardization of school knowledge in the interest of managing and controlling it; the increased call for standardized testing, and the devaluation of critical, intellectual work on the part of teachers and students for the primacy of practical considerations. In this view, teaching is reduced to training, and concepts are substituted by methods. Teaching in this view is reduced to a set of strategies and skills and becomes synonymous with a method or technique. Instead of learning to raise questions about the principles underlying different classroom methods, research techniques, and theories of education, teachers are often preoccupied with learning the "how to," with what works, or with mastering the best way to teach a given body of knowledge.

What is ignored in this retrograde view is any understanding of pedagogy as a moral and political practice that functions as a deliberate attempt to influence how and what knowledge, values, and identities are produced with particular sets of classroom social relations. What is purposely derided in conservative notions of teaching and learning is a view of pedagogy that in the most critical sense, illuminates the relationship among knowledge, authority, and power and draws attention to questions concerning who has control over the conditions for the production of knowledge. Pedagogy in this sense addresses and connects ethics, politics, power, and knowledge within practices that allow for generating multiple solidarities, narratives, and vocabularies as part of a broader democratic project. As Chandra Mohanty insists, pedagogy is not only about the act of knowing, but also about how knowledge is related to the power of self-definition, understanding one's relationship to others, and one's understanding and connection to the larger world.[18] In the end, pedagogy is not, as many conservatives argue, about immersing young people in predefined and isolated bits of information, but about the issue of agency and how it can be developed in the interest of deepening and expanding the meaning and purpose of democratization and the formative cultures that make it possible.

Technocratic and instrumental rationalities are also at work within the teaching field itself, and they play an increasing role in reducing teacher autonomy with respect to the development and planning of curricula and the judging and implementation of classroom instruction. In the past, this took the form of what was called "teacher-proof" curriculum packages. The underlying rationale in many of these packages views teacher work as simply the carrying out of predetermined content and instructional procedures. The method and aim of such packages was to legitimate what might be called "market-driven management pedagogies." That is, knowledge is broken down into discrete parts, standardized for easier management and consumption, and measured through predefined forms of assessment. Curricula approaches of this sort are management pedagogies because the central questions regarding teaching and learning are reduced to the problems of management, regulation, and control. Though such curricula are far from absent in many schools, they have been mostly replaced by modes of classroom instruction geared to a pedagogy of repression, defined through the rubric of accountability. This approach works to discipline both the body and mind in the interest of training students to perform well in high-stakes testing schemes. It defines quality teaching through reductive mathematical models.[19]

Pedagogy as an intellectual, moral, and political practice is now based on "measurements of value derived from market competition."[20] Mathematical utility has now replaced critical dialogue, debate, risk taking, the power of imaginative leaps, and learning for the sake of learning. A crude instrumental rationality now governs the form and content of curricula, and where content has the potential to open up the possibility of critical thinking, it is quickly shut down. This is a pedagogy that has led to the abandonment of democratic impulses, analytic thinking, and social responsibility. It is also a pedagogy that infantilizes both teachers and students. For instance, we have seen that the Texas GOP built into its platform the banning of critical thinking.[21] In addition, an increasing number of schools are tying teacher evaluation to reductionistic performance measures, banning critical thinking in history classes, and eliminating histories and cultures of subordinate groups, particularly for Latinos.[22] Texas, Florida, and Arizona, among other states, have not only banned any attempt at what can loosely be called critical interpretation in the curriculum but they have enforced a pedagogy of exclusion and oppression.

The soft underlying theoretical assumption that guides this type of pedagogy is that the behavior of teachers needs to be controlled and made consistent and predictable across different schools and student populations. The more hidden and hard assumption at work here is that teachers cannot be intellectuals, cannot think outside of conventional understanding, and cannot engage in forms of pedagogy that might enable students to think differently, critically, or more imaginatively. What is suppressed in this form of pedagogy are the pedagogical conditions necessary to enable students "to come to terms with their own power as individuals and social agents," to energize their civic imagination, and to expand their understanding of the relationship between themselves and the larger world. In the end, what these pedagogies of oppression reinforce is not only a crippling illiteracy but also what Paulo Freire has called a culture of silence.[23] The de-skilling of teachers, the reduction of reason to a form of instrumental rationality, and the disinvestment in education as a public good is also evident on a global level in policies produced by the World Bank that impose on countries forms of privatization and standardized curricula that undermine the potential for critical inquiry and engaged citizenship. Learning in this instance is depoliticized, prioritized as a method, and often reduced to teaching low-level skills, disciplinary-imposed behaviors, and corporate values. Neoliberal disciplinary measures now function to limit students to the private orbits in which they experience their lives while restricting the power of teachers to teach students to think rationally, judge wisely, and be able to connect private troubles to broader public considerations.

Public schools have become an object of disdain and teachers labor under educational reforms that separate conception from execution, theory from practice, and pedagogy from moral and social considerations. As content is devalued, history erased, and the economic, racial, and social inequities intensified, public schools are increasingly hijacked by corporate and religious fundamentalists. The effect is not only to de-skill teachers, to remove them from the processes of deliberation and reflection, but to routinize the nature of learning and classroom pedagogy. Needless to say, the principles underlying corporate pedagogies are at odds with the premise that teachers should be actively involved in producing curricular materials suited to the cultural and social contexts in which they teach.

More specifically, the narrowing of curricula choices to a back-to-basics format and the introduction of lock-step, time-on-task pedagogies operate from the theoretically erroneous assumption that all students can learn from the same materials, classroom instructional techniques, and modes of evaluation. The notion that students come from different histories and embody different experiences, linguistic practices, cultures, and talents is strategically ignored within the logic and accountability of management pedagogy theory. Curiosity is replaced by monotony and learning withers under the weight of dead time.

Teachers as Public Intellectuals

One way to rethink and restructure the nature of teacher work is to view teachers as public intellectuals. The category of intellectual is helpful in a number of ways. First, it provides a theoretical basis for examining teacher work as a form of intellectual labor, as opposed to defining it in purely instrumental or technical terms. Second, it clarifies the kinds of ideological and practical conditions necessary for teachers to function as intellectuals. Third, it helps to make clear the role teachers play in producing and legitimating various political, economic, and social interests through the pedagogies they endorse and utilize.

By viewing teachers as public intellectuals, we can illuminate the important idea that all human activity involves some form of thinking. No activity, regardless of how routinized it might become, can be abstracted from the functioning of the mind in some capacity. This is a crucial issue, because by arguing that the use of the mind is a general part of all human activity, we dignify the human capacity for integrating thinking and practice, and in doing so highlight the core of what it means to view teachers as reflective practitioners. Within this discourse, teachers can be seen not merely as "performers professionally equipped to realize effectively any goals that may be set for them. Rather [they should] be viewed as free men and women with a special dedication to the values of the intellect and the enhancement of the critical powers of the young."[24]

Viewing teachers as public intellectuals also provides a strong theoretical critique of technocratic and instrumental ideologies underlying educational theories that separate the conceptualization, planning, and design of curricula from the processes of implementation and execution. It is important to stress that teachers must take active responsibility for raising serious questions about what they teach, how they are to teach, and what the larger goals are for which they are striving. This means that they must take a responsible role in shaping the purposes and conditions of schooling. Such a task is impossible within a division of labor in which teachers have little influence over the conceptual and economic conditions of their work. This point has a normative and political dimension that seems especially relevant for teachers. If we believe that the role of teaching cannot be reduced to merely training in the practical skills, but involves, instead, the education of a class of engaged and public intellectuals vital to the development of a free society, then the category of intellectual becomes a way of linking the purpose of teacher education, public schooling, and in-service training to the principles necessary for developing a democratic order and society. Recognizing teachers as engaged and public intellectuals means that educators should never be reduced to technicians, just as education should never be reduced to training. Instead, pedagogy should be rooted in the practice of freedom—in those ethical and political formations that expand democratic underpinnings and principles of both the self and the broader social order.

By viewing teachers as intellectuals, we can begin to rethink and re-form the traditions and conditions that have prevented teachers from assuming their full potential as active, reflective scholars and practitioners. It is important not only to view teachers as public intellectuals, but also to contextualize in political and normative terms the concrete social functions that teachers have both to their work and to the dominant society.

A starting point for interrogating the social function of teachers as public intellectuals is to view schools as economic, cultural, and social sites that are inextricably tied to the issues of politics, power, and control. This means that schools do more than pass on in an objective fashion a common set of values and knowledge. On the contrary, schools are places that represent forms of knowledge, language practices, social relations, and values that are particular selections and exclusions from the wider culture. As such, schools serve to introduce and legitimate particular forms of social life. Rather than being objective institutions removed from the dynamics of politics and power, schools actually are contested spheres that embody and express struggles over what forms of authority, types of knowledge, forms of moral regulation, and versions of the past and future should be legitimated and transmitted to students.

Schools are always political because they produce particular kinds of agents, desires, and social relations, and they legitimate particular notions of the past, present, and future. The struggle is most visible in the demands, for example, of right-wing religious groups currently trying to inject creationism in the schools, institute school prayer, remove certain books from school libraries, and include certain forms of religious teachings in the curricula. Of course, different demands are made by feminists, ecologists, minorities, and other interest groups who believe that the schools should teach women's studies, courses on the environment, or black history. In short, schools are not neutral sites, and teachers cannot assume the posture of being neutral either.

Central to the category of public intellectual is the necessity of making the pedagogical more political and the political more pedagogical. Making the pedagogical more political means inserting schooling directly into the political sphere by arguing that schooling represents both a struggle to define meaning and a struggle over agency and power relations. Within this perspective, critical reflection and action become part of a fundamental social project to help students develop a deep and abiding faith in the struggle to overcome economic, political, and social injustices, and to further humanize themselves as part of this struggle. In this case, knowledge and power are inextricably linked to the presupposition that to choose life, to recognize the necessity of improving its democratic and qualitative character for all people, is to understand the preconditions necessary to struggle for it. Teaching must be seen as a political, civic, and ethical practice precisely because it is directive, that is, an intervention that takes up the ethical responsibility of recognizing, as Paulo Freire points out, that human life is conditioned but not determined.

A critical pedagogical practice does not transfer knowledge but creates the possibilities for its production, analysis, and use. Without succumbing to a kind of rigid dogmatism, teachers should provide the pedagogical conditions for students to bear witness to history, their own actions, and the mechanisms that drive the larger social order so that students can imagine the inseparable connection between the human condition and the ethical basis of our existence. Educators have a responsibility for educating students in ways that allow them to hold power accountable, learn how to govern, and develop a responsibility to others and a respect for civic life. The key here is to recognize that being a public intellectual is no excuse for being dogmatic. Although it is crucial to recognize that education has a critical function, the teacher's task is not to mold students but to encourage human agency, to provide the conditions for students to be self-determining and to struggle for a society that is both autonomous and democratic.

Making the political more pedagogical means treating students as critical agents; making knowledge problematic and open to debate; engaging in critical and thoughtful dialogue; and making the case for a qualitatively better world for all people. In part, this suggests that teachers as public intellectuals take seriously the need to give students an active voice in their learning experiences. It also means developing a critical vernacular that is attentive to problems experienced at the level of everyday life, particularly as they are related to pedagogical experiences connected to classroom practice. As such, the pedagogical starting point for such intellectuals is not the isolated student removed from the historical and cultural forces that bear down on their lives but individuals in their various cultural, class, racial, and historical contexts, along with the particularity of their diverse problems, hopes, and dreams.

As public intellectuals, teachers should develop a discourse that unites the language of critique with the language of possibility. In this instance, educators not only recognize the need to act on the world, to connect reading the word with reading the world, but also make clear that it is within their power individually and collectively to do so. In taking up this project, they should work under conditions that allow them to speak out against economic, political, and social injustices both within and outside of schools. At the same time, they should work to create the conditions that give students the opportunity to become critical and engaged citizens who have the knowledge and courage to struggle in order to make desolation and cynicism unconvincing and hope practical. Hope in this case is neither a call to social engineering nor an excuse to overlook the difficult conditions that shape both schools and the larger social order. On the contrary, it is the precondition for providing those languages and values that point the way to a more democratic and just world. As Judith Butler has argued, there is more hope in the world when we can question commonsense assumptions and believe that what we know is directly related to our ability to help change the world around us, though it is far from the only condition necessary for such change.[25] Hope provides the basis for dignifying our labor as intellectuals; it offers up critical knowledge linked to democratic social change, and allows teachers and students to recognize ambivalence and uncertainty as fundamental dimensions of learning. Ernst Bloch insists that hope is "not yet in the sense of a possibility; that it could be there if we could only do something for it."[26] Hope offers the possibility of thinking beyond the given—and lays open a pedagogical terrain in which teachers and students can engage in critique, dialogue, and an open-ended struggle for justice. As difficult as this task may seem to educators, if not to a larger public, it is a struggle worth waging. To deny educators the opportunity to assume the role of public intellectuals is to prevent teachers from gaining control over the conditions of their work, denying them the right to "push at the frontiers, to worry the edges of the human imagination, to conjure beauty from the most unexpected things, to find magic in places where others never thought to look,"[27] and to model what it means for intellectuals to exhibit civic courage by giving education a central role in constructing a world that is more just, equitable, and democratic in dark times.

What role might public school teachers play as public intellectuals in light of the brutal killings at Sandy Hook Elementary School? In the most immediate sense, they can raise their collective voices against the gun lobby and its poisonous influence in the media, political realm, and corporate world that enables it to inundate the country with deadly weapons. As Garry Wills argues, guns have become an object of reference in America, flooding the culture with killing machines that are readily available to most people and removed from any sensible set of regulations.[28] Guns and a powerful and influential formative culture of violence now mutually reinforce each other's existence, "embedded in the country's DNA" and central to "the very idea of America and 'freedom.'"[29] The economic, social, political, and cultural forces that underlie the epidemic of gun violence in America appear to exist beyond the boundaries of criticism, if not politics itself, in spite of the violence against children produced by a gun culture. Such violence becomes clear in a set of statistics that boggle the mind, yet fail to jolt the collective conscience. For example, "Since 1979 when gun data was first collected by age, a shocking 119,079 children and teens have been killed by gun violence . . . more child and youth deaths in America than American battle deaths in World War 1 (55,402) or in Vietnam (47,434) or in the Korean War (33,739) or in the Iraq War (3,517)," and yet there is no large-scale social movement, group of politicians, or political party willing "to protect children from pervasive gun violence here at home."[30] At the very least, educators can make clear that some of the biggest gun makers are owned by "private equity funds run by Wall Street titans."[31] By doing so, educators can bring out the pernicious and corrupt power of Wall Street as part of a larger campaign to mobilize investors and the public to organize a boycott against the holdings of those companies that trade and make profits off the machineries of death and violence. They can also illustrate new ways in which a neoliberal regime of corruption, violence, and greed operate and how they can be fought and held accountable by the American public. In the most general sense, this means challenging a neoliberal script that invests in violence rather than in children, one that sacrifices the safety of children to the sordid profits made by the commanding institutions that drive the culture of guns and violence.

Violence in America cannot be separated from the institutions, groups, media, intellectuals, and politicians that attempt to legitimate the conditions that make it possible. In the first instance, the proliferation of guns is made through the infantile argument that more guns mean more safety. In the face of mass shootings such as those that happened at Virginia Tech and the Sandy Hook Elementary School, gun advocates argue incredibly that we should arm teachers, students, and others in order to prevent further violence. Of course, more guns mean that problems that might have been handled peacefully or with even a fistfight are now handled with guns. More guns also legitimate the idea that violence is the most important mediating force to which individuals can resort. The presence of guns also accelerates the bonds of fear, not trust. When defense becomes a private matter—mimicking the logic of the market—the police and other agencies of domestic security equipped to act in the public interest lose their power. Personal security now trumps social and public security and increases a society filled with atomized individuals who now have the right to carry around weapons designed for warfare. The call to arm everyone in every sphere of activity is symptomatic of a society that has not only lost its moral compass, but truly has resorted to an ethic of barbarism in which fear becomes the only motivating force and weapons the only mark of security. These arguments and the interest they serve must be exposed and fought assiduously. This necessitates both an ideological campaign calling for gun regulation and a political campaign to do away with a market-driven society that trades in violence, profits from it, and undermines democracy because of the widespread suffering and carnage it produces.

At the same time, it is crucial that educators parents, politicians, and others show how the gun lobby and its culture of violence is only one part of a broader and all-embracing militarized culture of war, arms industry, and a Darwinian survival-of-the-fittest ethic, more characteristic of an authoritarian society than a democracy. The production of violence in a neoliberal society is complex and takes multiple forms. It extends from violent video games to films and television shows that glorify violence. Don Hazen provides a theoretical service in addressing these multiple causes behind the culture of violence in America:

> There is no one cause, or small number of causes, behind the culture of violence in America. There are many culprits but especially culpable are alcohol abuse, which often leads to violence; the war on drugs, which make drugs hugely valuable, increasing the violence; the return of hundreds of thousands of soldiers from two long and brutal wars, many trained killers, many with PTSD; the militarization of police departments, with heavy surveillance technology designed to make even a normal person paranoid; mass incarceration in prisons run frequently by companies trying to make a lot of profit off crime, and where for inmates, prison is

often a graduate course in more advanced crime, especially since there are no jobs and almost zero help in integrating ex-cons into productive lives after they leave prison; and high levels of unemployment, especially among the working class and those without college diplomas. [There is also] the emergence of the gun-toting Tea Party [that] has raised the specter of violence. There has been a marked increase in militia groups and right-wing extremists. [In addition], there is what is often called the "masculinity crisis." The changing roles of men, inspiring feelings of uselessness; the growing success and prominence of women and the increased maladaptiveness of many masculine traits, which are not so useful in day-to-day life in America in 2013 as they have been in the past. The end result, for whatever combination of reasons, is that virtually all the violence in America is executed by men.[32]

Hazen registers these problems as political problems, though in fact they are also pedagogical problems and demand that we not only understand them in relation to the realm of politics, power, and economics but also in terms of a cultural politics that functions as a power educational force—an amalgam of cultural/pedagogical forces for producing powerful market-driven values, desires, identities, and subject positions. In the face of such forces, educators can mobilize young people to stand up for teachers, students, and public education by advocating for policies that invest in public schools rather than in the military-industrial complex and its massive and expensive weapons of death. They can educate young people and a larger public to support gun regulation and the democratization of the culture industries that now trade in violence as a form of entertainment; they can speak out against the educational, political, and economic conditions in which violence has become a sport in America—one of the most valuable practices and assets of the national entertainment state. They can critically interrogate the emergence of a new hyper-masculinity and the violence it both celebrates and appears to perpetuate against women, gays, the homeless, and others considered weak and unworthy of human dignity. The violent screen culture of video games, extreme sports, violent Hollywood films, television dramas, and other cultural productions do not just produce entertainment, they are mainly teaching machines that instruct children in a sadistic culture in which killing is all right, violence is fun, and masculinity is defined increasingly through its propensity to make celebrities out of killers. This is a culture that serves as a recruiting tool for the military by making military force rather than democratic idealism the highest national ideal and war the most important organizing principle of society.

Public school teachers can join with parents, churches, synagogues, mosques, and other individuals and institutions to address the larger socioeconomic and ideological values and practices that legitimize a hyper-masculinity fueled by the death-dealing assumption that war and a primitive tribalism make men, irrespective of the violence they promote against women, gays, students, the homeless, and people with disabilities. America is obsessed with violence and death, and this fixation not only provides profits for Hollywood, the defense industries, and the weapons industries, it also reproduces a culture of war and cruelty that has become central to America's national identity—one that is as shameful as it is deadly to its children and others. American society has also become hardened since the 1980s under neoliberalism. We celebrate militarism, extreme competition, and a survival-of-the-fittest ethic while exhibiting disdain for any form of shared bonds, dependency, and compassion for others. As social bonds and the institutions that support them disappear from American society, the power of deadly violence becomes more attractive and serves as one of the few sources of pleasure left to the American public.[33]

Politics has become an extension of war and greed and, worse yet, corruption, and a culture of cruelty now defines some of the most commanding financial institutions in the United States. The sound of the cash register has replaced the echoes of the public, asserting their collective identities in spaces, places, and sites that affirm social bonds as a public good and crucial for participation in a democratic society. Atomization, fragmentation, and isolation are the collateral damage inflicted on the public economically and existentially by neoliberal reforms that extend "to every nook and cranny of human existence in a way that previous eras would not have believed possible."[34] Under such circumstances, it is impossible to disconnect the massacre at Sandy Hook Elementary School from attacks on the public sector, from schooling to mental health facilities to the lapse of the assault weapons ban. Jeff Sparrow captures the poisonous nature of neoliberalism and militarism and the social dislocations they produce, including rage murders, in his comment:

> This, it seems to me, provides a background to the proliferation of rage murder. On the one hand, ordinary Americans have been . . . experiencing a concerted assault from neoliberalism for some decades now, producing a profound social dislocation. The traditional bonds between people dissolve, with the normalization of an ideology of radical individualism. . . . [Moreover], the U.S. has been occupying Afghanistan for eleven years and Iraq for nine. You cannot maintain combat operations for that length of time without fostering, both deliberately and otherwise, a militarism closely connected to a sense of personal liberation through violence. War is carcinogenic to the body politic, and the cancers it generates appear in all kinds of unexpected ways. . . . In that setting, is it really so surprising that [the] joy of battle takes a certain proportion of damaged men by the throat, that some of those who know themselves to be among the detritus of a neoliberal order seek the power and clarity that comes from aiming a rifle and pulling its trigger? [35]

War psychosis and the war on public school teachers and children reached their tragic apogee with the brutal and incomprehensible killing of the young children at Sandy Hook Elementary School. What kind of country has the United States become in its willingness to allow this endless barrage of symbolic and material violence to continue? Why has violence become the most powerful mediating force shaping social relations in the United States? Why do we allow a government to use drones to kill young children abroad? Why does the American public remain silent in the face of a government that not only "permits the indefinite detention of American citizens" but also engages in a global assassination campaign that includes its own citizens?[36] Why does it allow the right-wing media and the mainstream press to constantly denigrate both teachers and young people? Why are the lives of young people one of our lowest national priorities? Why do we denigrate public servants such as teachers who educate, nurture, and safeguard young people? What kind of country betrays its teachers and denigrates public education? How does the violence against teachers and students destroy the connective tissue that makes possible the shared bonds of trust, compassion, and justice so necessary for education and democracy itself?

10.

Dangerous Pedagogy in
the Age of Casino Capitalism:
Reclaiming the Radical Imagination

ALL OVER THE WORLD, the forces of neoliberalism are on the march, dismantling the historically guaranteed social provisions provided by the welfare state, defining profit-making and market freedoms as the essence of democracy, and diminishing state regulation of the economy. At the same time that the forces of privatization, deregulation, and financial marketization tighten their grip on all aspects of society, the social state is transformed into the punishing state and increasingly violates civil liberties as part of an alleged war against terrorism. Echoing the ideology of Margaret Thatcher, advocates of neoliberalism appear secure in their dystopian vision that there are no alternatives to a market society as they work assiduously to undermine any viable notion of collective resistance, the public good, and democracy itself by celebrating the inevitability of economic laws in which the ethical ideal of intervening in the world gives way to the idea that we "have no choice but to adapt both our hopes and our abilities to the new global market."[1] Coupled with an ever-expanding culture of fear, a market-based notion of freedom seems securely grounded in a defense of national security and the institutions of finance capital. Under such circumstances, a neoliberal model now bears down on American society, threatening to turn it into an authoritarian state.

The script of the market fundamentalists is now familiar: there is no such thing as the common good; market values are the template for shaping all aspects of society; free, possessive individuals have no obligations to anything but their own self-interest; profit making is the essence of democracy; the government, and particularly the welfare state, is the archenemy of freedom; private interests trump public values; consumerism is the essence of citizenship; privatization is the essence of freedom; law and order is the new language for mobilizing shared fears rather than shared responsibilities; permanent war is the organizing principle for remaking society and the economy under market rule; and theocracy has become the legitimating code for punishing women, young people, the elderly, and those groups marginalized by class, race, and ethnicity when religious moralism is needed to shore up the war against all elements of the social order.[2]

Given the current crisis that has ensued from the ascendancy of market-based values, educators need a new political and pedagogical language for addressing the changing contexts and issues facing the world. Capitalism in its neoliberal incarnation now draws upon an unprecedented convergence of resources—financial, cultural, political, economic, scientific, military, and technological—to exercise powerful and diverse forms of control across all levels and sectors of society. If educators and others are to counter global capitalism's increased ability to separate the traditional reach of politics from the emerging transnational reach of corporate power, it is crucial to develop educational approaches that reject a collapse of the distinction between market liberties and civil liberties, a market economy and a market society. This suggests the need to develop forms of critical pedagogy capable of challenging neoliberalism and other anti-democratic traditions (such as the emerging religious fundamentalism in the United States), while resurrecting a radical democratic project that provides the basis for imagining a life beyond the nightmarish dream worlds of capitalism. To meet such a need, education must be viewed as more than testing or an obsession with accountability schemes and zero tolerance policies, or a site only for training students for the workforce. At stake here is recognizing the power of education to create the formative culture necessary to challenge the various threats being mobilized against the very ideas of justice and democracy, while also struggling for those public spheres and democratic ideals that offer alternative modes of identity, social relations, and politics.

As I have suggested throughout this book, the search for a new politics and a new critical language that can cross a range of theoretical divides must reinvigorate the relationship between democracy, ethics, and political agency by expanding both the meaning of the pedagogical as a political practice, and at the same time make the political more pedagogical. In the first instance, it is crucial to recognize that pedagogy has less to do with techniques and methods than it does with issues of language, politics, and power. Pedagogy is a moral and political practice that is always implicated in power relations and must be understood as a cultural endeavor that offers both a particular version and vision of civic life, the future, and how we might construct representations of ourselves, others, and our physical and social environment. As Roger Simon observes:

> As an introduction to, preparation for, and legitimation of particular forms of social life, education always presupposes a vision of the future. In this respect a curriculum and its supporting pedagogy are a version of our own dreams for ourselves, our children, and our communities. But such dreams are never neutral; they are always someone's dreams, and to the degree that they are implicated in organizing the future for others they always have a moral and political dimension. It is in this respect that any discussion of pedagogy must begin with a discussion of educational practice as a form of cultural politics, as a particular way in which a sense of identity, place, worth, and above all value is informed by practices which organize knowledge and meaning.[3]

An oppositional cultural politics can take many forms, but given the current assault by neoliberalism on all aspects of democratic public life, it seems imperative that educators renew the struggle to create conditions in which learning would be linked to social change in a wide variety of social sites, and pedagogy would take on the task of regenerating both a sense of social and political agency and a critical subversion of dominant power. Making the political more pedagogical rests on the assumption that education takes place at a variety of sites outside of the school. Under such circumstances, agency becomes the site through which power is not transcended, but reworked, replayed, and restaged in productive ways. Central to this position is the assumption that not only is politics about power, but also, as Cornelius Castoriadis points out, politics "has to do with political judgments and value choices."[4] For this reason, civic education and critical pedagogy—or learning how to become a skilled citizen—are central to the struggle over political agency and democracy. Critical pedagogy is important because it emphasizes critical reflexivity, bridging the gap between learning and everyday life, revealing the connection between power and knowledge, and extending democratic rights and identities by using the resources of history. However, among many educators and social theorists, there is a widespread refusal to recognize that this form of education is the foundation for expanding and enabling political agency, which must take place across a wide variety of public spheres mediated through the very force of culture itself. Matters of theory and critical thinking are also crucial for the ways in which teachers are taught, particularly in schools of education. There has been a systemic attempt on the part of wealthy elites such as Bill Gates, conservative think tanks such as the Heritage Foundation, and the Obama administration to develop alternative routes to teacher certification, based largely on data-driven approaches to teaching, such as "more on the job training." What is under attack here by academics such as David Steiner and Arnie Duncan, Obama's secretary of education, is the fear that if prospective teachers are exposed to critical, if not progressive views, about schooling, pedagogy, and broader social issues, they might reject the instrumentalized, stir-and-service recipes for teaching being pushed by conservatives. Pedagogy for this ilk is about teaching methods, eliminating the productive character of pedagogy as a moral and political practice, and educating teachers to be narrow technicians rather than engaged, public intellectuals who connect education to the most fundamental capacities needed to produce critical and thoughtful citizens.

One of the central tasks of any viable critical pedagogy is to make visible, as the Occupy movement is doing, alternative models of radical democratic relations in diverse sites across the broader society. These spaces can make *the pedagogical more political* by raising fundamental questions such as: What is the relationship between social justice and the distribution of public resources and goods? What are the conditions, knowledge, and skills that are a prerequisite for civic literacy, political agency, and social change? What kinds of identities, desires, and social relations are being produced and legitimated in the practice of teaching and learning? How might the latter prepare or undermine the ability of students to be self-reflective, exercise judgment, engage in critical dialogues, and assume some responsibility for addressing the challenges posed to democracy at a national and global level? Such a project will involve understanding and critically engaging dominant public transcripts and values within a broader set of historical and institutional contexts.

Making *the political more pedagogical* suggests producing modes of knowledge and social practices in a variety of sites that not only affirm oppositional thinking, dissent, and cultural work, but also offer opportunities to mobilize instances of collective outrage and collective action. Such a mobilization will oppose glaring material inequities and the growing cynical belief that the complexity of market forces and finance capital makes it impossible to address many of the major social problems facing both the United States and the larger world. Most important, such work points to the link among civic education, critical pedagogy, and modes of oppositional political agency, all of which are pivotal to creating a politics that promotes democratic values, relations, autonomy, and social change. Hints of such a politics are already evident in the various approaches the Occupy movement has taken in reclaiming the discourse of democracy and in collectively challenging the values and practices of a market-based social order. Borrowing a line from Rachel Donadio, the Occupy movement protesters are raising questions about "What happens to democracy when banks become more powerful than political institutions?"[5] We might add to this, what kind of education will it take both in and out of schools to recognize the dissolution of democracy and the emergence of an authoritarian state?

In taking up these questions and the challenges they pose, critical pedagogy proposes that education is a form of political intervention in the world that is capable of creating the possibilities for social transformation. Rather than viewing teaching as a technical practice, pedagogy in the broadest critical sense is premised on the assumption that learning is not about processing received knowledge, but about actually transforming it as part of a more expansive struggle for individual rights and social justice. This implies that any viable notion of pedagogy and resistance should illustrate how knowledge, values, desires, and social relations are always implicated in relations of power, and how such an understanding can be used pedagogically and politically by students to further expand and deepen the imperatives of social and political democracy. The key challenge facing educators within the current age of neoliberalism, militarism, and religious fundamentalism is to provide the conditions for students to address how knowledge is related to the power of both self-definition and social agency. In part, this means providing students with the skills, knowledge, and authority they need to inquire and act upon what it means to live in a substantive democracy, recognize anti-democratic forms of power, and fight against deeply rooted injustices in a society and world founded on systemic economic, racial, and gender inequalities.

The Responsibility of Educators as Public Intellectuals

In the age of irresponsible privatization, it is difficult to recognize that educators and other cultural workers bear an enormous responsibility in opposing the current threat to the planet and everyday life by bringing democratic political culture back to life. Although liberal democracy offers an important discourse around issues of "rights, freedoms, participation, self-rule, and citizenship," it has been mediated historically through the "damaged and burdened tradition" of racial and gender exclusions, economic injustice, and a formalistic, ritualized democracy that has substituted a swindle in place of the promise of democratic participation.[6] At the same time, liberal and republican traditions of Western democratic thought have given rise to forms of social and political criticism that at least contained a framework for addressing the deep gap between the promise of a radical democracy and the existing reality. With the rise of neoliberalism, any remaining referents for imagining even a weak democracy, or for that matter understanding the tensions between capitalism and democracy that animated political discourse through the twentieth century, appear to be overwhelmed by market discourses, identities, and practices, on the one hand, and a corrosive cynicism on the other.

In the current historical conjuncture, the United States is awash in a kind of political lunacy that testifies to the rise of a poisonous extremism in which the most important civic values, public spheres, and institutions necessary to sustain a working democracy are being eliminated. Democracy has now been reduced to a metaphor for the alleged "free" market, and in some cases to the image of a theocratic state. It is not that a genuine democratic public space once existed in some ideal form and has now been corrupted by the values of the market, but that these democratic public spheres, even in limited ways, no longer seem to be animating concepts for making visible the contradiction between the reality of existing democracy and the promise of a more fully realized substantive democracy. Part of the challenge of linking critical pedagogy with the process of democratization will mean constructing new locations of struggle, vocabularies, and subject positions that allow people in a wide variety of public spheres to become more than they are now, to question what it is they have become within existing institutional and social formations, and to give some thought to what it might mean to transform existing relations of subordination and oppression.

Critical Pedagogy as a Project of Intervention

If teachers, artists, activists, and others are to revitalize the language of civic education as part of a broader discourse of political agency and critical citizenship in a global world, they will have to consider grounding such a pedagogy in a defense of what I have called in chapter 8 *educated hope.*[7] Such hope is built upon recognizing pedagogy as part of a broader attempt to revitalize the conditions for individual and social agency, and simultaneously addressing critical pedagogy as a project informed by both a democratic political vision and the diverse ways such a vision gets mediated in different contexts. Such a project also suggests consciously recasting the relationship between the pedagogical and political as a project that is indeterminate, open to constant revision, and always in dialogue with its own assumptions. The project in this sense speaks to the directive nature of pedagogy: the recognition that any pedagogical practice presupposes some notion of the future, prioritizes some forms of identification over others, and upholds particular modes of social relations. Clearly, critical pedagogy presupposes a vision of the future in that it legitimates particular forms of knowledge, social relations, and values and as such is an introduction to, preparation for, and a legitimation of particular forms of social life. In doing so, it makes clear that education is about a generation's hopes for the future and a vision of agency that provides students with the capacities not only to prepare for the future but also to shape it. Rather than accept a dark future of draconian discipline, standardized testing, corporate values, and a pedagogy of conformity, ignorance, and oppression, critical pedagogy provides alternative forms of knowledge, connects student experience with learning itself, and encourages students to think beyond the given, to think otherwise in order to act otherwise. This is a form of teaching that teaches young people how to govern and not merely be governed. It is a pedagogy that has a long genealogy that can be found in the work of John Dewey, Paulo Freire, Maxine Greene, Ken Saltman, Deborah Britzmen, Roger Simon, myself, and others. At the same time, the normative nature of such a pedagogy does not offer guarantees as much as it recognizes that its own position is embedded in modes of authority, values, and ethical considerations that must be constantly debated for the ways in which they both open up and close down democratic relations, values, and identities. Central to keeping any notion of critical pedagogy alive is the recognition that it must address real social needs, be imbued with a passion for democracy, and provide the conditions for expanding democratic forms of political and social agency.

Critical Pedagogy in the Classroom: Contexts and Ethics

In opposition to the increasingly dominant views of education and cultural politics, I want to argue for a transformative pedagogy—rooted in the project of resurgent democracy—one that relentlessly questions the kinds of labor, practices, and forms of production that are enacted in public and higher education. Such an analysis should be relational and contextual, as well as self-reflective and theoretically rigorous. By relational, I mean that the current crisis of schooling must be understood in relation to the broader assault that is being waged against all aspects of democratic public life. As Jeffrey Williams has recently pointed out:

> The current restructuring of higher education is only one facet of the restructuring of civic life in the U.S. whereby previously assured public entitlements such as health care, welfare, and social security have evaporated or been "privatized," so no solution can be separated from a larger vision of what it means to enfranchise citizens of our republic.[8]

As important as such articulations are in understanding the challenges that public and higher education face in the current historical conjuncture, they do not go far enough. Any critical comprehension of those wider forces that shape public and higher education must also be supplemented by attentiveness to the conditional nature of pedagogy itself. Pedagogy should never be treated as a fixed set of principles and practices that can be applied indiscriminately across a variety of pedagogical sites. Pedagogy is not some recipe that can be imposed in the same way on all classrooms. On the contrary, it must always be contextually defined, allowing it to respond specifically to the ethical and political conditions, social issues formations, and economic problems that arise in various sites in which education takes place. Schools differ in their financing, quality of teachers, resources, histories, and cultural capital. Recognizing this, educators can address the purpose that schools might play in their relationship to the demands of the broader society, while simultaneously being sensitive to the distinctive nature of the issues educators address within the shifting contexts in which they interact with a diverse body of students, texts, and institutional formations.

Ethically, critical pedagogy requires an ongoing indictment of "those forms of truth-seeking which imagined themselves to be eternally and placelessly valid."[9] Simply put, educators need to cast a critical eye on those forms of knowledge and social relations that are defined through a conceptual purity and political innocence that cloud not only how they come into being, but also ignore that the alleged neutrality on which they stand is already grounded in ethico-political choices. Neutral, objective education is an oxymoron. Education cannot exist outside of relations of power, values, and politics. Thomas Keenan rightly argues that ethics on the pedagogical front demands an openness to the other, a willingness to engage a "politics of possibility" through a continuous critical engagement with texts, images, events, and other registers of meaning as they are transformed into public pedagogies.[10]

One consequence of linking pedagogy to the specificity of place is that it foregrounds the need for educators to rethink the cultural and political baggage they bring to each educational encounter. In other words, it highlights the necessity of educators being ethically and politically accountable for the stories they produce, the claims they make upon public memory, and the images of the future they deem legitimate. Pedagogy is never innocent, and if it is to be understood and problematized as a form of academic labor, educators must not only critically question and register their own subjective involvement in how and what they teach, but also resist all calls to depoliticize pedagogy through appeals to scientific objectivity or ideological dogmatism. Far from being disinterested or ideologically frozen, critical pedagogy is concerned about the articulation of knowledge to social effects and succeeds to the degree to which educators encourage critical reflection and moral and civic agency among students. Crucial to the latter position is the ongoing necessity for critical educators to be attentive to the ethical dimensions of their own practice.

Critical Pedagogy and the Promise of Democratization

As an act of intervention, critical pedagogy needs to be grounded in a project that not only problematizes its own location, mechanisms of transmission, and effects, but also functions as part of a larger effort to contest various forms of domination and to help students think more critically about how existing social, political, and economic arrangements might be better suited to address the promise of a radical democracy as an anticipatory rather than messianic goal. The late Jacques Derrida suggested that the social function of intellectuals as well as any viable notion of education should be grounded in a vibrant politics that makes the promise of democracy a matter of concrete urgency. For Derrida, making visible a democracy which is to come, as opposed to that which presents itself in name only, provides an opening for both criticizing what parades as democracy here and now—"the current state of all so-called democracy"—and critically assessing the conditions and possibilities for democratic transformation.[11] Derrida sees the promise of democracy as the explication of a political ethics, and suggests that when higher education is engaged and articulated through the project of democratic social transformation, then it functions as a vital public sphere for critical learning, ethical deliberation, and civic engagement.

The utopian dimension of pedagogy articulated through the project of radical democracy also offers the possibility of resistance to the increasing depoliticization of the citizenry. It does so by providing a language to challenge the politics of accommodation, which increasingly connects education to the logic of privatization, commodification, religious dogma, and instrumental knowledge. A transformative pedagogy refuses to define the citizen as simply a consuming subject and actively opposes the view of teaching as market-driven practice and of learning as a form of training. Utopianism in this sense is not an antidote to politics, a nostalgic yearning for a better time or for some "inconceivably alternative future." To the contrary, it is an "attempt to find a bridge between the present and future in those forces within the present which are potentially able to transform it."[12]

Critical pedagogy poses an important challenge to dominant forms of education and pedagogy that simply reproduce the present with no thought for the future, while scorning ethical principles and reducing the essence of democracy to the imperatives of the bottom line. Critical pedagogy takes as one of its core concerns how to provide students with the competencies they need to cultivate the capacity for critical judgment, thoughtfully connect politics to social responsibility, and expand their own sense of agency in order to curb the excesses of dominant power, revitalize a sense of public commitment, and expand democratic relations. Animated by a sense of critique and possibility, critical pedagogy at its best attempts to provoke students to deliberate, resist, and address various oppressions using a range of capacities that enable them to move beyond the world they already know without insisting on a fixed set of meanings.

Defending the Critical Role of Public Schools and Higher Education

Against the current onslaught to privatize public schools and corporatize higher education, educators need to defend public and higher education as resources vital to the democratic and civic life of the nation. Central to such a task is the challenge for academics, young people, the Occupy movement, labor unions, and other groups to find ways to join together in broad-based social movements and oppose the transformation of the public schools and higher education into commercial spheres—that is, to resist turning schools into what Bill Readings has called consumer-oriented corporations more concerned about accounting than accountability.[13] The crisis of public schooling and higher education—while having different registers—needs to be analyzed in terms of the wider configurations of economic, political, and social forces that exacerbate tensions between those who value such institutions as public goods and those ideologues of neoliberalism who see market culture as a master design for all human affairs. The threat corporate power poses can be seen in the ongoing attempts by neoliberals and other hyper-capitalists to subject all forms of public life, including public and higher education, to the dictates of the market, while simultaneously working to empty democracy itself of any vestige of ethical, political, and social considerations. What educators must challenge is the attempt on the part of neoliberals to define democracy exclusively as a liability and to enervate its substantive ideals by reducing it to the imperatives and freedoms of the marketplace. This requires that educators consider the political and pedagogical importance of struggling over the meaning and definition of democracy, as well as situate such a debate within an expansive notion of human rights, social provisions, civil liberties, equity, and economic justice. What must be challenged at all costs are the increasingly dominant views propagated by neoliberal gurus such as Ayn Rand and Milton Friedman that selfishness is the supreme value in shaping human agency, profit making is the most important practice in a democracy, and accumulating private assets is the essence of the good life.

Defending public and higher education as vital democratic spheres will be necessary to develop and nourish the proper balance between public values and commercial power, and between identities founded on democratic principles and identities steeped in forms of competitive, self-interested individualism that celebrate profiteering and greed. Educators must also reconsider the advocacy roles they might take up within public and higher education so as to enable them to oppose those approaches to schooling that corporatize, privatize, and bureaucratize the teaching process. A critical pedagogy should, in part, be premised on the assumption that educators must vigorously resist any attempt on the part of either liberals or conservatives to reduce their critical role in schools to that of technician or corporate pawn. Instead, educators themselves must take the initiative to define their role as that of the engaged public intellectual capable of teaching students the language of critique and possibility as a precondition for social agency.[14] Such a redefinition of educational purpose, meaning, and politics suggests that educators should critically interrogate the fundamental links between knowledge and power, pedagogical practices and social consequences, and authority and civic responsibility. It also means working to eliminate existing modes of corporate governance in the public schools and higher education that reduce teachers to the status of clerks and technicians, or in the case of higher education to a subaltern class of part-time workers with little power, few benefits, and excessive teaching loads.

By redefining the purpose and meaning of schooling as part of a broader attempt to struggle for a radical democratic social order, educators can begin to challenge a number of dominant assumptions and policies currently structuring public and higher education, including but not limited to the ongoing attempts by corporate culture to define educators as multinational operatives; the escalating efforts by colleges and universities to deny students the loans, resources, and public support they need to have access to a quality education; the mounting pressures brought to bear by corporate interests to compel universities to reward forms of scholarship that generate corporate profits; the increasing attempts to deny women and students of color access to higher education through the reversal of affirmative action policies; the never-ending policy of skyrocketing increases in tuition costs; and the growing emphasis on classroom pedagogies designed to create marketable products and mindless consumers. Rather than providing students with an opportunity to learn how to shape and govern public life, formal systems of education are increasingly being vocationalized, reduced to a commodity that provides privileges for a few students and low-skill industrial training for the rest, especially those who are marginalized due to class and race. One example of the threat facing critical educators was Republican Party presidential candidate Rick Santorum's claim that public education is a form of government intrusion and higher education is simply irrelevant because it is doing the work of Satan by allowing leftist educators to indoctrinate students.[15] That such ideological and political idiocy passes as a legitimate discourse in a presidential candidacy race tells us something about the devalued state of public and higher education, not to mention how vulnerable it is to the most extreme authoritarian pressures and policies.

What has become clear in this current climate of religious fundamentalism and casino capitalism is that the corporatization of education functions so as to cancel out the democratic values, impulses, and practices of a civil society by either devaluing or absorbing them within the logic of the market. Educators need a critical language to address these challenges to public and higher education. They also need to join with other groups outside of the spheres of public and higher education in order to create a national movement that links the defense of non-commodified education with a broader struggle to deepen the imperatives of democratic public life. The quality of educational reform can, in part, be gauged by the caliber of public discourse concerning the role that education plays in furthering *not* the market-driven agenda of corporate interests, but the imperatives of critical agency, social justice, and an operational democracy. In this capacity, educators need to develop a language of possibility and new pedagogical practices for raising critical questions about both the aim of schooling and the purpose of what and how educators teach. In doing so, pedagogy will draw attention to engaging classroom practice as a moral and political consideration animated by a fierce sense of commitment to expanding the range of individual and collective capacities that enable students to become critical agents capable of linking knowledge, responsibility, and democratic social transformation.

Approaching pedagogy as a critical and political practice suggests that educators must refuse all attempts to reduce classroom teaching exclusively to matters of technique and method. In opposition to such approaches, educators can highlight the performative character of education as an act of intervention in the world—focusing on the work that pedagogy does as a deliberate attempt to influence how and what knowledge and experiences are produced within particular sets of classroom relations. Within this perspective, critical pedagogy foregrounds the diverse conditions under which authority, knowledge, values, and subject positions are produced and interact within unequal relations of power. It also problematizes the ideologically laden and often contradictory roles and social functions that educators assume within the classroom. Pedagogy in this view can also be reclaimed as a form of academic labor that bridges the gap between individual considerations and public concerns, affirms bonds of sociality and reciprocity, interrogates the relationship between individual freedom and privatized notions of the good life, and defends the social obligations and collective structures necessary to support a vibrant democracy.

Classroom Authority and Pedagogy as the Outcome of Struggles

The question of what educators teach is inseparable from what it means to be located in public discourses and to be willing to invest in public commitments. Implicit in this position is the assumption that the responsibility of critical educators cannot be separated from the consequences of the roles they have been assigned, the knowledge they produce, the social relations they legitimate, and the ideologies they disseminate to students. Educational work at its best represents a response to questions and issues posed by the tensions and contradictions of the broader society. It is an attempt to understand and intervene in specific problems that emanate from those sites that people concretely inhabit and in which they actually live out their lives and everyday existence. Teaching in this sense becomes performative and contextual, and it highlights considerations of power, politics, and ethics fundamental to any form of teacher-student-text interaction.

It is crucial to reiterate that any pedagogy that is alive to its own democratic implications is always cautious concerning its need to resist totalizing certainties and answers. Refusing the pull of dogmatism, ideological purity, and imperious authority, educators must grasp the complexity and contradictions that inform the conditions under which they produce and disseminate knowledge. Recognizing that pedagogy is the outgrowth of struggles that are historically specific—as are the problems, questions, and issues that guide what and how we teach—should not suggest that educators renounce their authority. On the contrary, it is precisely by recognizing that teaching is always an act of intervention inextricably mediated through particular forms of authority that teachers can offer students a variety of analytic tools, diverse historical traditions, a wide-ranging knowledge of dominant and subaltern cultures, and a consideration of how each of these things influence one another. This is a far cry from suggesting that critical pedagogy either define itself within the grip of a self-righteous mode of authority or completely remove itself from any sense of commitment whatsoever. On the contrary, what is important here is the need to insist on modes of authority that are directive but not imperious, linking knowledge to power in the service of self-production and encouraging students to go beyond the world they already know in order to expand their range of human possibilities.

Educators must deliberate, make decisions, and take positions, and in doing so recognize that authority "is the very condition for intellectual work" and pedagogical interventions.[16] Authority in this perspective in not on the side of oppression; rather, it is used to intervene and shape the space of teaching and learning so as to provide students with the means for challenging society's commonsense assumptions and for analyzing the interface between their own everyday lives and those broader social formations that bear down on them. Authority, at best, becomes both a stance for legitimating a commitment to a particular vision of pedagogy and a critical referent for a kind of auto-critique. In other words, critical pedagogy demands consideration of how authority functions within specific relations of power regarding its own promise to provide students with a public space where they can learn, debate, and engage critical traditions in order to imagine otherwise and develop discourses that are crucial for defending vital social institutions as a public good. Such a task not only demands pedagogies that are critical and transformative but also institutional spaces where the conditions for such emancipatory modes of teaching and learning can take place. This would demand a complete restructuring of public education so as to provide a funding base that would ensure a quality education for all students and not just those from rich neighborhoods. A democratic pedagogy and the formative culture it promotes has to be accompanied by a school system in which class and racial barriers are eliminated. This is as much a structural issue that seeks to eliminate the class-based inequities that fund public schooling as it is an ideological challenge.

Although pedagogy can be understood performatively as an event when many things can happen in the service of learning, it is crucial to stress the importance of democratic classroom relations that encourage dialogue, deliberation, and the power of students to raise questions. Such relations do not signal a retreat from teacher authority as much as they suggest using authority reflexively to provide the conditions for students to exercise intellectual rigor, theoretical competence, and informed judgment. Thus students can think critically about the knowledge they gain and what it means to act on such knowledge in order to expand their sense of agency as part of a broader project of increasing both "the scope of their freedoms" and "the operations of democracy."[17] What students learn and how they learn should amplify what it means to experience democracy from a position of possibility, affirmation, and critical engagement. In part, this suggests that educators develop pedagogical practices that open up the terrain of the political, while simultaneously encouraging students to "think better about how arrangements might be otherwise."[18]

At its best, critical pedagogy must be interdisciplinary and contextual; it must engage the complex relationships between power and knowledge, critically address the institutional constraints under which teaching takes place, and focus on how students relate to the imperatives of critical social citizenship. Education is not simply about the transmission of knowledge: it is more accurately about the production of subjects, identities, and desires. This is no small matter when one recognizes what such a struggle suggests about preparing students for the future. Once again, critical pedagogy must be self-reflexive about its aims and practices, conscious of its ongoing project of democratic transformation, and openly committed to a politics that does not offer any guarantees. But refusing dogmatism does not suggest that educators descend into a laissez-faire pluralism or benign relativism, or adopt methodologies designed to neutralize politics by "teaching the conflicts." On the contrary, it suggests that in order to make the pedagogical more political, educators must afford students with diverse opportunities to understand and experience how politics, power, commitment, and responsibility work on and through them both within and outside of schools. This, in turn, enables students to locate themselves within an interrelated confluence of ideological and material forces as critical agents who can influence such forces and simultaneously be held responsible for their own views and actions. Within this perspective, relations between institutional forms and pedagogical practices are acknowledged as complex, open, and contradictory—though always situated within unequal relations of power.[19]

Making the Pedagogical More Meaningful

Any analysis of critical pedagogy must stress the importance of addressing the role that affect and emotion play in the formation of individual identity and social agency. Any viable approach to critical pedagogy must take seriously those maps of meaning, affective investments, and sedimented desires that enable students to connect their own lives and everyday experiences to what they learn. Pedagogy in this sense becomes more than a mere transfer of received knowledge, an inscription of a unified and static identity, or a rigid methodology; it presupposes that students are moved by their passions and motivated, in part, by the affective investments they bring to the learning process. This suggests, as Paulo Freire points out, the need for a theory of pedagogy willing to develop a "critical comprehension of the value of sentiments, emotions, and desire as part of the learning process."[20] Not only do students need to understand the ideological, economic, and political interests that shape the nature of their educational experiences, but they must also address the strong emotional investments they may bring to such beliefs.

Educators must similarly acknowledge the role of desire in both ignorance and learning. "Teaching," explains Shoshana Felman, "has to deal not so much with lack of knowledge as with resistances to knowledge. Ignorance, suggests Jacques Lacan, is a 'passion.' Inasmuch as traditional pedagogy postulated a desire for knowledge, an analytically informed pedagogy has to reckon with the passion for ignorance."[21] Felman elaborates further on the productive nature of ignorance, arguing: "Ignorance is nothing other than a desire to ignore: its nature is less cognitive than performative . . . it is not a simple lack of information but the incapacity—or the refusal—to acknowledge one's own implication in the information."[22] If students are to move beyond the issue of understanding to an engagement with the deeper affective investments that make them complicit with oppressive ideologies and capable of empathizing with others' suffering, they must be positioned to address and formulate strategies of transformation through which their individualized beliefs and affective investments can be articulated with broader public discourses that extend the imperatives of democratic public life. An unsettling pedagogy in this instance would engage student identities and resistances to learning from unexpected vantage points, such as reading history from the perspective of oppressed groups, and articulate how these are connected to existing material relations of power. At issue here is not only a pedagogical practice that recalls how knowledge, identifications, and subject positions are produced, unfolded, and remembered, but also an understanding of how students and teachers become part of an ongoing process, more strategic, so to speak, of mediating and challenging existing relations of power.

Conclusion

As the twenty-first century unfolds, the concept of the social state and the common good are being refigured and displaced as constitutive categories for making democracy operational and political agency the condition for social transformation. The notions of "the social" and "the public" are not being eradicated as much as they are being reconstructed under circumstances in which public forums for serious debate, including public education, are being used to different ends. Within the ongoing logic of neoliberalism, teaching and learning are removed from the discourse of democracy and civic culture, their public purposes eroded as they are redefined as purely private affairs. How else to explain Santorum's rants against higher education, public schools, and that old phantom, the liberal media? Divorced from the imperatives of a democratic society, pedagogy is reduced to a matter of taste, individual choice, homeschooling, and job training. Pedagogy as a mode of witnessing—a public engagement in which students learn to be attentive and responsible to the memories and narratives of others—disappears within a corporate-driven notion of learning in which the logic of the market devalues the opportunity for students to make connections with others through social relations that foster a mix of compassion, ethical decision making, and hope. The current crisis of the social is further amplified by the withdrawal of the state as a guardian of the public trust and the state's growing lack of investment in those sectors of social life that promote the public good. With the Supreme Court ruling that now makes school vouchers constitutional, a deeply conservative government will be given full rein to renege on the government's long-standing responsibilities to provide every child with an education that affirms public life, embraces the need for critical citizenship, and supports the truism that political agency is central to the possibility of democratic life.

The greatest threat to our children does not come from lowered educational standards, the absence of privatized choice schemes, or the lack of rigid testing measures. On the contrary, it comes from a society that refuses to view children as a social investment, one that consigns 16.3 million children to live in poverty, reduces critical learning to massive testing programs, promotes policies that eliminate most crucial health and public services, and defines masculinity through the degrading celebration of a gun culture, extreme sports, and the spectacles of violence that permeate corporate-controlled media industries. Students are not at risk because of the absence of market incentives in the schools: they are at risk because as a country the United States supports an iniquitous class-based system of funding public education and has more recently become intent on completely destroying it precisely because it is public. Children and young adults are under siege in both public and higher education because far too many of these institutions have become breeding grounds for commercialism, racism, sexism, homophobia, and consumerism, spurred on by the right-wing discourse of the Republican Party, conservative pundits, religious fundamentalists, and a weak mainstream media. We live in a society in which a culture of punishment and intolerance has replaced a culture of social responsibility and compassion. Within such a climate of harsh discipline and contempt for our collective well-being, it is easier for states such as California to set aside more financial resources to build prisons than to support higher education.

Within this context, the project of critical pedagogy needs to be taken up both within and outside of public and higher education. Pedagogy is not a practice that only takes place in schools. When linked to the ongoing project of democratization, it is perhaps more importantly a public mode of teaching, that is, a public intellectual practice that incorporates a range of cultural apparatuses extending from television networks to print media to the Internet. As a central element of a broad-based cultural politics, critical pedagogy in its various forms can provide opportunities for educators and other cultural workers to redefine and transform the connections among language, desire, meaning, everyday life, and material relations of power as part of a broader social movement to reclaim the promise and possibilities of democratic public life. Such forms of pedagogy are dangerous because they not only provide the intellectual capacities and ethical norms for students to fight against poverty, ecological destruction, and the dismantling of the social state, but also hold the potential for instilling in students a profound desire for a "real democracy based on relationships of equality and freedom."[23] Given the current economic crisis, a growing authoritarian populism, the rise of religious dogmatism, the failure of democratic governance, a political system largely controlled by bankers and corporations, and a massive education deficit in the United States, critical pedagogy becomes a reminder not only of something precious that has been lost under a regime of casino capitalism, but also of a democratizing project and practice that needs to be reclaimed, reconfigured, and made a central part of our current political lives and those of future generations.

Notes

INTRODUCTION

1. Zygmunt Bauman, "Has the Future a Left?," *Soundings*, 35 (2007). Online: http://www.lwbooks.co.uk/journals/articles/bauman07.html.

2. David Blacker, *The Falling Rate of Learning and the Neoliberal Endgame* (London: Zero Books, 2013), 3.

3. Charles H. Ferguson, *Predator Nation: Corporate Criminals, Political Corruption, and the Hijacking of America* (New York: Crown Business, 2012), 21. See, for example, Bill McKibben, *The End of Nature* (New York: Random House, 2006); Chalmers Johnson, *Dismantling the Empire: America's Last Hope* (New York: Metropolitan Books, 2010); and Angela Davis, *Are Prisons Obsolete?* (New York: Seven Stories Press, 2003).

4. Henry A. Giroux, *Against the Terror of Neoliberalism* (Boulder, CO: Paradigm, 2008); Colin Crouch, *The Strange Non-Death of Neoliberalism* (London: Polity, 2011).

5. Glenn Greenwald, *With Liberty and Justice for Some: How the Law Is Used to Destroy Equality and Protect the Powerful* (New York: Metropolitan Books, 2011); Jeff Madrick, *The Age of Greed* (New York: Vintage, 2012). On the issue of inequality there is an abundance of research. Some recent work includes Joseph E. Stiglitz, *The Price of Inequality* (New York: W. W. Norton, 2012); and a brilliant essay by Michal D. Yates, "The Great Inequality," *Monthly Review* 63/10 (March 2012), http://monthlyreview.org/2012/03/01/the-great-inequality.

6. See Pierre Bourdieu and Jean-Claude Passeron, *Reproduction in Education, Society and Culture*, 2nd ed. (Thousand Oaks, CA: Sage, 1991); *Stanley*

Aronowitz and Henry A. Giroux, Education Still Under Siege, 2nd ed.(New York: Praeger, 1993).

7. See, for example, Thomas E. Mann and Norman J. Ornstein, "Let's Just Say It: The Republicans Are the Problem," *Washington Post,* April 27, 2012, http://www.washingtonpost.com/opinions/lets-just-say-it-the-republic-ans-are-the-problem/2012/04/27/gIQAxCVUlT_story.html.

8. Jane Mayer, "Ayn Rand Joins the Ticket," *The New Yorker,* August 11, 2012, http://www.newyorker.com/online/blogs/newsdesk/2012/08/paul-ryan-and-ayn-rand.html.

9. Rick Santorum, "Video: Town Hall Meeting," C-Span, January 4, 2012, http://c-spanvideo.org/program/SantorumTo. Santorum believes that the "moochers," code for the young, elderly, low-income poor, and disadvantaged minorities, are draining the public coffers. What he ignores, as Larry Bartels points out, is that "programs serving heavily minority and poor populations are not where the money is. According to the Census Bureau's Consolidated Federal Funds Report, less than 8 percent of federal spending in 2010 was for unemployment benefits, food stamps, housing assistance, student aid, and the earned-income tax credit. Almost half was for salaries and wages, grants, and procurement; most of the rest consisted of Social Security and Medicare payments. Large-scale reductions in government spending would require significant cuts in big-ticket programs that mostly benefit the middle class." See Bartels, "The Narcotic of Government Dependency," *The Monkey Cage,* February 13, 2012, http://themonkeycage.org/blog/2012/02/13/the-narcotic-of-government-dependency/.

10. Robert Reich, "Romney-Ryan Will Bring Back Social Darwinism," *Kansas City Star,* August 14, 2012, http://www.kansascity.com/2012/08/14/3762436/robert-b-reich-romney-ryan-will.html.

11. Robert O. Self, "The Antisocial Contract," *New York Times,* August 25, 2012,http://campaignstops.blogs.nytimes.com/2012/08/25/the-antiso-cial-contract/.

12. George Lakoff and Glenn W. Smith, "Romney, Ryan and the Devil's Budget," *Huffington Post,* August 22, 2012, http://www.huffingtonpost.com/george-lakoff/romney-ryan-and-the-devil_b_1819652.html.

13. Ibid.

14. Books on the public sphere almost constitute an industry. The classic is Jürgen Habermas's *The Structural Transformation of the Public Sphere* (Cambridge, MA: MIT Press, 1991). For an excellent reader on seminal articles on the public sphere, see Jostein Gripsrud, Hallvard Moe, Anders Molander, Graham Murdock, eds., *The Idea of the Public Sphere: A Reader* (Boulder, CO: Lexington Books, 2010). For some recent interesting work, see Ian Angus, *Emergent Publics: An Essay on Social Movements and Democracy* (Winnipeg, MB: Arbeiter Ring Publishing, 2001); Daniel Drache, *Defiant Publics*

(London: Polity Press, 2008); Dan Hind, *The Return of the Public* (London: Verso, 2010); and Michael Hardt and Antonio Negri, *Commonwealth* (Cambridge, MA: Belknap, 2009).

15.   Proinnsias Reathnach, "Casino Capitalism and Global Recession: Historical Background and Future Outlook," *Irish Left Review,* September 15, 2009, http://www.irishleftreview.org/2009/09/15/casino-capitalism-global-recession-historical-background-future-outlook/. The term "casino capitalism" was first coined by Susan Strange, in *Casino Capitalism* (Manchester: Manchester University Press, 1997). Also see Hans-Werner Sinn, *Casino Capitalism: How the Financial Crisis Came About and What Needs to Be Done Now* (New York: Oxford University Press, 2010); and Susmit Kuman, *Casino Capitalism: The Collapse of the U.S. Economy and the Transition to Secular Democracy in the Middle East* (Bloomington, IN: iUniverse, 2012).

16.   Editorial, "How to Profit in Our Casino Economy," *Casino Capitalism,* September 8, 2010, http://www.casinocapitalism.com/about/.

17.   Ibid.

18.   Zygmunt Bauman, *Living on Borrowed Time: Conversations with Citlali Rovirosa-Madrazo* (Cambridge: Polity Press, 2010), 132.

19.   See Jeffrey R. Di Leo, Henry A. Giroux, Sophia A. McClennen, and Kenneth J. Saltman, *Neoliberalism, Education, Terrorism: Contemporary Dialogues* (Boulder, CO: Paradigm, 2012).

20.   Chris Mooney, *Republican Brain: The Science of Why They Deny Science—and Reality* (New York: Wiley, 2012). See also Joseph Stiglitz, *The Price of Inequality: How Today's Divided Society Endangers Our Future* (New York: W. W. Norton, 2012); Michelle Alexander, *The New Jim Crow: Mass Incarceration in the Age of Colorblindness* (New York: New Press, 2012); and Dorothy Roberts, *Fatal Invention: How Science, Politics, and Big Business Re-Create Race in the Twenty-first Century* (New York: New Press, 2011).

21.   Ferguson, *Predator Nation.*

22.   Henry A. Giroux, *Zombie Politcs in the Age of Casino Capitalism* (New York: Peter Lang, 2011).

23.   Democracy is a complicated concept and one of the most useful books I have read mapping its divergent theories is Frank Cunningham, *Theories of Democracy: A Critical Introduction* (New York: Routledge, 2002). See also David Held, *Models of Democracy,* 3rd ed. (Stanford, CA: Stanford University Press, 2006); Marc Stears, *Demanding Democracy* (Princeton: Princeton University Press, 2010).

24.   Angela Davis, "The 99%: A Community of Resistance," *The Guardian,* November 15, 2011, http://www.guardian.co.uk/commentisfree/cifamerica/2011/nov/15/99-percent-community-resistance.

25.   Stanley Aronowitz, "The Winter of Our Discontent," *Situations* 4/2 (Spring 2012): 40, 60.

26. For a history of such experiments, see Paul Avrich, *The Modern Schools Movement* (Oakland, CA: AK Press, 2005); and Allen Graubard, *Free the Children;: Radical Reform and the Free School Movement* (New York: Pantheon, 1972).

27. Stanley Aronowitz, "The Winter of Our Discontent," *Situations* 4/2 (Spring 2012): 68.

28. One particularly important source among the many dealing with the emerging authoritarianism in the United States is Sheldon S. Wolin, *Democracy Incorporated: Managed Democracy and the Specter of Inverted Totalitarianism* (Princeton: Princeton University Press, 2008). See also Henry A. Giroux, *Against the New Authoritarianism: Politics After Abu Ghraib* (Winnipeg, MB: Arbieter Ring Publishing, 2005); Tony Judt, "What Is Living and What Is Dead in Social Democracy?," *New York Review of Books* 56/ 20 (December 17, 2009), http://www.nybooks.com/articles/23519.

29. Paul Virilio, "The Suicidal State," in *The Virilio Reader*, ed. J. DerDerian (New York: Oxford University Press, 1998), 29–45.

1. BEYOND THE POLITICS OF THE BIG LIE

1. Tony Judt, *Reappraisals: Reflections on the Forgotten Twentieth Century* (New York: Penguin, 2008), 420.

2. Raymond Williams, "Preface to Second Edition," *Communications* (New York: Barnes and Noble, 1967), 15.

3. Ibid.

4. Robert Jenson, "Florida's Fear of History: New Law Undermines Critical Thinking," *CommonDreams.org*, July 17, 2006, http://www.commondreams.org/views06/0717-22.htm.

5. Jessica LaGreca, "Texas GOP Platform Opposes Teaching 'Critical Thinking Skills' in Schools., *Daily Kos*, June 27, 2012, http://www.dailykos.com/story/2012/06/27/1101959/-Texas-GOP-Platform-to-ban-teaching-Critical-Thinking-Skills-in-schools-The-stupid-IT-BURNS.

6. Steve Horn, "Three States Pushing ALEC Bill to Require Teaching Climate Change Denial in Schools," *DeSmogBlog.com*, January 31, 2012, http://www.desmogblog.com/print/6851.

7. Hannah Arendt, "Thinking and Moral Considerations: A Lecture," *Social Research* 38/3 (Fall 1970): 417.

8. Zygmunt Bauman, *The Individualized Society* (London: Polity Press, 2001), 55.

9. Zygmunt Bauman, "Freedom From, In and Through the State: T. H. Marshall's Trinity of Rights Revised," *Theoria* (December 2005), http://www.berghahnbooksonline.com/journals/th/abs/2005/52-3/TH520303.html.

10. Zygmunt Bauman, *Liquid Times: Living in an Age of Uncertainty* (London: Polity Press, 2007), 103.

11. Charles Pierce, "Democracy vs. Money in Wisconsin," *ReaderSupport-edNews*, June 2, 2012, http://readersupportednews.org/opinion2/277-75/11728-focus-democracy-vs-money-in-wisconsin.

12. Peter Baker, "Lobby E-Mails Show Depth of Obama Ties to Drug Industry," *New York Times*, June 8, 2012, http://www.nytimes.com/2012/06/09/us/politics/e-mails-reveal-extent-of-obamas-deal-with-industry-on-health-care.html?_r=1&hp.

13. Ibid.

14. Bill Moyers and Michael Winship, "Pity the Poor Billionaires," *Common-Dreams.org*, June 1, 2012, http://www.commondreams.org/view/2012/06/01-11.

15. Manfred B. Steger and Ravi K. Roy, *Neoliberalism: A Very Short Introduction* (Oxford: Oxford University Press, 2010), 60–62.

16. Cited in Amy Goodman, "How Citizens United Helped Scott Walker in Wisconsin," *The Guardian*, June 7, 2012, http://www.guardian.co.uk/commentisfree/2012/jun/07/citizens-united-helped-scott-walker-win-wisconsin?newsfeed=true.

17. Sheldon S. Wolin, "Inverted Totalitarianism: How the Bush Regime Is Effecting the Transformation to a Fascist-Like State," *The Nation*, May 19, 2003, 14. Wolin develops his theory of inverted totalitarianism in great detail in his *Democracy Incorporated: Managed Democracy and the Specter of Inverted Totalitarianism* (Princeton: Princeton University Press, 2008).

18. Ibid., 14–15.

19. For an excellent analysis of media in late modernity, see Nick Couldry, *Media, Society, World: Social Theory and Digital Media Practice* (London: Polity, 2012).

20. Robert W. McChesney, *The Political Economy of Media: Enduring Issues, Emerging Dilemmas* (New York: Monthly Review Press, 2008); Bill Press, *Toxic Talk: How the Radical Right Has Poisoned America's Airwaves* (New York: Thomas Dunne Books, 2010); David Brock, Ari Rabin-Havt, and Media Matters for America, *The Fox Effect: How Roger Ailes Turned a Network into a Propaganda Machine* (New York: Anchor, 2012).

21. James Petras, "The Politics of Language and the Language of Political Regression," *Global Research*, May 24, 2012, http://www.globalresearch.ca/index.php?context=va&aid=31018.

22. Stuart Hall and Les Back, "In Conversation: At Home and Not at Home," *Cultural Studies* 23/4 (July 2009): 679.

23. For an excellent analysis of the impact of philanthropy on education, see Kenneth Saltman, *The Gift of Education: Public Education and Venture Philanthropy* (New York: Palgrave Macmillan, 2010). See also Kenneth Saltman, *Capitalizing on Disaster: Taking and Breaking Public Schools* (Boulder, CO: Paradigm, 2007); Philip E. Kovacs, *The Gates Foundation and the Future*

of US *"Public" Schools* (New York: Routledge, 2010); Diane Ravitch, *The Death and Life of the Great American School System: How Testing and Choice Are Undermining Education* (New York: Basic Books, 2010).

24. Henry A. Giroux, *Education and the Crisis of Public Values* (New York: Peter Lang, 2012).

25. David Hursh, *High-Stakes Testing and the Decline of Teaching and Learning: The Real Crisis in Education* (Boulder, CO: Rowman and Littlefield, 2008).

26. I have taken up this issue in detail in Henry A. Giroux, *The University in Chains: Confronting the Military-Industrial-Academic Complex* (Boulder, CO: Paradigm Publishers, 2007).

27. Full text of "The Powell Memo," see: http://reclaimdemocracy.org/powell_memo_lewis/.

28. Francis Fox Piven, "The War Against the Poor," *TomDispatch.com,* November 6, 2011, http://www.tomdispatch.com/archive/175463/.

29. See the many examples in S. E. Smith, "Police Handcuffing 7-Year-Olds? The Brutality Unleashed on Kids with Disabilities in Our School Systems," *Alternet,* May 22, 2012, http://www.alternet.org/story/155526/police_handcuffing_7-year-olds_the_brutality_unleashed_on_kids_with_disabilities_in_our_school_systems.

30. Douglas Montero, Lorena Mongelli, and Jamie Schram, "Cops Handcuff and Interrogate Boy, 7, for Hours Over Missing $5," *New York Post* (January 30, 2012), http://www.nypost.com/p/news/local/cops_are_cuff_guys_with_kid_eaRQ39892kXQndMJkDgY9J.

31. Yasha Levine, "Malcolm Gladwell Unmasked: A Look into the Life & Work of America's Most Successful Propagandist," *The Exiled,* June 6, 2012, http://exiledonline.com/malcolm-gladwell-unmasked-a-look-into-the-life-work-of-america%E2%80%99s-most-successful-propagandist/.

32. Ibid.

33. Charles Ferguson, "The Sellout of the Ivory Tower, and the Crash of 2008," *Huffington Post,* May 22, 2012, http://www.huffingtonpost.com/charles-ferguson/academic-corruption_b_1532944.html.

34. Ibid.

35. Bill Moyers, "Interview with William K. Black," *Bill Moyers Journal,* PBS, April 23, 2010, http://www.pbs.org/moyers/journal/0423010/transcript4.html.

36. Amy Goodman, "How Citizens United Helped Scott Walker in Wisconsin," http://www.guardian.co.uk/commentisfree/2012/jun/07/citizens-united-helped-scott-walker-win-wisconsin?newsfeed=true.

37. Ibid.

38. For a brilliant analysis of the effects of casino capitalism on those marginalized by race and class, see Dorothy Roberts, *Fatal Intervention: How Science, Politics, and Business Re-Create Race in the Twenty-first Century* (New York:

New Press, 2011). For a sustained and convincing argument for equality in the service of democracy, see Richard Wilkinson and Kate Pickett, *The Spirit Level: Why Equality Is Better for Everyone* (New York: Penguin, 2010). See also Tony Judt, *Ill Fares the Land* (New York: Penguin, 2010).

39.   William Deresiewicz, "Capitalists and Other Psychopaths," *New York Times,* May 12, 2012.

40.   Paul K. Piff, Daniel M. Stancato, Stephane Cote, Rodolfo Mendoza-Denton, and Dacher Keltern, "Higher Social Class Predicts Increased Unethical Behavior," *Proceedings of the National Academy of Sciences* (February 27, 2012, http://www.pnas.org/cgi/doi/10.1073/pnas.1118373109. A summary of these reports appears in Thomas B. Edsall, "Other People's Suffering," *New York Times,* March 4, 2012, http://campaignstops.blogs.nytimes.com/2012/03/04/other-peoples-suffering/.

41.   Joseph Stiglitz, "Politics Is at the Root of the Problem," *The European,* April 23, 2012, http://theeuropean-magazine.com/633-stiglitz-joseph/634-austerity-and-a-new-recession.

42.   Joseph E. Stiglitz, "The 1 Percent's Problem," *Vanity Fair,* May 31, 2012, http://www.vanityfair.com/politics/2012/05/joseph-stiglitz-the-price-on-inequality.

43.   Reuters, "Nearly Half of Americans Struggling to Stay Afloat," *CommonDreams.org,* November 23, 2011, http://www.commondreams.org/headline/2011.11.23-0?print. For the most recent statistics, see the State of Working America at http://stateofworkingamerica.org/.

44.   Tony Judt, "I Am Not Pessimistic in the Very Long Run," *The Independent,* March 24, 2010, http://www.independent.co.uk/arts-entertainment/books/features/tony-judt-i-am-not-pessimistic-in-the-very-long-run-1925966.html.

45.   Randy Martin, cited in Patricia Ticineto Clough and Craig Willse, *Beyond Biopolitics: Essays on the Governance of Life and Death* (Durham, NC, and London: Duke University Press, 2011), 3.

46.   See, for example, Laurie Bennett, "Ivy League Presidents Find Time for Corporate Boards," *Maced,* June 30, 2010, http://news.muckety.com/2010/06/30/ivy-league-presidents-find-time-for-corporate-boards/26921; Jack Stripling and Andrea Fuller, "College Presidents Serving on Boards of Trustees' Companies," *MAICgregator,* January 16, 2012, http://maicgregator.org/post/45. Charles Ferguson develops this theme in his Academy Award–winning film *Inside Job* and in his book *Predator Nation* by focusing on prominent economists such as Larry Summers, Martin Feldstein, and Glenn Hubbard, all of whom appear shameless in their complicity with corporate power, greed, and corruption.

47.   There are endless lists of such lies on the Internet. See, for example, Sandy Screeds, "Short List of GOP Lies," *Daily Kos,* June 8, 2012, http://www.dai-

lykos.com/story/2012/06/08/1098424/-SHORT-LIST-OF-GOP-LIES-work-in-progress. See also Chris Mooney, "Reality Bites Republicans," *The Nation,* June 4, 2012: 6–8.

48. Jess Coleman, "Five Lies from Mitt Romney," *Huffington Post,* May 24, 2012, http://www.huffingtonpost.com/jess-coleman/five-lies-from-mitt romne_b_1540942.html.

49. See the extensive list of Romney's lies in Yosef 52, "Every Romney Lie in One Place!," April 12, 2012, http://www.dailykos.com/story/2012/04/12/1082975/-EVERY-Romney-Lie-In-One-Place-UP-DATED.

50. Diane Ravitch, "The Miseducation of Mitt Romney," *New York Review of Books,* June 5, 2012, http://www.nybooks.com/blogs/nyrblog/2012/jun/05/miseducation-mitt-romney/.

51. Robert Reich, "Romney's Lying Machine," *ReaderSupportedNews,* August 24, 2012, http://readersupportednews.org/opinion2/277-75/13091-focus-romneys-lying-machine.

52. Ibid.

53. Ibid.

54. See, for example, Jeffrey R. Di Leo, Walter Jacobs, and Amy Lee, "The Sites of Pedagogy," *Symploke* 10/1–2 (2002): 7–12; Dilip Parameshwar Gaonkar and Elizabeth A. Provinelli, "Technologies of Public Forms: Circulation, Transfiguration, Recognition," *Public Culture* 15/3 (2003): 385–97; Lewis Lapham, "Tentacles of Rage: The Republican Propaganda Mill, a Brief History," *Harper's Magazine,* September 2004: 31–41; Henry A. Giroux, "The Politics of Public Pedagogy," in *If Classrooms Matter: Place, Pedagogy and Politics,* ed. Jeffrey Di Leo et al. (New York: Routledge, 2005), 15–36; and Henry A. Giroux, "Neoliberalism as Public Pedagogy," in *Handbook of Public Pedagogy,* ed. Jennifer Sandlin, Brian Schultz, and Jane Burdick (New York: Routledge, 2010), 486–99.

55. Cornelius Castoriadis, "The Greek Polis and the Creation of Democracy," in *Philosophy, Politics, Autonomy: Essays in Political Philosophy* (New York: Oxford University Press, 1991), 102.

56. James Baldwin, "A Talk to Teachers," *The Saturday Review,* December 21, 1963: 44.

57. Ibid.

2. THE SCORCHED EARTH POLICY OF AMERICA'S
FOUR FUNDAMENTALISMS

1. Tom Engelhardt, "The American Lockdown State: Post-Legal Drones, the Bin Laden Tax, and Other Wonders of Our American World," *TomDispatch.com,* February 5, 2013, http://www.tomdispatch.com/post/175646/tomgram%3A_engelhardt%2C_paying_the_bin_laden_tax/. See also

Dana Priest and William M. Arkin, *Top-Secret America: The Rise of the New American Security State* (Boston: Back Bay Books, 2012); Stephen Graham, *Cities Under Siege: The New Military Urbanism* (New York: Verso, 2012); Loic Wacquant, *Punishing the Poor: The Neoliberal Government of Social Insecurity* (Durham, NC: Duke University Press, 2009); Christian Parenti, *Lockdown America* (New York: Verso, 2008).

2.   Jonathan Turley, "10 Reasons the U.S. Is No Longer the Land of the Free," *Washington Post,* January 13, 2012, http://www.washingtonpost.com/opinions/is-the-united-states-still-the-land-of-the-free.

3.   There are too many sources on this issue to cite. For a recent commentary, see Paul Harris, "Drone Wars and State Secrecy—How Barack Obama Became a Hardliner," *The Guardian,* June 2, 2012, http://www.guardian.co.uk/world/2012/jun/02/drone-wars-secrecy-barack-obama.

4.   Glen Greenwald, "Obama's Illegal Assaults," *In These Times,* August 26, 2011, http://www.inthesetimes.com/article/11787/obamas_illegal_assaults/.

5.   Glenn Greenwald, *With Liberty and Justice for Some: How the Law Is Used to Destroy Equality and Protect the Powerful* (New York: Metropolitan Books, 2011).

6.   Jim Garrison, "Obama's Most Fateful Decision," *Huffington Post,* December 12, 2011, http://www.huffingtonpost.com/jim-garrison/obamas-most-fateful-decis_b_1143005.html.

7.   See, for example, Rania Khalek, "6 Creepy New Weapons the Police and Military Use to Subdue Unarmed People," *AlterNet,* August 1, 2011, http://www.alternet.org/story/151864/6_creepy_new_weapons_the_police_and_military_use_to_subdue_unarmed_people?page=0%2C3.

8.   Jonathan Schell, "Cruel America," *The Nation,* September 28, 2011, http://www.thenation.com/article/163690/cruel-america.

9.   Erik Hoffner, "Punishing Protest, Policing Dissent: What Is the Justice System For?," *Common Dreams,* February 11, 2012, http://www.commondreams.org/view/2012/02/12-6.

10. Chris McGreal, "The US Schools with Their Own Police," *The Guardian,* January 9, 2012, http://www.guardian.co.uk/world/2012/jan/09/texas-police-schools.

11. Cited in ibid.

12. John O'Connor and Sarah Gonzalez, "Many Florida Schools Use Seclusion Rooms for Students with Disabilities," *StateImpact,* April 9, 2012, http://stateimpact.npr.org/florida/2012/08/09/many-florida-schools-use-seclusion-rooms-for-students-with-disabilities.

13. See John O'Connor and Sarah Gonzalez, "Many Florida Schools Use Seclusion Rooms for Students With Disabilities."

14. Aviva Shen, "Ohio and Florida Public Schools Lock Mentally Disabled Children in Closets," *ThinkProgress,* August 9, 2012, http://thinkprogress.org/education/2012/08/09/667931/ohio-florida-school-closets/.

15. Ibid.

16. Annie-Rose Strasser, "Mississippi Schools Sending Kids to Prison for Mis-behaving in the Classroom," *ThinkProgress*, August 13, 2012, http://think-progress.org/justice/2012/08/13/681261/mississippi-schools-sending-kids-to-prison-for-misbehaving-in-the-classroom/.

17. Joao Biehl, *Vita: Life in a Zone of Social Abandonment* (Berkeley: University of California Press, 2005), 4.

18. I have borrowed this idea of school as a repressive institution from Stanley Aronowitz, "Paulo Freire's Pedagogy: Not Mainly a Teaching Method," in *Paulo Freire's Intellectual Roots: Toward Historicity in Praxis*, ed. Robert Lake and Tricia Kress (New York: Continuum, 2012). 10.

19. Ibid., 10–11, 14.

20. Sheldon S. Wolin, *Democracy Incorporated: Managed Democracy and the Specter of Inverted Totalitarianism* (Princeton: Princeton University Press, 2008); Chris Hedges, *American Fascists: The Christian Right and the War on America* (New York: Free Press, 2008).

21. Henry A. Giroux, *Youth in a Suspect Society: Democracy or Disposability?* (New York: Palgrave, 2010); Sarah Jane Forman, "Countering Criminal-ization: Toward a Youth Development Approach to School Searches," *The Scholar* 14/2 (2011): 302–73. Also online: http://thescholarlawreview.org/wp-content/uploads/Forman.pdf.

22. See Henry A. Giroux, "Why Teaching People to Think for Themselves Is Repugnant to Religious Zealots and Rick Santorum," *Truthout*, February 22, 2012, http://www.truthout.org/why-teaching-people-think-themselves-re-pugnant/1329847441.

23. Frank Rich, "I Saw Jackie Mason Kissing Santa Claus," *New York Times*, De-cember 25, 2005.

24. Paul Krugman, "Looting the Future," *New York Times*, December 5, 2003.

25. Robert Kuttner, "The War on America," *The American Prospect* 22/8 (2011): 3.

26. Frank Rich, "The Year of Living Indecently," *New York Times*, February 6, 2005.

27. Katherine Stewart, "Is Texas Waging War on History?" *AlterNet*, May 21, 2012, www.alternet.org/story/155515/is_texas_waging_war_on_history/.

28. Sandhy A. Somashekhar, "Karen Santorum: Rick's Presdential Run Is 'God's Will,'" *Washington Post*, February 26, 2012, http://www.washingtonpost.com/blogs/election-2012/post/karen-santorum-husbands-presidential-run-is-gods-will/2012/02/23/gIQAhCkdWR_blog.html.

29. Amy Goodman, "The Paul Ryan Vision of America: Ban Abortion, Defund Contraception, Outlaw In Vitro Fertilization," *Democracy Now*, August 13, 2012, http://www.democracynow.org/2012/8/13/the_paul_ryan_vision_of_america.

30. Robert Reich, "The Sad Race for Bottom on the Loony Right," *AlterNet*,

February 28, 2012, http://www.alternet.org/teaparty/154321/the_sad_race_for_bottom_on_the_loony_right_/.

31.   Kenneth J. Saltman, David A. Gabbard, eds., *Education as Enforcement: The Militarization and Corporatization of Schools* (New York: Routledge, 2010); Annette Fuentes, *Lockdown High: When the Schoolhouse Becomes a Jail House* (New York: Verso Press, 2013).

32.   Henry A. Giroux, *Youth in a Suspect Society* (New York: Palgrave, 2009).

33.   John W. Whitead, "Is High-Tech Surveillance in Schools a Security Need or a Money Scam?," *Huffington Post*, December 4, 2012, http://www.huffington-post.com/john-w-whitehead/the-fight-against-schools_b_2232112.html.

34.   See Henry A. Giroux, *Education and the Crisis of Public Values* (New York: Peter Lang, 2012).

35.   On the relationship between democracy and iniquitous wealth, see Robert W. McChesney and John Nichols, *Dollarocracy: How Billionaires Are Buying Our Democracy and What We Can Do About It* (New York: Nation Books, 2013), forthcoming.

36.   Robert McChesney and John Nichols, *Our Media, Not Theirs: The Democratic Struggle against Corporate Media* (New York: Seven Stories, 2002), 52–53.

37.   Of course, they also take advantage of the realistic anxieties that the system produces, providing easy answers. One of the problems is that institutions such as labor unions that might counter this have been absorbed into the dominant ideological discourse.

38.   Andrew J. Bacevich, *The New American Militarism* (New York: Oxford University Press, 2005), 1. See also the more recent Andrew J. Bacevich, ed., *The Short American Century: A Postmortem* (Cambridge: Harvard University Press, 2012).

39.   Tony Judt, "The New World Order," *New York Review of Books* 52/12 (July 14, 2005): 16

40.   Cited in ibid., 6. See Cornel West, *Democracy Matters: Winning the Fight against Imperialism* (New York: Penguin, 2004).

41.   David Price, *Weaponizing Anthropology* (Petrolia, CA: AK Books, 2011).

42.   Michael Hardt and Antonio Negri, *Multitude: War and Democracy in the Age of Empire* (New York: Penguin, 2004), 12–13.

3. VIOLENCE, USA

1.   Melinda Cooper, *Life as Surplus: Biotechnology & Capitalism in the Neoliberal Era* (Seattle: University of Washington Press, 2008), 92.

2.   Andrew Bacevich, "After Iraq, War Is US," *ReadersNewsService*, December 20, 2011, http://readersupportednews.org/opinion2/424-national-security/9007-after-iraq-war-is-us.

3.   bmazlish, "Blog #18: Why bombs, not books," *Activism*, May 7, 2012, http://www.bmazlish.blog.com/.

4.   Henry A. Giroux, "'Instants of Truth': The 'Kill Team' Photos and the Depravity of Aesthetics," *Afterimage: Journal of Media Arts and Cultural Criticism* (Summer 2011): 4–8.

5.   Thom Shanker and Graham Bowley, "Images of GIs and Remains Fuel Fears of Ebbing Discipline," *New York Times,* April 18, 2012, http://www.nytimes. com/2012/04/19/world/asia/us-condemns-photo-of-soldiers-posing-with-body-parts.html.

6.   Craig Whitlock and Carol Morello, "U.S. Army Sergeant Faces 17 Murder Counts in Afghan Killings," *Toronto Star,* March 22, 2012, http://www.the-star.com/printarticle/1150698.

7.   Mark Selden and Alvin Y. So, eds., *War and State Terrorism: The United States, Japan, and the Asia-Pacific in the Long Twentieth Century* (Denver, CO: Rowman & Littlefield, 2004); Jeremy Brecher, Jill Cutler, and Brendan Smith, eds., *In the Name of Democracy: American War Crimes in Iraq and Beyond* (New York: Macmillan, 2005); Jordan J. Paust, *Beyond the Law: The Bush Administration's Unlawful Responses in the "War" on Terror* (New York: Cambridge University Press, 2007); and Andrew Bacevich, *Washington Rules: America's Path to Permanent War* (New York: Metropolitan Books, 2010).

8.   Common Dreams Staff, "Report: US Soldiers Bringing Their Violence Home from Overseas," *CommonDreams.org,* January 20, 2012), https:// www.commondreams.org/headline/2012/01/20-1; Mary Slosson, "Violent Sex Crimes by U.S. Army Soldiers Rise: Report," Reuters, January 19, 2012, http://www.reuters.com/article/2012/01/20/us-army-health-report-idUSTRE80J01C20120120.

9.   Joachim J. Savelsberg and Ryan D. King, *American Memories: Atrocities and the Law* (New York: Russell Sage Foundation, 2011); Carl Boggs, *The Crimes of Empire: The History and Politics of an Outlaw Nation* (London: Pluto Press, 2010).

10.   See Nick Turse's new book, *Kill Anything that Moves,* which shows how systematic murder of civilians was in Vietnam. Wars are now conceived in efficient production terms, with dead bodies as the output. Nick Turse, *Kill Anything that Moves: The Real American War in Vietnam* (New York: Metropolitan Books, 2013).

11.   A. O. Scott, "Finding Comfort in Easy Distinctions," *New York Times* (February 28, 2013), http://www.nytimes.com/interactive/2013/03/03/arts/critics-on-violence-in-media.html?nl=todaysheadlines&emc=edit_th_20130303

12.   See, for example, Catherine A. Lutz, *Homefront: A Military City and the American Twentieth Century* (Boston: Beacon Press, 2002); Carl Boggs, ed., *Masters of War: Militarism and Blowback in the Era of the America Empire* (New York: Routledge, 2003); Chalmers Johnson, *The Sorrows of Empire:*

Militarism, Secrecy, and the End of the Republic (New York: Metropolitan Books, 2004); Andrew J. Bacevich, *The New American Militarism* (New York: Oxford University Press, 2005); Nick Turse, *How the Military Invades Our Everyday Lives* (New York: Metropolitan Books, 2008); and Bacevich, *Washington Rules.*

13. Joel Klein and Condoleezza Rice, *U.S. Education Reform and National Security* (Washington, D.C.: Council on Foreign Relations, 2012), http://www.cfr.org/united-states/us-education-reform-national-security/p27618. For a brilliant critique of this right-wing warmongering screed, which is really a front for privatizing schools, see Jennifer Fisher, "'The Walking Wounded': Youth, Public Education, and the Turn to Precarious Pedagogy," *Review of Education, Pedagogy & Cultural Studies* 33/5 (November–December 2011): 379–432.

14. John Whitehead, "Arrested Development: The Criminalization of America's Schoolchildren," *NJToday.net,* May 7, 2012, http://njtoday.net/2012/05/07/arrested-development-the-criminalization-of-americas-schoolchildren.

15. Ibid.

16. Etienne Balibar, *We, The People of Europe? Reflections on Transnational Citizenship* (Princeton: Princeton University Press, 2004), 120.

17. Editorial comment, "Big Bang Theories: Violence on Screen," *New York Times,* February 28, 2013, http://www.nytimes.com/interactive/2013/03/03/arts/critics-on-violence-in-media.html.

18. I want to thank Grace Pollock for this idea. See also Henry A. Giroux, "The 'Suicidal State' and the War on Youth," *Truthout,* April 10, 2012, http://truth-out.org/opinion/item/8421-the-suicidal-state-and-the-war-on-youth.

19. A. O. Scott, "Superheroes, Super Battles, Super Egos," *New York Times,* May 3, 2012, http://www.nytimes.com/2012/05/04/movies/robert-downey-jr-in-the-avengers-directed-by-joss-whedon.html.

20. Ibid.

21. Ibid.

22. See the classic text, Theodor Adorno, Else Frenkel-Brunswik, Daniel J. Levinson, and R. Nevitt Sanford, *The Authoritarian Personality* (New York: W. W. Norton, 1993).

23. Chris Hedges, "Murder Is Not an Anomaly in War," *TruthDig.com,* March 19, 2012, http://www.truthdig.com/report/item/murder_is_not_an_anomoly_in_war_20120319/.

24. Stephen Foley, "NBC Rejects Calls to Cancel Show that 'Glorifies War,'" *The Independent,* August 15, 2012, http://www.independent.co.uk/news/media/tv-radio/nbc-rejects-calls-to-cancel-show-that-glorifies-war-8046789.html.

25. See the show's website: http://www.nbc.com/stars-earn-stripes/.

26. Foley, "NBC Rejects Calls to Cancel Show that 'Glorifies War.'"

27. Jody Williams, Desmond Tutu, Mairead Maguire, Shirin Ebadi, José Ramos-Horta, Adolfo Pérez Esquivel, Oscar Arias Sanchez, Rigoberta Menchú Tum, and Betty Williams, "NBC's 'Stars Earn Stripes' Continues an Inglorious Tradition of Glorifying War," *The Guardian* (August 14, 2012. http://www.guardian.co.uk/commentisfree/2012/aug/14/nbc-stars-earn-stripes-continues-inglorious-tradition.

28. For a critical rendering of the current age of greed, see Jeff Madrick, *Age of Greed: The Triumph of Finance and the Decline of America, 1970 to the Present* (New York: Random House, 2012).

29. Phil Stewart, "Death Penalty Possible in Afghan Massacre: Panetta," Reuters, March 12, 2012, http://www.reuters.com/article/2012/03/13/us-afghanistan-usa-panetta-idUSBRE82C05320120313.

30. Ibid.

31. Hedges, "Murder Is Not an Anomaly."

32. Robert Johnson, "Pentagon Offers U.S. Police Full Military Hardware," *ReaderSupportedNews,* December 11, 2011, http://readersupported-news.org/news-section2/323-95/8758-focus-pentagon-offers-us-police-full-military-hardware.

33. Dana Priest and William Arkin, *Top Secret America: The Rise of the New American Security State* (New York: Little, Brown, 2011).

34. Andrew Becker and G. W. Schulz, "Cops Ready for War," *ReaderSupportedNews,* December 21, 2011, http://readersupportednews.org/news-section2/316-20/9023-focus-cops-ready-for-war.

35. David Theo Goldberg, *The Threat of Race: Reflections on Racial Neoliberalism* (Malden, MA: Wiley-Blackwell, 2009), 334.

36. John W. Whitehead, "Invasion of the Body Searchers: The Loss of Bodily Integrity in an Emerging Police State," *The Rutherford Institute,* January 14, 2013, https://www.rutherford.org/publications_resources/john_whiteheads_commentary/invasion_of_the_body_searchers_the_loss_of_bodily_integrity_in_an_emer.

37. Richard McAdam, "On Bounties and the Integrity of Professional Sports," *SportsCardForum,* April 2012, http://www.sportscardforum.com/articles/2012/04/on-bounties-and-the-integrity-of-professional-sports/.

38. Ibid.

39. Gary Younge, "America's Deadly Devotion to Guns," *The Guardian,* April 16, 2012, www.guardian.co.uk/world/2012/apr/16/americas-deadly-devotion-guns.

40. Ibid.

41. David and Lucille Packard Foundation, "Children, Youth, and Gun Violence: Analysis and Recommendations," *The Future of Children* 12/2 (2002), http://futureofchildren.org/futureofchildren/publications/docs/.

42. Jean and John Comaroff, "Criminal Obsessions, After Foucault: Postcoloniality, Policing, and the Metaphysics of Disorder," *Critical Inquiry* 30 (Summer 2004): 803–4.

43. Ibid., 804, 808.

44. Stanley Aronowitz, "The Winter of Our Discontent," *Situations* 4/2 (Spring 2012): 57.

45. The complete findings of the study are available at http://costsofwar.org.

46. David Rothkopf, *Power, Inc.: The Epic Rivalry between Big Business and Government—and the Reckoning that Lies Ahead* (New York: Farrar, Straus & Giroux, 2012), 258.

47. For an excellent article on inequality, see Michael D. Yates, "The Great Inequality," *Monthly Review* 63/10 (March 2012), http://monthlyreview.org/2012/03/01/the-great-inequality; Paul Krugman, "America's Unlevel Field," *New York Times,* January 8, 2012; Nicholas Lemann, "Evening the Odds: Is There a Politics of Inequality?," *The New Yorker,* April 23, 2012, http://www.newyorker.com/arts/critics/atlarge/2012/04/23/120423crat_atlarge_lemann. See also Charles M. Blow, "Inconvenient Income Inequality," *New York Times,* December 16, 2011, http://www.nytimes.com/2011/12/17/opinion/blow-inconvenient-income-inequality.html; David Moberg, "Anatomy of the 1%," *In These Times,* December 15, 2011, http://www.inthesetimes.com/article/12409/anatomy_of_the_1_percent/; and Hope Yen and Laura Wides-Munoz, "U.S. Poorest Poor at Record Highs," *ReaderSupportedNews,* November 4, 2011, http://readersupportednews.org/newssection2/320-80/8235-us-poorest-poor-at-record-highs.

48. Yates, "The Great Inequality."

49. Michelle Brown, *The Culture of Punishment: Prison, Society and Spectacle* (New York: New York University Press, 2009), 194.

50. Alain Badiou, *The Rebirth of History* (London: Verso, 2012), 12.

51. Ibid., 13.

52. Ibid.

53. Aronowitz, "The Winter of Our Discontent," 69.

54. Nick Turse, "Empire of Bases 2.0," *South Asia Times,* January 12, 2011, http://www.atimes.com/atimes/South_Asia/MA12Df01.html.

55. C. Wright Mills, "The Cultural Apparatus," *The Politics of Truth: Selected Writings of C. Wright Mills* (New York: Oxford University Press, 2008), 204.

56. Bernard Harcourt, "Occupy's New Grammar of Political Disobedience," *The Guardian,* November 30, 2011, http://www.guardian.co.uk/commentisfree/cifamerica/2011/nov/30/occupy-new-grammar-political-disobedience.

57. Patricia Ticento Clough and Craig Willse, "Beyond Biopolitics: The Governance of Life and Death," in *Beyond Biopolitics,* ed. Clough and Willse (Durham, NC: Duke University Press, 2011), 3.

58. Aronowitz, "The Winter of Our Discontent," 68.

59. Brown, *The Culture of Punishment*, 207.

4. HOODIE POLITICS

1. I take this up in great detail in Henry A. Giroux, *Youth in a Suspect Society: Democracy or Disposability?* (New York: Palgrave, 2010).

2. Michelle Alexander, "Michelle Alexander, The Age of Obama as a Racial Nightmare," *Tom Dispatch,* March 25, 2012, http://www.tomdispatch.com/post/175520/best_of_tomdispatch%3A_michelle_alexander,_the_age_of_obama_as_a_racial_nightmare/.

3. Ibid.

4. Andrew Sum et al., *The Consequences of Dropping Out of High School: Joblessness and Jailing for High School Dropouts and the High Cost for Taxpayers* (Boston: Center for Labor Market Studies, Northeastern University, 2009), http://www.clms.neu.edu/publication/documents/The_Consequences_of_Dropping_Out_of_High_School.pdf.

5. Ibid.

6. Lindsey Tanner, "Half of US Kids Will Get Food Stamps, Study Says," *Chicago Tribune,* November 2, 2009, http://www.chicagotribune.com/news/chi-ap-us-med-children-food,0,6055934.story.

7. Mary Otto, "For Lack of a Dentist," *Washington Post,* February 28, 2007, http://www.washingtonpost.com/wp-dyn/content/article/2007/02/27/AR2007022702116.html.

8. Cited in Jean Comaroff, "Beyond Bare Life: AIDs, (Bio)Politics and the Neoliberal Order," *Public Culture* 19/1 (Winter 2007): 213.

9   Rich Menjamin, "The Gated Community Mentality," *New York Times,* March 30, 2012.

10. James Carroll, "A Nation Lost," *Boston Globe,* April 22, 2003, http://www.commondreams.org/views03/0422-02.htm.

11. Jorge Mariscal, "Lethal and Compassionate: The Militarization of Culture," *CounterPunch,* May 3, 2003, http://www.counterpunch.org/mariscal0502003.html.

12. Zygmunt Bauman, *Wasted Lives* (New York: Polity Press, 2004), 92–93.

13. Erica Goode, "Many in U.S. Are Arrested by Age 23, Study Finds," *New York Times,* December 19, 2011, http://www.nytimes.com/2011/12/19/us/nearly-a-third-of-americans-are-arrested-by-23-study-says.html.

14. Reuters, "45% Struggle in US to Make Ends Meet," MSNBC, *Business Stocks and Economy,* November 22, 2011, http://www.msnbc.msn.com/id/45407937/ns/business-stocks_and_economy/#.T3SxhDEgd8E. For a range of statistics that provide an overall picture of the myth of the postracial society, see Michael D. Yates, "It's Still Slavery by Another Name," *Cheap Motels and a Hot Plate: An Economist's Travelogue,* February 23, 2012,

http://cheapmotelsandahotplate.org/2012/02/23/slavery-by-another-name/.

15. Etienne Balibar, "Outline of a Topography of Cruelty: Citizenship and Civility in the Era of Global Violence," in *We, The People of Europe? Reflec tions on Transnational Citizenship* (Princeton: Princeton University Press, 2004), 128.

16. Steve Herbert and Elizabeth Brown, "Conceptions of Space and Crime in the Punitive Neoliberal City," *Antipode* (2006) 757.

17. Glen Ford, "Vilification of Young Black Youth Deeply Embedded in American Culture," *The Real News*, April 1, 2012, http://therealnews.com/t2/index.php?option=com_content&task=view&id=31&Itemid=74&jumiv al=8150.

18. Patricia Ticento Clough and Craig Willse, "Beyond Biopolitics: The Governance of Life and Death," in *Beyond Biopolitics*, ed. Clough and Willse (Durham, NC: Duke University Press, 2011), 3.

5. THE "SUICIDAL STATE" AND THE WAR ON YOUTH

1. Alex Honneth, *Pathologies of Reason* (New York: Columbia University Press, 2009), 188.

2. Robert Reich, "The Fable of the Century," *Robert Reich's Blog*, April 6, 2012, http://robertreich.org/post/20538393444.

3. Some useful sources on neoliberalism include Lisa Duggan, *The Twilight of Equality* (Boston: Beacon Press, 2003); David Harvey, *A Brief History of Neoliberalism* (New York: Oxford University Press, 2005); Wendy Brown, *Edgework: Critical Essays on Knowledge and Politics* (Princeton: Princeton University Press, 2005); Alfredo Saad-Filho and Deborah Johnston, eds., *Neoliberalism: A Critical Reader* (London: Pluto Press, 2005); Neil Smith, *The Endgame of Globalization* (New York: Routledge, 2005); Aihwa Ong, *Neoliberalism as Exception: Mutations in Citizenship and Sovereignty* (Durham, NC: Duke University Press, 2006); Randy Martin, *An Empire of Indifference: American War and the Financial Logic of Risk Management* (Durham, NC: Duke University Press, 2007); Naomi Klein, *The Shock Doctrine: The Rise of Disaster Capitalism* (New York: Alfred A. Knopf, 2007); Henry A. Giroux, *Against the Terror of Neoliberalism* (Boulder, CO: Paradigm Publishers, 2008); David Harvey, *The Enigma of Capital and the Crisis of Capitalism* (New York: Oxford University Press, 2010); and Gerard Dumenil and Dominique Levy, *The Crisis of Neoliberalism* (Cambridge, MA: Harvard University Press, 2011).

4. Paul Virilio, "The Suicidal State," in *The Virilio Reader*, ed. J. Derderian (New York: Oxford University Press, 1998), 29–45.

5. Ibid.

6. Giovanna Borradori, ed., "Autoimmunity: Real and Symbolic Suicides—A

Dialogue with Jacques Derrida," *Philosophy in a Time of Terror: Dialogues with Jürgen Habermas and Jacques Derrida* (Chicago: University of Chicago Press, 2004), 94.

7. Susan Searls Giroux, "Generation Kill: Nietzschean Meditations on the University, Youth, War and Guns," in *Academic Freedom in the Post-9/11 Era*, ed. Edward J. Carvalho and David B. Downing (New York: Palgrave Macmillan, 2010), 130–31.

8. Colin Crouch, *The Strange Non-Death of Neoliberalism*, Cambridge: Polity Press, 2011), 7.

9. Bill Moyers and Michael Winship, "The Best Congress the Banks' Money Can Buy," *CommonDreams*, April 6, 2012, http://www.commondreams.org/view/2012/04/06?print.

10. Andrew J. Bacevich, *Washington Rules: America's Path to Permanent War* (New York: Metropolitan Books, 2010), 25.

11. For an insightful list of some of these antidemocratic forces, see Les Leopold, "Ten Ways Our Democracy Is Crumbling around Us," *AlterNet*, April 5, 2012, http://www.alternet.org/story/154884/10_ways_our_democracy_is_crumbling_around_us?akid=8543.40823.8x8jfR&rd=1&t=8.

12. Harvey, *A Brief History of Neoliberalism*, 19.

13. Virilio, "The Suicidal State," 29.

14. Anne-Marie Cusac, *Cruel and Unusual: The Culture of Punishment in America* (New Haven: Yale University Press, 2009).

15. A number of important books address this issue. See, most recently, Michelle Alexander, *The New Jim Crow: Mass Incarceration in the Age of Colorblindness* (New York: New Press, 2010).

16. Matt Taibbi, "Bloomberg's New York: Cops in Your Hallways," *Rolling Stone*, April 5, 2012, http://www.rollingstone.com/politics/blogs/taibblog/mike-bloombergs-new-york-cops-in-your-hallways-20120403.

17. These themes are taken up in Lawrence Grossberg, *Caught in the Crossfire: Kids, Politics, and America's Future* (Boulder, CO: Paradigm, 2005); Henry A. Giroux, *Youth in a Suspect Society* (New York: Routledge, 2009).

18. See, for example, Jean and John Comaroff, "Reflections of Youth, from the Past to the Postcolony," *Frontiers of Capital: Ethnographic Reflections on the New Economy*, ed. Melissa S. Fisher and Greg Downey (Durham, NC: Duke University Press, 2006), 267–81.

19. Zygmunt Bauman, *Liquid Times: Living in an Age of Uncertainty* (Cambridge: Polity Press, 2007), 14.

20. Sharon Stephens, ed., *Children and the Politics of Culture* (Princeton: Princeton University Press, 1995), 19.

21. Zygmunt Bauman, "Downward Mobility Is Now a Reality," *The Guardian*, May 31, 2012, http://www.guardian.co.uk/commentisfree/2012/may/31/downward-mobility-europe-young-people. Bauman develops this theme in

detail in his *On Education* (Cambridge: Polity Press, 2012) and *This Is Not a Diary* (Cambridge: Polity Press, 2012).

22. Zygmunt Bauman, *Wasted Lives* (London: Polity, 2004), 76.

23. Ibid.

24. Zygmunt Bauman, *On Education* (Cambridge: Polity Press, 2012), 47.

25. Ibid.

26. Lawrence Grossberg, *Caught in the Crossfire: Kids, Politics, and America's Future* (Boulder, CO: Paradigm, 2005), 38–39.

27. I have borrowed the term "zones of social abandonment" from João Biehl, *Vita: Life in a Zone of Social Abandonment* (Berkeley: University of California Press, 2005). See also Henry A. Giroux, *Disposable Youth* (New York: Routledge, 2012); and Michelle Alexander, *The New Jim Crow* (New York: Free Press, 2012).

28. Angela Y. Davis, "State of Emergency," in *Racializing Justice, Disenfranchising Lives,* ed. Manning Marable, Keesha Middlemass, and Ian Steinberg (New York: Palgrave, 2007), 324.

29. Bauman, 76–77.

30. Zygmunt Bauman, *In Search of Politics* (Stanford, CA: Stanford University Press, 1999), 8.

31. Leo Lowenthal, *False Prophets: Studies in Authoritarianism* (New Brunswick, NJ: Transaction Books, 1987), 181–82.

32. See, for example, Annette Fuentes, *Lockdown High: When the Schoolhouse Becomes a Jailhouse* (New York: Verso, 2011). Also see Henry A. Giroux, *Youth in a Suspect Society: Democracy or Disposability?* (New York: Palgrave, 2010).

33. On the rise of the punishing state, see Loic Wacquant, *Punishing the Poor: The Neoliberal Government of Social Insecurity* (Durham, NC: Duke University Press, 2009).

34. Bauman, *Wasted Lives*, 92–93.

35. Cusac, *Cruel and Unusual*, 175.

36. Lindsey Tanner, "Half of U.S. Kids Will Get Food Stamps, Study Says," *Chicago Tribune,* November 2, 2009, http://www.chicagotribune.com/news/chi-ap-us-med-children-food,0,6055934.story.

37. John Van Houdt, "The Crisis of Negation: An Interview with Alain Badiou," *Continent* 1/4 (2011), http://continentcontinent.cc/index.php/continent/article/viewArticle.

38. Stanley Aronowitz, "The Winter of Our Discontent," *Situations* 4/2 (Spring 2012): 37–76.

6. RELIGIOUS FUNDAMENTALISM, THE ATTACK ON PUBLIC
SCHOOLS, AND THE CRISIS OF REASON

1. Editors, "Open Thread for Night Owls: Texas Republicans Write Their Platform," *Daily Kos*, June 27, 2012, http://www.dailykos.com/story/2012/06/27/1103721/-Open-thread-for-night-owls-Texas-Republicans-write-their-platform.

2. Bill Moyers, "Messing with Texas Textbooks," *Moyers and Company*, PBS, June 29, 2012, http://billmoyers.com/content/messing-with-texas-textbooks/.

3. James C. McKinley Jr., "Texas Conservatives Win Curriculum Change," *New York Times*, March 12, 2010.

4. Ibid.

5. Ibid.; Moyers, "Messing with Texas Textbooks."

6. Frank Rich, "Banishing Akin Won't Cure the Stag Party," *New York*, August 22, 2012. http://readersupportednews.org/off-site-opinion-section/72-72/13089-focus-banishing-akin-wont-cure-the-stag-party.

7. Adele M. Stan, "Agenda for the Dark Ages: GOP Frontrunner Rick Santorum's 5 Most Extremist Themes," *AlterNet*, February 28, 2012), http://www.alternet.org/news/154242/agenda_for_the_dark_ages%3A_gop_frontrunner_rick_santorum's_5_most_extremist_themes_.

8. Ibid.

9. There is a long tradition in American thought that has made this visible. See, for instance, Richard Hofstadter, *Anti-Intellectualism in American Life* (New York: Vintage, 1966). More recently, see Susan Jacoby, *The Age of Unreason* (New York: Vintage, 2009).

10. Mark Slouka, "A Quibble," *Harper's Magazine*, February 2009, 9–11, online at: http://www.harpers.org/archive/2009/02/0082362.

11. Will Bunch, *The Backlash: Right-Right Radicals, High-Def Hucksters, and Paranoid Politics in the Age of Obama* (New York: HarperCollins, 2010); Paul Street and Anthony DiMaggio, *Crashing the Tea Party* (Boulder, CO: Paradigm, 2011); and Anthony DiMaggio, *The Rise of the Tea Party* (New York: Monthly Review Press, 2011).

12. On the book-banning incident in Arizona, see "Disposable Knowledge and Disposable Bodies: Book Burning in Arizona," in Henry A. Giroux, *Youth in Revolt: Reclaiming a Democratic Future* (Boulder, CO: Paradigm, 2013), chap. 4.

13. I take up this issue in great detail in Henry A. Giroux, *Youth in a Suspect Society: Democracy or Disposability?* (New York: Palgrave, 2010).

14. Chris McGreal, "The U.S. Schools with Their Own Police," *The Guardian*, January 9, 2012, http://www.guardian.co.uk/world/2012/jan/09/texas-police-schools.

15. Ibid.

16. Kenneth J. Saltman and David A. Gabbard, eds., *Education as Enforcement: The Militarization and Corporatization of Schools* (New York: Routledge,

2010); Henry A. Giroux, *Education and the Crisis of Public Values* (New York: Peter Lang, 2012).

17. Rosalind Rossi, "'Flaming Hot' Chips, Gum, Other 'Infractions' Costly at Some Schools," *Sun Times*, February 14, 2012, http://www.suntimes.com/news/metro/10626363-418/flaming-hot-chips-gum-other-infractions-costly-at-some-schools.html.

18. I have paraphrased and quoted in this instance from an unpublished 46-page paper by a talented graduate student, Tyler J. Pollard, "Schools, Students and the Intensification of Market Reforms and Punishment in the Age of Neoliberalism" (McMaster University, February 29, 2012).

19. Editors, "End Zero Tolerance Policies in Chicago," *Advancement Project Alert*, March 5, 2012, https://mail.google.com/mail/#inbox/135e4750fc179906.

20. Rossi, "'Flaming Hot' Chips."

21. Associated Press, "Chicago School Draws Scrutiny over Student Fines," February 20, 2012, http://abcnews.go.com/US/wireStory/chicago-school-draws-scrutiny-student-fines-15753004?page=2#.TOO3t_Egcsc.

22. Bill Moyers, "Discovering What Democracy Means," *TomPaine*, February 12, 2007, http://www.tompaine.com/articles/2007/02/12/discovering_what_democracy_means.php.

23. Jacques Derrida, "The Future of the Profession or the Unconditional University," in *Derrida Downunder*, ed. Laurence Simmons and Heather Worth (Auckland, NZ: Dunmore Press, 2001), 233.

24. See, for instance, Paulo Freire, *Pedagogy of the Oppressed* (New York: Continuum, 2009); and Paulo Freire, *Pedagogy of Freedom* (Boulder, CO: Rowman and Littlefield, 2000).

25. Stanley Aronowitz, "Paulo Freire's Pedagogy: Not Mainly a Teaching Method," in *Paulo Freire's Intellectual Roots: Toward Historicity in Praxis*, ed. Robert Lake and Tricia Kress (New York: Continuum).

26. Edward Said, *Reflections on Exile and Other Essays* (Cambridge, MA: Harvard University Press, 2001), 501.

27. Stanley Aronowitz, "Introduction," in Freire, *Pedagogy of Freedom*, 10–11.

28. Zygmunt Bauman and Keith Tester, *Conversations with Zygmunt Bauman* (Malden, MA: Polity, 2001), 4.

29. Chandra Mohanty, "On Race and Voice: Challenges for Liberal Education in the 1990s," *Cultural Critique* (Winter 1989–1990): 192.

30. Cornelius Castoriadis, "Democracy as Procedure and Democracy as Regime," *Constellations* 4/1 (1997); 5.

31. See, for instance, John Keane, *The Life and Death of Democracy* (New York: W. W. Norton, 2009). See also John Dewey, *Democracy and Education* (New York: Simon and Brown, 2012).

32. Erich Fromm, *Escape from Freedom* (New York: Henry Holt, 1994).

7. GATED INTELLECTUALS AND FORTRESS AMERICA

1. Jane Mayer, "Covert Operations: The Billionaire Brothers Who Are Waging a War against Obama," *The New Yorker*,. August 30, 2010, http://www.newyorker.com/reporting/2010/08/30/100830fa_fact_mayer.
2. Zygmunt Bauman, *Liquid Fear* (London: Polity Press, 2006), 113.
3. Greg Smith, "Why I Am Leaving Goldman Sachs," *New York Times*, March 14, 2012.
4. Maureen Dowd, "Don't Tread on Us," *New York Times*, March 14, 2012.
5. Robert O. Self, "The Antisocial Contract," *The New York Times*, August 25, 2012, http://campaignstops.blogs.nytimes.com/2012/08/25/the-antisocial-contract/; and George Lakoff and Glenn W. G. Smith, "Romney, Ryan and the Devil's Budget," *Reader Supported News*, August 22, 2012, http://blogs.berkeley.edu/2012/08/23/romney-ryan-and-the-devils-budget-will-america-keep-its-soul.
6. David Theo Goldberg, *The Threat of Race: Reflections on Racial Neoliberalism* (Malden, MA: Wiley-Blackwell, 2009), 338–39.
7. Zygmunt Bauman, "Has the Future a Left?," *Review of Education/Pedagogy/Cultural Studies* (2007): 2.
8. Irving Howe, "This Age of Conformity," *Selected Writings 1950–1990* (New York: Harcourt Brace Jovanovich, 1990), 31.
9. I take this up in detail in Henry A. Giroux, *Education and the Crisis of Public Values: Challenging the Assault on Teachers, Students, and Public Education* (New York: Peter Lang, 2012).
10. Steve Benen, "Political Animal," *Washington Monthly*, March 26, 2011, http://www.washingtonmonthly.com/archives/individual/2011_03/028621.php.
11. Editors, "A Conversation with David Harvey," *Logos: A Journal of Modern Society & Culture* 5/1 (2006), http://www.logosjournal.com/issue_5.1/harvey.htm.
12. See, for instance, a list of ten important Occupy movement websites at http://www.makeuseof.com/tag/10-occupy-movement-websites-check/.
13. Quoted in Burton Bollag, "UNESCO Has Lofty Aims for Higher Education Conference, but Critics Doubt Its Value," *Chronicle of Higher Education*, September 4, 1998, A76.

8. THE OCCUPY MOVEMENT AND THE POLITICS OF EDUCATED HOPE

1. See, for example, Richard Wolff in conversation with David Barsamian, *Occupy the Economy* (San Francisco: City Lights, 2012).
2. Colin Crouch, *The Strange Non-Death of Neoliberalism* (London: Polity, 2011), viii–ix.
3. David Harvey, *The Enigma of Capital and the Crises of Capitalism* (New York: Oxford University Press, 2010).

4.   Manfred B. Steger and Ravi K. Roy, *Neoliberalism: A Very Short Introduction* (New York: Oxford University Press, 2010). See also Stuart Hall, "The Neo-Liberal Revolution," *Cultural Studies*, 25/6 (November 2011): 705–28. What should be noted is that neoliberalism divorces itself from neoclassical economics which says that all this self-interest promotes the public interest.

5.   João Biehl, *Vita: Life in A Zone of Social Abandonment* (Los Angeles: University of California Press, 2005), 20.

6.   Eric Cazdyn, "Bioeconomics, Culture, and Politics after Globalization," in *Cultural Autonomy: Frictions and Connections*, ed. Petra Rethmann, Imre Szeman, William D. Coleman (Vancouver, BC: UBC Press, 2010), 60.

7.   Ibid., 64.

8.   Joy James, "The Dead Zone: Stumbling at the Crossroads of Party Politics, Genocide, and Postracial Racism," *South Atlantic Quarterly: Africana Thought*, 108/3 (Summer 2009): 464–65.

9.   This theme is taken up particularly well in Jacques Rancière, *Hatred of Democracy* (London: Verso Press, 2006).

10.   Jean Comaroff, "Beyond Bare Life: AIDS, (Bio)Politics, and the Neoliberal Order," *Public Culture* 19/1 (Winter 2007): 197–219.

11.   I take up this issue in detail in Henry A. Giroux, *The Twilight of the Social: Resurgent Politics in the Age of Disposability* (Boulder, CO: Paradigm, 2012).

12.   For a brilliant theoretical framework and wealth of empirical work for understanding the militarization of American society, see Stephen Graham, *Cities under Siege: The New Military Urbanism* (London: Verso, 2010).

13.   For the full report by the Partnership for Civil Justice on FBI surveillance of Occupy, see http://www.justiceonline.org/commentary/fbi-files-ows.html. See the excellent reporting on this issue done by Jason Leopold, for instance, "DHS Turns Over Occupy Wall Street Documents to Truthout," March 20, 2012, http://truth-out.org/news/item/8012-dhs-turns-over-occupy-wall-street-documents-to-truthout. See also, Naomi Wolf, "Revealed: How the FBI Coordinated the Crackdown on Occupy," *The Guardian*, December 29, 2012, http://www.guardian.co.uk/commentisfree/2012/dec/29/fbi-coordinated-crackdown-occupy.

14.   Jacques Rancière, "Democracy, Republic, Representation," *Constellations* 13/3 (2006) 299–300.

15.   Theodor W. Adorno and Max Horkheimer, *Dialectic of Enlightenment* (London: Verso Press, 1989), 243; Theodor W. Adorno, *The Culture Industry: Selected Essays on Mass Culture*, ed. J. M. Bernstein (London: Routledge, 1991), 292.

16.   Richard D. Wolff, "Capitalism Is Taboo in America," *Truthout*, May 15, 2012, http://truth-out.org/opinion/item/9139-capitalism-is-taboo-in-america.

17.   Ellen Willis, "Three Elegies for Susan Sontag," *New Politics* 10/3 (Summer 2005), http://www.wpunj.edu/newpol/issue39/cont39.htm.

18. Stanley Aronowitz, "The Winter of Our Discontent," *Situations* 4/2 (Spring 2012): 68.

19. Ibid.

20. Zygmunt Bauman, *Does Ethics Have a Chance in a World of Consumers* (Cambridge, MA: Harvard University Press, 2008).

21. Zygmunt Bauman, "Has the Future a Left?," *Soundings* 35 (2007). Online: http://www.compassonline.org.uk/news/item.asp?n=546.

22. Biehl, *Vita*, 10–11.

23. Chris Hedges, "Colonized by Corporations," *Truthdig*, May 14, 2012, http://www.truthdig.com/report/item/colonized_by_corporations_20120514.

24. Slavoj Žižek, "Occupy Wall Street: What Is to Be Done Next?," *The Guardian*, April. 24, 2012, http://www.guardian.co.uk/commentisfree/cifamerica/2012/apr/24/occupy-wall-street-what-is-to-be-done-next.

25. On the related issues of hope and pedagogy, see Mark Coté, Richard J. F. Day, and Greig de Peuter, eds., *Utopian Pedagogy: Radical Experiments against Neoliberal Globalization* (Toronto: University of Toronto Press, 2007).

26. Andrew Benjamin, *Present Hope: Philosophy, Architecture, Judaism* (New York: Routledge, 1997), 1.

27. Alain Touraine, *Beyond Neoliberalism* (London: Polity, 2001), 6.

28. Zygmunt Bauman, *Work, Consumerism and the New Poor* (Philadelphia: Open University Press, 1998), 98.

29. Ron Aronson, "Hope after Hope?" *Social Research* 66/2 (Summer 1999); 489.

30. Zygmunt Bauman and Keith Tester, *Conversations with Zygmunt Bauman* (Malden, MA: Polity, 2001), 4.

31. Zygmunt Bauman, *Liquid Life* (London: Polity, 2005), 213.

32. Elisabeth Young-Bruehl, *Why Arendt Matters* (New York: Integrated Publishing Solutions, 2006), 6.

33. Sources that address this issue include Henry A. Giroux, *Youth in Revolt* (Boulder, CO: Paradigm, 2013); and Manuel Castells, *Networks of Outrage and Hope: Social Movements in the Internet Age* (Cambridge, MA: Polity, 2012).

9. NEOLIBERALISM'S WAR AGAINST TEACHERS IN DARK TIMES

1. Adam Bessie, "Public Teaches: America's New 'Welfare Queens," *Truthout*, March 6, 2011, http://truth-out.org/news/item/175:public-teachers-americas-new-welfare-queens-2.

2. For a list of such humiliations, see VetGrl, "Here Are Your Parasites and Terrorists, M*therf*ckers," *Daily Kos*, December 15, 2012, http://www.dailykos.com/story/2012/12/15/1170268/-Here-are-your-parasites-and-terrorists-m-therf-ckers.

3.   Manfred B. Steger and Ravi K. Roy, *Neoliberalism: A Very Short Introduction* (Oxford University Press, 2010); Henry A. Giroux, *Against the Terror of Neoliberalism* (Boulder, CO: Paradigm, 2008); David Harvey, *A Brief History of Neoliberalism* (New York: Oxford University Press, 2005).

4.   Kenneth Saltman, *The Gift of Education: Public Education and Venture Philanthropy* (New York: Palgrave Macmillan, 2010); Diane Ravitch, "The People Behind the Lawmakers Out to Destroy Pubic Education: A Primer— What You Need to Know about ALEC," *CommonDreams*, May 2, 2012,https://www.commondreams.org/view/2012/05/02-0.

5.   See Henry A. Giroux, *Education and the Struggle for Public Values* (Boulder, CO: Paradigm, 2012); Ken Saltman, *The Failure of Corporate School Reform* (New York: Palgrave, 2012); Diane Ravitch, *The Death and Life of the Great American School System* (New York: Basic Books, 2011); Alex Means, *Schooling in the Age of Austerity* (New York: Palgrave, 2013); Philip Kovacs, *The Gates Foundation and the Future of U.S. 'Public' Schools* (New York: Routledge, 2010).

6.   On the corruption of Wall Street, see, for example, Jeff Madrick, *Age of Greed: The Triumph of Finance and the Decline of America, 1970 to the Present* (New York: Vintage, 2011); Charles Ferguson, *Predator Nation* (New York: Crown Business, 2012); Henry A. Giroux, *Zombie Politics in the Age of Casino Capitalism* (New York: Peter Lang, 2010).

7.   I am not just talking about right-wing Republicans but also about the Obama administration policy on education, which has reproduced the worst dimensions of the former Bush administration's policies on educational reform, which are as reactionary as they are detrimental to the quality, if not future, of public education in the United States.

8.   Mustafha Marruchi, "The Value of Literature as a Public Institution," *College Literature* 33/4 (Fall 2006): 176.

9.   Sara Robinson, "How the Conservative Worldview Quashes Critical Thinking—And What that Means for Our Kids' Future," *AlterNet*, May 20, 2012, http://www.alternet.org/education/155469/how_the_ conservative_worldview_quashes_critical_thinking_--_and_what_that_ means_for_our_kids%27_future?page=entire.

10.   Martha C. Nussbaum, "Education for Profit, Education for Freedom," *Liberal Education* (Summer 2009): 6. Also see Martha C. Nussbaum, *Not for Profit: Why Democracy Needs the Humanities* (Princeton: Princeton University Press, 2010).

11.   Stanley Aronowitz, "Paulo Freire's Pedagogy: Not Mainly a Teaching Method," in *Paulo Freire's Intellectual Roots: Toward Historicity in Praxis,* ed. Robert Lake and Tricia Kress (New York: Continuum, 2012).

12.   Noam Chomsky, "The Assault on Public Education," *TruthOut*, April 4, 2012, http://truth-out.org/opinion/item/8305-the-assault-on-public-education.

13.   Les Leopold, "Hey Dad, Why Does This Country Protect Billionaires, and Not Teachers?," *AlterNet*, May 5, 2010, http://www.alternet.org/module/printversion/146738.

14.   Ken Saltman and David A. Gabbard, eds., *Education as Enforcement: The Militarization and Corporatization of Schools*, 2nd ed. (New York: Routledge, 2010); David A. Gabbard and E. Wayne Ross, eds., *Education under the Security State (Defending Public Schools)* (New York: Teachers College Press, 2008).

15.   Henry Giroux, *Youth in a Suspect Society: Democracy or Disposability* (New York: Palgrave, 2009).

16.   Ibid.; Robinson, "How the Conservative Worldview Quashes Critical Thinking."

17.   There is a great deal of literature written about zero tolerance policies. For a brilliant academic discussion, see Christopher Robbins, *Expelling Hope: The Assault on Youth and the Militarization of Schooling* (New York: SUNY Press, 2009); Julianne Hing, "The Shocking Details of a Mississippi School-to-Prison Pipeline," *TruthOut*, December 3, 2012, http://truth-out.org/news/item/13121-the-shocking-details-of-a-mississippi-school-to-prison-pipeline; Donna Lieberman, "Schoolhouse to Courthouse," *New York Times*, December 8, 2012, http://www.nytimes.com/2012/12/09/opinion/sunday/take-police-officers-off-the-school-discipline-beat.html.

18.   Chandra Mohanty, "On Race and Voice: Challenges for Liberal Education in the 1990s," *Cultural Critique* (Winter 1989–1990): 192.

19.   See, for example, Sam Dillon, "Formula to Grade Teachers' Skill Gains in Use, and Critics," *New York Times*, August 31, 2010.

20.   Michael Collins, "Universities Need Reform—But the Market Is Not the Answer," *OpenDemocracy*, November 23, 2010, http://www.opendemocracy.net/ourkingdom/michael-collins/universities-need-reform-but-market-is-not-answer.

21.   Danny Weil, "Texas GOP Declares: No More Teaching of 'Critical Thinking Skills' in Texas Public Schools," *Truthout*, July 7, 2012, http://truth-out.org/news/item/10144-texas-gop-declares-no-more-teaching-of-critical-thinking-skills-in-texas-public-schools.

22.   See, for instance, Henry A. Giroux, "Book Burning in Arizona," *Truthout*, February 8, 2012, http://truth-out.org/news/item/6548:book-burning-in-arizona.

23.   Paulo Freire, *Pedagogy of the Oppressed* (New York: Continuum, 1964); also see what I think is Freire's best book, *Pedagogy of Freedom* (Boulder,CO: Rowman and Littlefield, 2000).

24.   Israel Scheffler, *Reason and Teaching* (New York: Routledge, 1973), 92.

25.   Cited in Gary Olson and Lynn Worsham, "Changing the Subject: Judith Butler's Politics of Radical Resignification," *JAC* 204 (200): 765.

26.   Ernst Bloch, "Something's Missing: A Discussion between Ernst Bloch and Theodor W. Adorno on the Contradictions of Utopian Longing,"

in Ernst Bloch, *The Utopian Function of Art and Literature: Selected Essays* (Cambridge, MA: MIT Press, 1988), 3.

27. Arundhati Roy, *Power Politics* (Cambridge, MA: South End Press, 2001), 1.

28. Garry Wills, "Our Moloch," *New York Review of Books*, December 15, 2012, http://www.nybooks.com/blogs/nyrblog/2012/dec/15/our-moloch/.

29. Frank Rich, "America's Original Sin," *New York*, December 17, 2012, http:// nymag.com/daily/intelligencer/2012/12/frank-rich-americas-other- original-sin.html.

30. Marian Wright Edelman, "Dear God! When Will It Stop?" *CommonDreams*, December 15, 2012, www.commondreams.org/view/ 2012/12/15-0?print.

31. Andrew Ross Sorkin, "Wall Street, Invested in Firearms, Is Unlikely to Push for Reform," *New York Times*, December 17, 2012.

32. Don Hazen, "We Are a Country Drenched in Bloodshed: Some Hard Truths about Violence in the Media," *AlterNet*, December 20, 2012, http:// www.alternet.org/media/we-are-country-drenched-bloodshed-some- hard-truths-about-violence-media.

33. I take up this issue in Henry A. Giroux, *Youth in a Suspect Society* (Boulder, CO: Paradigm, 2013).

34. Jeff Sparrow, "When the Burning Moment Breaks: Gun Control and Rage Massacres," *Overland*, August 6, 2012, http://overland.org.au/blogs/new- words/2012/08/when-the-burning-moment-breaks-gun-control-and- rage-massacres/.

35. Ibid.

36. Noam Chomsky and Eric Bailey, "Noam Chomsky: America, Moral Degenerate," *Reader Supported News*, December 14, 2012, http:// readersupportednews.org/opinion2/277-75/15019-focus-noam- chomsky-america-moral-degenerate.

10. DANGEROUS PEDAGOGY IN THE AGE OF CASINO CAPITALISM

1. Stanley Aronowitz, "Introduction," in Paulo Freire, *Pedagogy of Freedom* (Lanham. MD: Rowman and Littlefield, 1998), 7.

2. For an excellent analysis of contemporary forms of neoliberalism, see Stuart Hall, "The Neo-Liberal Revolution," *Cultural Studies* 25/6 (November 2011): 705–28. See also David Harvey, *A Brief History of Neoliberalism* (Oxford: Oxford University Press, 2005); and Henry A. Giroux, *Against the Terror of Neoliberalism* (Boulder, CO: Paradigm, 2008).

3. Roger Simon, "Empowerment as a Pedagogy of Possibility," *Language Arts* 64/4 (April 1987): 372.

4. Cornelius Castoriadis, "Institutions and Autonomy," in *A Critical Sense*, ed. Peter Osborne (New York: Routledge, 1996), 8.

5. Rachel Donadio, "The Failing State of Greece," *New York Times*, February 26, 2012.

6.   John Brenkman, "Extreme Criticism," in *What's Left of Theory,* ed. Judith Butler, John Guillary, and Kendal Thomas (New York: Routledge, 2000), 123.

7.   I develop the notion of educated hope in greater detail in Henry A. Giroux, *Public Spaces, Private Lives: Democracy beyond 9/11* (Lanham, MD: Rowman and Littlefield, 2003).

8.   Jeffrey Williams, "Brave New University," *College English* 61/6 (1999); 749.

9.   Paul Gilroy, *Against Race* (Cambridge, MA: Harvard University Press, 2000), 69.

10. For a brilliant discussion of the ethics and politics of deconstruction, see Thomas Keenan, *Fables of Responsibility: Aberrations and Predicaments in Ethics and Politics* (Stanford, CA: Stanford University Press, 1997), 2.

11. Jacques Derrida, "Intellectual Courage: An Interview," trans. Peter Krapp, *Culture Machine* 2 (2000): 9.

12. Terry Eagleton, *The Idea of Culture* (Malden, MA: Basil Blackwell, 2000), 22.

13. Bill Readings, *The University in Ruins* (Cambridge, MA: Harvard University Press), 11, 18.

14. On the role of the public intellectual, there is an abundance of excellent literature. Some of the more important succinct sources include: Noam Chomsky, "The Responsibility of Intellectuals," *New York Review of Books,* February 23, 1967, http://www.chomsky.info/articles/19670223.htm; Russell Jacoby, *The Last Intellectuals* (New York: Basic Books, 1982); Zygmunt Bauman, *Legislators and Interpreters: On Modernity, Post-Modernity and Intellectuals* (London: Polity, 1989); Stanley Aronowitz, "On Intellectuals," *The Politics of Identity: Class, Culture, Social Movement,* (New York: Routledge, 1992), 125–74; C. Wright Mills, *The Sociological Imagination* (Oxford: Oxford University Press, 2000); Edward W. Said, *Representations of the Intellectual* (New York: Pantheon, 1994); Pierre Bourdieu, "For a Scholarship with Commitment," *Profession* (2000): 40–45; Noam Chomsky, "Paths Taken, Tasks Ahead," *Profession* (2000): 32–39. Henry A. Giroux, *Public Spaces, Private Lives* (Boulder, CO: Rowman and Littlefield, 2004).

15. Scott Jaschik, "Santorum's Attack on Higher Education," *Inside Higher Education,* February 27, 2012, http://www.insidehighered.com/news/2012/02/27/santorums-views-higher-education-and-satan.

16. This expression comes from John Michael, *Anxious Intellects: Academic Professionals, Public Intellectuals, and Enlightenment Values* (Durham, NC: Duke University Press, 2000), 2.

17. Cornel West, "The New Cultural Politics of Difference," in *Out There,* ed. Russell Fergusen, Martha Geever, Trinh T. Minh-ha, and Cornel West (Cambridge, MA: MIT Press, 1991), 35.

18. Jodi Dean, "The Interface of Political Theory and Cultural Studies," in *Cultural Studies and Political Theory*, ed. Jodi Dean (Ithaca, NY: Cornell University Press, 2000), 3.

19. Alan O'Shea, "A Special Relationship? Cultural Studies, Academia and Pedagogy," *Cultural Studies* 12/4 (1998): 513–27.

20. Paulo Freire, *Pedagogy of Freedom* (Lanham, MD: Rowman and Littlefield, 1999), 48.

21. Shoshana Felman, *Jacques Lacan and the Adventure of Insight: Psychoanalysis in Contemporary Culture* (Cambridge, MA: Harvard University Press, 1987), 79. For an extensive analysis of the relationship between schooling, literacy, and desire, see Ursula A. Kelly, *Schooling Desire: Literacy, Cultural Politics, and Pedagogy* (New York: Routledge, 1997); and Sharon Todd, *Learning Desire: Perspectives on Pedagogy, Culture, and the Unsaid* (New York: Routledge, 1997).

22. Ibid., Felman, 79.

23. Michael Hardt and Antonio Negri, *Multitude: War and Democracy in the Age of Empire* (New York: Penguin, 2004), 67.

Index

1

38 *Index*

Williams, Jeffrey, 191
Williams, Raymond, 30–31, 143
Wills, Garry, 175
Willse, Craig, 87, 100
Winship, Michael, 36
Wolin, Sheldon, 36–37, 55

Yates, Michael D., 82–83
Younge, Gary, 81

Zimmerman, George, 91, 94, 95, 98–99